J.L. BLACK is a member of the Department of History at Laurentian University, Sudbury, and the editor of *Essays on Karamzin: Russian Man of Letters, Political Commentator, Historian (1766-1826)*.

Nicholas Karamzin (1766-1826) was a remarkably active thinker and writer during a time that was trying to all Europeans. A first-hand witness to the French Revolution, Napoleonic suzerainty over Europe, the burning of Moscow, and the Decembrist revolt in St Petersburg, he presented in his voluminous correspondence and published writings a world view that recognized the weaknesses of the Russian Empire and at the same time foresaw the dangers of both radical change and rigid autocracy. Russian conservatism owes much to this man, even though he would have agreed with very few of those who came after him and were called conservative: he supported autocracy, but was committed to enlightenment; he supported serfdom, but hated despotism; he placed faith in rule of law, but abhorred constitutions. The fact that his writing had lasting significance has rarely been challenged, but the social and political nature of that contribution has never before been demonstrated. Previous studies of Karamzin have dealt with his literary career. This monograph focuses on the final third of his life, on his career at court (1816-26) and on the cultural heritage he left to the Russian Empire. As the historian of Russia most widely read by his and later generations, his historical interpretations mirrored and helped shape the image Russians had of themselves. Professor Black's study of Karamzin is crucial to any examination of Russia's enlightenment, conservatism, historical writing, and national self-consciousness.

J. L. BLACK

Nicholas Karamzin and Russian Society in the Nineteenth Century: A Study in Russian Political and Historical Thought

UNIVERSITY OF TORONTO PRESS
TORONTO AND BUFFALO

© University of Toronto Press 1975
Toronto and Buffalo
Printed in Canada

Library of Congress Cataloging in Publication Data

Black, Joseph Laurence, 1937–
   Nicholas Karamzin and Russian society in the nine-
teenth century.
   Bibliography: p.
   Includes index.
   1. Karamzin, Nikolaĭ Mikhaĭlovich, 1766-1826.
   2. Russia – Historiography.   3. Political science –
History – Russia.   4. Russia – History – 19th century.
   I. Title.
   DK38.7.K35B57   947′.07′0924 [B]   75-20146
   ISBN 0-8020-5335-1

Contents

To Milos Mladenovic

Acknowledgements

A number of people and institutions have contributed in various ways to the completion of this book, but among the individuals to whom I am most indebted, Professor Milos Mladenovic of McGill University stands out as critic and guide. For that reason, this book is dedicated to him with my sincere appreciation. I am also grateful to the staffs at McGill University Library, the Lenin Library in Moscow, Helsinki University Library, Yale University Library, and the Russian and East European Research Centre at the University of Illinois, Champaigne-Urbana. I would also like to express appreciation to the trustees of the Senator McConnell awards, McGill University, to the Canada Council for three grants, and to Laurentian University, for financial assistance which made this effort possible.

Last, but certainly not least, to my wife, Janice, and to my three children, thanks for their patience during the many hours which I spent closeted with this manuscript.

This book has been published with the assistance of a grant from the Humanities Research Council of Canada, using funds provided by the Canada Council, and with the assistance of the Publications Fund of the University of Toronto Press, using a grant from the Andrew W. Mellon Foundation.

Transliteration and System of Citing Dates

The translation of Russian names and titles in the text has been based on a slightly modified Library of Congress system, and according to the ISO Recommendation R9, 2nd edition, 1968. In the case of Russian names ending in 'ii,' a simple 'y' has been substituted because of traditional English-language usage. Russian names have all been transcribed from the original except where close English equivalents are available (eg, Alexander, Nicholas). The familiar English form also has been employed for commonly used words and names, like Boyar, Rurik, Capodistrias. Titles of books in Russian are listed in the form in which they were first published.

The 'Old Style,' or Julian calendar, which was used in the Russian Empire, was twelve days behind the Gregorian calendar in the nineteenth century. The 'New Style' (Gregorian) dating system was adopted by the government of the USSR, and has been used throughout this book.

Introduction

The year 1766 was a momentous one for the Russian nobility. In December of that year, Catherine II issued a manifesto calling for the establishment of a commission to consider legal and political changes in the Russian Empire. Her *Nakaz*, or 'Instructions,' which was designed to provide philosophical guidelines for the discussion to follow, provoked the admiration of Russians and Europeans alike. It acknowledged ideas from the best thinkers of the times and apparently made it possible for Russians to dwell on matters once regarded as the prerogative of the autocrat. Although the potential of this commission was never reached, nor perhaps was it intended to do so, it did help to usher in a new era for Russian nobility and gentry. Already partially freed from obligatory service to the state, many now looked forward to sharing authority with their ruler. Nevertheless, in retrospect, a number of them eventually came to see another event of the same month as one of far greater lasting import for their class, that is, the birth of Nicholas Karamzin.

Karamzin was a remarkably active thinker and writer during a trying time for all Europeans. Having begun his literary career just prior to the French Revolution, to which he was a witness in France, he subsequently observed at close hand the phenomena of Napoleonic suzereignty over Europe, the burning of Moscow and, finally, the Decembrist revolt in St Petersburg. As one of the best educated Russians of the era and a political thinker of the highest calibre, his observations on and conclusions about these events are of great value to any student of modern European history. For students of Russian history, he represents a way of thinking that was similar to, but not exactly like that of his Western European counterparts, Burke and de Maistre. As the historian of Russian most widely read by his and later generations, Karamzin helped incorporate many traditional ideals into lay matters. In so doing, he became one of the leading exponents of a secular conservatism which was to replace Orthodoxy as the dominant ideology of the Russian Empire.

Professor Richard Pipes of Harvard rightly suggested in 1959 that a study of Karamzin's *Memoir on Ancient and Modern Russia* (*Zapiska o drevnei i novoi Rossii*, 1811) could enable one to reach a clearer understanding of nineteenth-century Russian conservative tradition. It is undoubtedly true that the *Memoir* represented a concensus among a large cross-section of the Russian élite, yet that particular essay reached few readers during the first half of the century. On the other hand, Karamzin's greatest work, the *History of the Russian State* (*Istoriia gosudarstva Rossiiskago*, 12 volumes, 1818-29), was known to all members of the educated classes in Russia and so it both reflected and helped to shape a national state of mind. The key question asked by Pipes was, why did Russian conservatives remain so 'loyal to the institution of autocracy'? An awareness of Karamzin's historical themes and the extent of their acceptance by large segments of Russian society may go a long way towards answering that query.

In the 1820s Karamzin's image, sometimes far more than his actual ideas, became a focal point for debate between protagonists of opposing social and political ideologies and remained so until the 1870s. During that half-century, polemics were waged for and against him with equal passion. Isaiah Berlin once wrote of the period 1838-48 as the 'marvellous Decade,' the embryo era of the Russian intelligentsia, of Belinsky, Herzen, and others. There was another side to that intellectual coin, for the literary and political heritage of the long-deceased Karamzin was an integral part of the same decade. His importance was such that in 1841 M.P. Pogodin explained his own literary position to opponents by saying, 'I grew up with Karamzin. I belong to the older generation.' More than thirty years later, N.N.

Strakhov wrote of the forties and said, 'I grew up with Karamzin.' And Dostoevsky exclaimed, 'I too grew up with Karamzin.' Goncharov echoed the sentiment. In the sixties, the radical writers Chernyshevsky, Dobroliubov, and others had blamed Karamzin for creating a heartless and insincere attitude among the gentry and nobility; they were repudiated by nobles and bourgeoisie who saw in Karamzin an embodiment of Russian humane philanthropy and of Russian enlightenment. In the seventies, the conservatives Strakhov and Dostoevsky defended Karamzin from the liberals, Alexander Pypin and M.E. Saltykov.[1]

Westernizers respected his talents but rebuked him for laying the groundwork for Slavophilism. Most Slavophiles praised him, but some, especially in the early part of the century, accused him of a too strong Western orientation. In the latter half of the century, others charged him with deism or cynicism. Apart from those directly involved in argument about him, however, there was a multitude, indeed generations, who revered him as part of their national heritage. The government recognized propaganda value in this and made Karamzin a mainstay of the Russian educational system, using his *History* to train youth to be 'ideal' citizens.

No attempt will be made in this monograph to define Karamzin's place in the history of Russian letters. His literary career, which A.G. Cross has defined as the period between 1783 and 1803, has been thoroughly studied by Cross, Nebel, Rothe, Lotman, and others in fairly recent years. The present study will look at those years only to find in them the roots of his political ideas, of his interpretation of Russian history, and to see the gradual crystallization of his world view.

The main focus of this book will be the final third of the writer's life, the years usually ignored in other studies, and the continuing relevance of his ideas after his death. Karamzin's voluminous correspondence with friends during that time, along with published writings, represent one of our most important commentaries on the reign of Alexander I. Together they also represent a world view, a 'liberal-conservatism' that recognized the weaknesses of the Russian Empire and at the same time foresaw the dangers of both radical change and of rigid autocracy. The same attitude refused to countenance rapid, untimely reform and change. Karamzin contributed enormously to the genesis and formulation of Russian conservatism, but would have agreed with very few who came after him and were called conservative. He supported autocracy, but was committed to enlightenment; he supported serfdom, but sympathized with peasants in their plight. The fact that his writings had lasting significance has rarely been challenged, but the social and political nature of that contribution has never been demonstrated. I hope that this book will serve that purpose.

KARAMZIN'S LIFE AND IDEAS

I
Creative Writer to Historian
1766 – 1800

Prin also?

On 28 September 1803, after almost two decades of remarkably successful and prolific literary activity, Nicholas Karamzin applied to Alexander I for the rank of Imperial Historiographer. He was granted that position a month later, and so gave up purely literary writing in order to compile a national history, a task which he expected to finish in five years but which was not fully completed at the time of his death twenty-three years later.

Karamzin had been fascinated by history from his youth and so the transition to historical writing was in keeping with his general frame of mind. His interest in such matters had been accelerated by the flowering of national consciousness in Russia during the final decade of Catherine II's reign. Attracted by the nationalist ideas of his contemporaries, the writers Novikov, Fonvizin, Sumarokov, and Kheraskov and the historians Boltin and Shcherbatov, Karamzin found it easy to take up the current pastime of looking to the past in order to find some meaning for his nation in the present. But the initial stimuli for the 'sudden' turn to historical writing were political events in post-1789 Europe. The widespread insecurity of the revolutionary era and the seeming instability of society everywhere forced both the liberally and conservatively inclined thinkers of the time to come to grips with their feelings about existing social and political structures. Karamzin turned to history to find his answers, but not before he had already drawn certain conclusions about the society in which he hoped to live.[1]

The change in interest was also in keeping with the finalization of Karamzin's attitude towards the purpose of literature in general, and of historical writing in particular. By the turn of the century, he had become convinced that, to be good, all literature must have a pragmatic aim. As the contemporary political scene became more and more chaotic in Europe and despotic in Russia after 1789, his faith in the value of literature as an educative medium, his strong nationalism, and his self-confidence as a writer evolved to such an extent that he felt duty-bound to use his talents to advise Russian rulers and people alike. Indeed, for Karamzin, the turn to history was not merely a product of political or patriotic zealousness; rather it marked the finalization of his *Weltanschauung*. The subsequent body of writing that came from Karamzin was in itself a plea for national policies that would produce truly educated men and an enlightened, patriotic citizenry.

Born into a provincial gentry family near Buzuluko in 1766, Karamzin spent most of his youth near Simbirsk, on the Volga River.[2] His father, who had obtained the rank of captain in the military branch of state service, lived comfortably although not in wealthy circumstances. He had foresight enough to provide his sons with a western-type education, but not of the superficial, boorish kind lampooned so bitterly by Kantemir, Fonvisin, and Pushkin. Young Nicholas came into contact with German and French cultures at a very early age, and at the same time was constantly in touch with Russian tradition as it was exemplified by the provincial nobility. Thus, when he moved to Moscow in the eighties he was well suited to the pro-Russian, anti-Voltairian, but still western-looking cultural milieu of that city.

According to his own account, the early years in the provinces instilled in him a healthy respect for his class, a 'middle' gentry from which he professed to have 'borrowed Russian friendliness, the spirit of Russia, and a pride ... [he] later did not find among the upper nobility.' It was also from members of the local gentry, many of whom were accustomed to meeting at his father's home for conversation, that he claimed to have derived an interest in Russian history. He was later to recall the emphasis in those discussions on 'anecdotes of the past,'[3] on the glories of ancient Russia, and about the inspiration such tales gave to him. Of all the noteworthy experiences of his early days, however, the one that remained implanted on his mind for the longest time was an incident that he rarely mentioned, the Pugachev rebellion of 1774-5. That event, which nearly brought disaster to his family, was the first of a number of large-scale upheavals which helped determine his social and political viewpoint, but had meaning for him only as part of a series of major occurrences. Seen later in the light of the French Revolution, Napoleon's invasion of Russia, and the Decembrist Revolt, the Pugachev affair appeared to Karamzin as part of a natural, but irrational, side of life that could only be avoided by the creation of an educated citizenry.

In the late seventies, Karamzin was sent to Moscow, where he studied for a few years in a private school run by a German, J.M. Schaden, who was at the same time a professor at the University of Moscow. According to I.I. Dmitriev (1760-1837), a Russian poet and long-time friend of Karamzin, Schaden was 'one of the best professors' of that institution. He was also singled out for praise as a lecturer and as a fine man by Fonvisin and I.F. Timkovsky. Yet, though Karamzin once said of Schaden that 'he loved me and I loved him,' it is still difficult, if not impossible, to estimate the degree to which the teacher impressed his own ideas upon the pupil. It is probable, however, that Schaden's faith in education as the means to most ends, his interest in the past, and above all, his monarchical views were absorbed by Karamzin. If nothing else, Karamzin learned German and French and was made aware of most of the intellectual trends then sweeping Europe.[4]

After a short period of military service and a brief stay at home in Simbirsk, Karamzin returned to Moscow in early 1785 to act as a translator for the Friendly Learned Society (Druzheskoe uchenoe obshchestvo), a group dominated by N.I. Novikov (1744-1818), J.G. Schwartz (d 1784), and their Freemason colleagues. Although many systems of thought were embraced by members of the society, the two main ones were a highly mystical sentiment sponsored by Schwartz and A.M. Kutuzov (1749-97), and a more pragmatic position on life taken by Novikov. Consistent to both these points of view was the belief that the key to Russia's future lay in a forward-looking educational system.[5]

The Freemason movement in Moscow had taken its strength partly in reaction against the atheistic and skeptical overtones of eighteenth-century rationalism, and partly in reaction against the somewhat superficial posturing of the St Petersburg Masons. It became a centre for an attack on the preponderance of foreign customs, especially French ones, in St Petersburg's social life. Following the initiative of European pre-Romantics and idealists, its members stressed the need to rehabilitate the ancient culture of their native land. While giving lip service to what government officials came to believe were subversive, liberal views, most Russian Masons had been so shocked by Pugachev's rebellion that they did not demand any striking changes in the current class structure. Their most uniform social ambition involved little more than the addition of an humanitarian face to existing institutions. They idealized the Russian peasantry in their writings but did not suggest that they be raised above their bonded station. Freedom and happiness were matters of the soul, they said, and so need not be discussed in real terms. For the Moscow Freemasons, the republicanism that they praised in their musings represented a utopia in which there were no vices or evil men, and which had little connection with contemporary dialogue about political equality. Karamzin's associates were far removed in spirit from the 'repentant' noblemen of Alexander Radishchev's (1749-1802) ilk, although they travelled in the same circles and read virtually the same literature.

Karamzin came into contact with most of the cross-currents of enlightened and mystical beliefs of his time and was immensely impressed by the intellectual ferment of Moscow. Novikov's vast and exciting publishing enterprises, the struggle of M.M. Kheraskov (1733-1809) and others to create a national literature, the constant battle against foreign influences in dress and language, sporadic attempts to portray the national history, an atmosphere of philanthropic reformism and its inevitable self-righteousness, all made Moscow an exciting place in which to live. The very timeliness of Karamzin's arrival in that city, before the lid was put on by Catherine, was certainly one of the most fortunate happenstances of his life.

Swayed by Rousseau and by Herder, almost all of the Masons in Moscow, and particularly Novikov, were interested in Russian history, ancient legends, ballads, and popular myths. The attention given to the Russian past by Moscovites must have been to Karamzin's liking, for M.P. Pogodin reported that the future historian already in the 1780s was conscious of antiquity, 'often used legends ... and made analogies to the ancient world. Russian history also attracted his attention and he was well versed in its main events, probably from Tatishchev, Shcherbatov, Boltin ... Müller and Novikov.'[6] Some of Karamzin's early works did reveal knowledge at least of V.N. Tatishchev and G.F. Müller, but it was undoubtedly the proximity to Novikov that made him more than usually aware of Russia's history.[7]

Among Novikov's many publications was *Readings for Children* (*Detskoe chtenie*), a journal in which he proposed history and fables as the best means to enlighten the youth of Russia and by which he tried to foster in them a sense of Russian patriotism.[8] Founded in 1785, the *Readings for Children* was apparently co-edited by Karamzin and his friend, A.A. Petrov (d 1793), during its last years, 1787-9. In it, young Karamzin expressed complete agreement with Novikov's aim and, like him, bewailed the fact that 'our readers are probably more practised in the study of the French language than in Russian.' Karamzin continued, 'the study of good French books ... is fine for children; we hope, however, that they read more Russian books.'[9] He was not simply following Novikov's editorial guidelines on this topic, for this was to be a consistently recurring idea in his own works.

A number of well-qualified Russian writers in the nineteenth century credited Novikov for much of Karamzin's intellectual progress. Ivan Dmitriev and Pogodin, two of Karamzin's most ardent admirers, were the first to testify to Novikov's overall contribution to Karamzin's education. A. Nezelenov and the famous Slavophile, Khomiakov, attributed most of Karamzin's historical consciousness to Novikov; another Slavophile, Ivan Kireevsky, claimed that the latter writer provided the young student with taste and with a 'philosophy'; the social critic, N.G. Chernyshevsky, said that Karamzin was educated by the famous publisher. But these assumptions were rarely given analytic support by their proponents and, at first sight anyway, Novikov would not appear to have made any appreciable impression on Karamzin's political outlook.

What Novikov and his colleagues did bring to Karamzin, however, was the framework for the maturation of his social and political

viewpoint. They brought him into contact with the humanistic notions that were permeating the aristocratic and near-aristocratic
societies of his time. By the 1780s, in Russia at any rate, the practical
musings of the Philosophes and the more revolutionary trends of the
Enlightenment had become intertwined with a growing religiosity, so
that the rampant rationalism that came from France in the mid-eighteenth century was being slowly submerged by mysticism. The aristocracy, after all, could hardly be expected to carry the new ideas
beyond that certain point where their intellectual pursuits challenged
their own way of life. Karamzin, as a young and exceedingly active
thinker, found himself at the crossroads between the reforming bent
of Novikov and the mystical leanings of his own class. He spent the
next fifteen years trying to find a comfortable mean between these
two directions.

In political matters Karamzin held some opinions that were at
complete variance to those of Novikov, particularly in his feelings
about the nature of government and on the validity of serfdom. In
another of his publications, *Moscow Gazette* (*Moskovskie vedomosti*),
Novikov had supported the American republicans in their war against
the British monarchy and had implied disapproval of serfdom.[10]
Karamzin, on reading accounts of the American Revolution while in
Schaden's school, had demonstrated a preference for the British
cause[11] and rarely suggested anything but behavioural changes in the
relationship between serfs and their landlords. Still, both believed in
a republic of the Platonic type, that is, a society guided by an educated élite, where people could live passively and in harmony with
those who were best trained to govern them. In his later writings,
Karamzin often praised Novikov for his tenacity in advocating enlightenment and in 1790 'sang in praise of Nikander [Novikov] when
he, defenceless, was the defender of truth....'[12]

Novikov's constant attention to the matter of educating Russia's
youth could not help but have a lasting meaning for Karamzin. In
1783, the same year in which Catherine prescribed a text for schools
entitled, *On the Duties of Man and Citizen*, Novikov printed an essay,
'On the Upbringing and Instruction of Children.' No advocate of
social mobility here, he drew a picture of proper upbringing with
which Catherine could have no quarrel. Proper education, he said,
should instill in Russia's youth an 'inclination to virtue, a habit of

order ... a patriotic feeling, a noble national pride ... a contempt for weakness and [ostentation] ... Men and women must be educated according to their sex, and each particular class of society must be taught to fulfill its proper function.' His argument for education in the face of increasing government restrictions was typically Masonic, for he insisted that education would help preserve and not undermine the status quo. It would make autocracy work. In a fully educated society, he wrote, 'the laws will be universally obeyed ... and citizens of every class will be true to their station in life.' Like Rousseau and so many of his enlightened contemporaries, Novikov believed that a child began life with a blank mind, which need only be moulded as if from a lump of clay. The aim of pedagogy, then, is to 'educate the children to be happy people and useful citizens.' The degree of knowledge which a child should be granted depended upon the social class to which he belonged, 'for the benefit of the state and his own contentment.'[13] Karamzin subscribed to these principles throughout his life.

Furthermore, there can be no doubt that the historicism of Novikov's writing, which had the parallel aims of reviving Russian national feeling and of subverting 'Gallomania,' also made a considerable impression upon Karamzin. Both regarded historical writing as the ideal means with which to comment on the present, and their views on education were so similar that, in 1853, L.N. Tolstoi mistakenly attributed to Karamzin an editorial written by Novikov in 1777.[14]

Karamzin's closest friend throughout his life was Dmitriev, whom he first came to know well in 1781.[15] Among others whom he counted as friends were A.A. Petrov, Kutuzov, J. Lenz, and members of the Pleshcheev family. Each of these helped direct his reading and aesthetic interests. Petrov and Kutuzov, who were much more idealistic and mystical than Karamzin ever became, were especially fond of English poetry and drama and it was undoubtedly through them that the younger Karamzin developed a liking for Ossian, Sterne, and Shakespeare. Lenz, a one-time friend of Goethe and a devotee of *Sturm und Drang*, was also inclined toward English works and induced Karamzin's translation of Shakespeare's *Julius Caesar*.[16] Of all his friends from that time, Petrov probably exerted the most influence upon Karamzin's feelings about life and letters. It was probably Petrov, not Novikov, who forced Karamzin to take himself and his work more seriously and it was Petrov who, in 1785, told Karamzin that the only way one could escape the doldrums evoked by political pressure was to busy himself with literary activity and scholarship. Like Karamzin, Petrov was somewhat disenchanted with the abstract notions of his colleagues, and above all else hoped to bring more knowledge to the attention of the Russians. Thus, when Karamzin began to edit the *Moscow Journal* (*Moskovskii zhurnal*) in 1791, Petrov was one of his few former associates who were delighted with the project. He approved because it was 'generally useful.'[17] Petrov consistently emphasized utility and in this way may have been a model for Karamzin's similar inclination at the end of the century. Certainly, Karamzin had no reservations about his debt to Petrov, with whom he spent entire nights reading Ossian, Shakespeare, and Bonnet.[18]

The absence of any well-defined political convictions in Karamzin's writings of the 1780s has been cited often as proof that he looked at life in the same utopian manner as his Masonic friends. But, surely, an apolitical writer at least represents satisfaction with the status quo. As a matter of fact, his translations of Albrecht von Haller's *Vom Ursprung des Übels* (1786), Shakespeare's *Julius Caesar* (1787), and G.E. Lessing's *Emilia Galotti* (1788) each carried a clear, if superficial political message. Along with his own poem, 'Poetry' ('Poeziia,' 1787), they served as precedents for his later tendency to use literature as a lesson-carrying medium. Karamzin was already searching for an explanation of the real world. As he wrote the Swiss philosopher Johann Lavater (1741-1801) in 1788, 'we should observe ... how everything comes about,' not 'how everything might come about.'[19]

Karamzin agreed with Haller's suggestion that all the forces of education and enlightenment should be directed towards creating sensible and virtuous men rather than to changing existing society. Yet he did not accept the accompanying idea that man's free will was the cause of all evil. Foreshadowing his characteristically ambivalent notion of society, Karamzin admitted the potential dangers of free will but added that it was still 'the most precious gift from the creator.' It was in this study as well that Karamzin demonstrated his idealistic impression of the arcadian-like existence of Swiss shepherds who lived in a republic.[20] A similar contradiction appeared in a foreword to his translation of Shakespeare, where he remarked that the 'char-

acter Brutus is best' and implied that a citizen was obligated to overthrow despotism. Although the Russian government was soon to see
this work as an affront to tsarism, the comment was not really intended as a challenge to the existing political system. Although it is
unlikely that he intended any more than praise for Shakespeare's
characterization in this particular instance, Karamzin always managed
to register his displeasure with any irrational use of authority whether
by Jacobins or by autocrats.

It was in 'Poetry' that Karamzin first revealed his views on mankind and enlightenment, and gave early signs of his sense of history.
Exclaiming over the romantic qualities of the past, 'incomparable'
Ossian, and the 'flow' of centuries, he insisted that positive human
qualities had been kept alive since the 'fall of man' only by a few enlightened sages. On this note, he expressed what was to become his
most consistent idea on the value and purpose of literature and, subsequently, history: 'in all countries, holy Poetry is the teacher of
people.' Poetry, by which he meant literature in general, could be the
source and saviour of wisdom which, in turn, would lead to widespread calm and its corollary, human happiness.[21] Herein lay the first
manifestation of Karamzin's desire to harness, by means of the written
word, uneducated man's natural bent for violence. Written two years
before the outbreak of the French Revolution, the worldliness of the
poem demonstrates clearly that Karamzin was not much affected by
the mysticism of Freemasonry. In these years he believed that it had
been poets who had carried and disseminated the wisdom of the ages;
later he was to assign this role to historians and practise it himself.

The political dualism common to Karamzin's first efforts was especially apparent in the translation of *Emilia Galotti*. Illustrating an
ambiguity in his thinking when it came to matters of the state on the
one hand and individual rights on the other, Karamzin expressed a
desire for freedom and justice. But he was convinced of the need for
strong monarchy and law even when it meant sacrificing the rights of
an individual. Agreeing with the main tenets of the play which, for
him, centred on the comment, 'great or small: a ruler is a ruler...,'
Karamzin later utilized it as an example of the way in which literature could be used to shape social mores.[22]

An important medium for Karamzin's general views in the 1780s
was the *Readings for Children*, the first Russian-language journal for

children.[23] The most frequently translated European writer during Karamzin's tenure as editor was Mme de Genlis (1746-1830), from whose writings he adopted a number of tales. Although her works contained what could be construed as 'liberal' phrases, neither she nor the *Readings for Children* attacked the social structure of contemporary Europe; rather they provided a new, 'enlightened' rationale for the status quo. Genlis was fully committed to monarchy and idealized serfdom and hoped for a society in which everyone was morally, if not socially, equal. Complete with stricture against rabid nationalism, her sentiments were remarkably like Karamzin's whole argument of the 1790s in defence of the Enlightenment. Above all, her emphasis on education which, she felt, revealed the 'real differences between people,' paralleled Karamzin's way of thinking. Even in the eighties, when Karamzin was purported by some later writers to be of liberal bent, he rejected political equality because then everyone 'would suffer hunger ... and would not love one another.'[24] In the translations of Genlis's works, to which Karamzin added Russian colour, the predominance of aristocrats in society was justified by their better education and virtue, while those who still lived in slavery did so because for persons 'with many vices ... slavery is almost inevitable.'[25] Even the 'enlightened' members of the eighteenth-century nobility promised more paternalism than social change. The sentimental philanthropy of the journal was spread widely among the children of the gentry, so that Karamzin helped add an aura of legitimacy and righteousness to convictions already taught them in their homes. Like many of her aristocratic friends, Genlis also gave an extremely idyllic picture of peasants who, she said, were happy, independent, and satisfied with simple things and so must not be ruined by being the recipients of 'too much.'[26]

The parallel between the political feelings of Mme Genlis and Karamzin was revealed in his story, 'The Hermit' ('Pustynnik,' 1788), which only recently has been attributed to him. Although expressed indirectly, the author demonstrated a high regard for the British constitutional régime and the Swiss republics, but added that the success of both systems was due not to their form, but to an educated citizenry. The ideal political structure remained enlightened monarchy because it alone provided people with 'reliable tranquility.'[27] Sometime later, Karamzin was to take great pains in his *History of the Russian State* to prove this to be the case for Russia.

In May 1789, Karamzin left Moscow and set out on a trip through Europe that lasted for a year and a half. He later claimed that his aim had been to see 'those great men whose creations had so activated my feelings,'[28] but his main purpose in making the journey remains uncertain. Obviously disturbed by the ever-increasing mysticism of his friends, a dissatisfaction with which he was to proclaim loudly soon after his return, he now wished to embark upon a literary and philosophical career of his own.[29]

It may be, however, that Karamzin had some other reason for so carefully disassociating himself from his former colleagues. The Russia that he left behind was one in which men of letters had standing in society and a certain degree of immunity from political pressures. It was a relatively open society where even the empress would argue and accept, albeit ungraciously, mild reproof from the intellectuals among her subjects. But such days were obviously numbered even before the Revolution in France. By the time Karamzin returned to Moscow, change was readily discernable. The Revolution was the reigning topic for conversation, and the flow of ideas from Europe, which had begun under Catherine's own tutelage, was now regarded by her with considerable suspicion. The new class of emancipated nobility, freed from state service between 1762 and 1785, found that their intellectual diversions held unforeseen dangers. The Masons were suspected of subversive activity by the Russian government and, since it was assumed by many at the time that Karamzin had been sent abroad as an agent of Novikov's society,[30] he felt it necessary to disclaim that impression. It was perhaps for that reason that the *Moscow Journal*, which he founded shortly after his return (September 1790), was advertised as a counter to mysticism.[31]

The attack on mysticism may also have stemmed from the mutual animosity between him and his former associates, many of whom mistrusted Karamzin's newly-found self-confidence. Since he hoped to enlighten Russians by filling the *Moscow Journal* with good foreign literature, he was taken to task for being unpatriotic by the editors of *The Spectator* (*Zritel'*) and by individual Masons like N.N. Trubetskoi, M.I. Bagriansky, and Kutuzov. Even his close friends, the Pleshcheevs, worried that he had become anti-Russian and hoped that he would not publish the journal. In particular, they objected to his proposal to include a serialized description of his Grand Tour.[32]

They need not have worried. The journal had spectacular success and, appearances to the contrary, the tour of Europe had stimulated in Karamzin a latent patriotism and an interest in Russian history. Reacting to the obvious disregard for Russian history on the part of Europeans and realizing the attention given to the national past in those countries which he visited, Karamzin became convinced of the need for a national history of Russia. The *Moscow Journal* was therefore filled with patriotic historical nuances and his monarchist bias was clearly visible. Within a short time, few Masons were suspicious of Karamzin's intentions, at least as far as his patriotism was concerned, and many even became contributors, thereby joining such well-known writers as Derzhavin, Kheraskov, Iu. A. Neledinsky-Meletsky, and Dmitriev. Following Lomonosov, Novikov, and Boltin, Karamzin hoped to stimulate national consciousness[33] by praising Russia's past, but still could see the advantage of European examples. It was for this concerted, and largely successful, early effort that Prince P.A. Viazemsky later was to praise him for breaching the 'Chinese wall that separates us from Europe.'[34] Karamzin, then, was part of a new generation of Russians who were able to combine rational westernism with an awareness of the singular needs, characteristics, and history of their own nation.

Only twenty-five years old when he began editing the *Moscow Journal*, Karamzin was self-confident enough, or, as his enemies and even some of his friends insisted, arrogant enough, to give it a clearly educative content. Karamzin had not yet completely formulated his view of life, so his advice to readers was not always consistent, nor was the extent to which it was political very obvious. But, at the risk of appearing too selective, one can turn to his review of Jean Jacques Barthélemy's seven-volume *Voyage du jeune Anacharsis en Grèce dans le milieu du quatrième Siècle avant l'Ère vulgaire* for a preview of the way in which he was to use literature to shape the thinking of his readers.[35] Spread over three issues, this review marked the first time that Karamzin used history to illustrate an important political contention, ie, that republics, in this case Athens, are inevitably doomed to failure because of their susceptibility to demagoguery. In fact, the periodical had a constant political and didactic tone and Karamzin's image of his own role as editor and main contributor was perhaps best exemplified by his inscription for book seven, taken from Shaftesbury:

> *Poets, in the early days, were look'd upon as authentic sages, for dictating rules of life, and teaching manners and good sense; how they may have lost their pretensions, I cannot say.*

Dominating the *Moscow Journal* (1791-2) were his famous *Letters of a Russian Traveller* (*Pis'ma russkago puteshestvennika*), the promised observations on Europe. For Karamzin, the *Letters* had, among other things, an aim to instruct.[36] He described in them foreign values, customs, literature, ideas, and art, and used these descriptions to convey lessons to his readers. The *Letters* form an important part of the body of European and Russian sentimental literature; they also show us the gradual maturation of Karamzin the political thinker. Since the *Letters* were written, rewritten, and revised over the entire decade 1791-1801, they reflect both the beginnings and the finalization of his attempt to formulate a consistent world view for himself.

His conclusions, or lessons, fall into two general categories. The first was political and his message in that regard was simply that no country could be a model for another when it came to political systems. All political forms except anarchy were valid, but only autocracy was suitable for Russia. By the time that he published his last letter, Karamzin had decided that even the English system, which he admired, 'would be bad in another country.'[37] His second general lesson, which like the first permeated all his writings, was that only enlightenment can provide a panacea for the ills of mankind. By enlightenment Karamzin meant education in citizenship; the subject must learn how and why to obey, the monarch must learn to rule firmly and wisely. In this regard, the pages of the *Moscow Journal*, in a somewhat faltering way, carried the premises that became the very essence of his periodical of the next decade, the *Messenger of Europe* (*Vestnik evropy*).

Especially significant for an understanding of why Karamzin was to concentrate on historical writing during the nineteenth century were the constant, if oblique, signs of political awareness throughout the *Letters*. There were no references whatsoever to the French Revolution until a letter dated 29 July, when he had already passed through Prussia and Switzerland, fifteen days after the fall of the Bastille. So the first parts of this publication have frequently been used to support the hypothesis that he was indifferent to contemporary political events. Yet it was in these very years that he first began to demonstrate the 'liberal-conservative' premises that were the essence of his subsequent political attitude.

It has been pointed out in a fairly recent study that politics were of little concern to most Russians of Karamzin's class and education.[38] But this does not mean that they were indifferent to the larger question of the political order. Though Karamzin consciously encouraged the former impression himself, an important clue to his real turn of mind appeared in one of the first of the *Letters*, in which he outlined what he felt were the ideal qualities in a monarch. On making judgements about the relative merits of rulers, Karamzin maintained 'one must consider only those acts which benefit the state ... not erudition, wit, or authorship.' Following up this none-too-subtle allusion to Catherine II he added in pure Machiavellian that 'kings do not act according to those rules which must be the law for us private citizens,'[39] to show that he had no reservations about monarchy as the best guardian of Russia's interest. Even the offhandedness of his initial reference to the French Revolution was belied in the same letter by a review of Schiller's play, *Fiesco*. In that work, a citizen waivers between remaining loyal to his monarchical fatherland and participating in an attempt to turn it into a republic. To a certain extent, *Fiesco* had as a theme the inevitable decline of republics into some form of tyranny, so Karamzin demanded, unequivocally, 'Choose the first!'[40]

Karamzin's concern with the political order was hardly surprising. He had already pondered the seeming contradictions of life and nature of the eighties, as his correspondence with Lavater attests. In Schaden's school, and with his friends, he had studied German and English literature, through which he gained some immunity to the temptations of French-style enlightenment. The doctrine of natural law as it was interpreted by the philosophers of German *Aufklärung* stressed the duties and obligations which individuals had in their societies. Rights were described by them as privileges to be earned by the fulfillment of responsibilities towards one's fellow man. Karamzin and most of Russia's noblemen easily adopted such a doctrine of man in society, for service had long been part of their cultural and social heritage. Furthermore, the major proponents of German philosophy had been taught in Russia's schools ever since Peter I had become so intrigued with the writings of Pufendorf, Wolff, and Leibnitz. Peter had ordered the translation of Pufendorf's *De Officiis hominis* in 1724, and it appeared in Russian as *On the Duties of Man and Citizen* (*O dolzhnostiakh cheloveka i grazhdanina*) two years later. Wolff and Leibniz had advised the emperor on educational matters, and all three were constantly referred to by Russia's educators throughout the century.

In Karamzin's day, the pre-romantic concept of nature being made up of competing good and evil forces and of the existence of fate as an irrational power inclined many towards a faith in a firm, ordered political community which could keep the destructive side of man's nature in check. Their anxieties and their assumptions were confirmed with a vengeance when the French Revolution deteriorated into anarchy and terror.

In the same issue of the *Moscow Journal* in which he reviewed Schiller's play, Karamzin also examined Voltaire's *Henriade*. It is coincidental, but nonetheless interesting, that Catherine II wrote Melchior Grimm that year (1791) and told him that she had been reading *Henriade* and hoped that the French 'ragamuffins' would do the same thing. Both Karamzin and his empress believed that the message of the poem lay in its dedication to Henry IV, the 'hero who ruled over France' by right of conquest and birth and who calmed it in a time of division and chaos. Catherine wished for a new Henry and predicted that republicanism would merely arouse a desire on the part of Frenchmen for a return to monarchy. Karamzin was later to announce that very circumstance, which he also believed to be inevitable, in the *Messenger of Europe*.[41]

Before arriving in France, Karamzin wrote that he had sensed with distaste an authoritarian and military aura in the Prussian state. In contrast, the *Letters* seemed to go to extremes in their enthusiasm for freedom when he arrived in Switzerland from Germany.[42] Commenting favourably on the democratic atmosphere at Basel and praising it as a republic 'undistrubed by tyrannical passions,' Karamzin went on to divulge his interpretation of true republicanism and liberty while in Zurich and in Berne. In those Swiss communities, the epithet 'citizen' applied to a small group of people, so that democracy was in reality a privilege reserved for a minority.[43] At all times, Karamzin kept the reader conscious of the potential dangers of unbridled freedom, intimating that lack of control in the republics would lead to ultimate disaster. He even belittled the Genevan republic as a 'plaything.'[44] In an aside on poorly-disciplined Swiss children, he said that 'the young imps will grow up in time and will scatter in their homeland a perilous moral disease from which ... freedom perishes in republics.' Karamzin expressed this opinion in 1791.[45]

After a few months in Switzerland, Karamzin lamented that the only immediate concern of wealthy Swiss was whether or not they would lose money invested in France. Complaining that the Swiss were so absorbed with material things that they were not even 'aware of the fact that Russia and Sweden are at war,' he actually regretted having left Germany.[46] The idyllic republican bubble had obviously been broken as far as he was concerned.

The nature and validity of republicanism was a recurring topic in the *Moscow Journal* and, indeed, throughout Karamzin's other publications. In March 1791, he reviewed Thomas More's *Utopia* and suggested that a republic of the Platonic type may well be an ideal worth striving for, but that there was little likelihood of one ever surviving in real life.[47] Karamzin was quite plainly anxious over the disorder implicit in the events in France, but not yet worried enough to condemn the Revolution. A favourable note on Benjamin Franklin, published in December 1791, substantiates this impression. Most Russians of his class were apprehensive over the implications of revolution, and they were still reeling from the furor sparked by Radishchev's *Journey from St Petersburg to Moscow* and his subsequent imprisonment. Karamzin, however, was quite willing to ignore the Radishchev case and to praise Benjamin Franklin for giving 'freedom to almost all of America.'[48]

In a recent article, A.G. Cross has shown how the idyll, *Palemon and Dafnis* (1791), was actually intended as a warning to Karamzin's countrymen not to fall into the same trap as the French had done. Cross interpreted the idyll as a plea to Russians to be content with the status quo.[49] Yet Karamzin continued to claim indifference to political events. He was 'bored' when regaled with tales of the storm-ing of the Bastille, and later was to insist that he had looked 'on the excitement with a quiet mind.'[50] At a time when most of the Russian press was attacking French republicans, Karamzin promised informa-tion from the *Mercure de France* and reported on French drama and books, several of which were critical of church and nobility under the *ancien régime*.[51] He even reviewed a work on the taking of the Bastille, although he suggested that it would be of little interest to anyone outside Paris.[52] Similarly, he criticized a play in Lyons for so overdramatizing contemporary events that they would 'bore anyone, even the French.'[53]

In 1792, Karamzin favourably reviewed Comte de Volney's *Les Ruines ou méditations sur les révolutions des empires* (1791) and a study on Rousseau by L.S. Mercier. Both condemned institutions of the *ancien régime* whose counterparts were still considered sacred in Russia.[54] Karamzin was not yet cowed by growing repression in Rus-sia, a fact illustrated by scarcely veiled criticism of government prac-tices in several short poems.[55] In one of them, he praised Rousseau and incurred the wrath of some Freemasons and of the government for what seemed to be an irreligious attitude.[56]

Although he appeared calm enough about events in Europe, Karamzin began looking into Russia's past with the expressed hope of finding some tradition of order that might prove any similar anar-chism to be irrelevant for his own country. Simultaneously, he began to demonstrate his particular brand of nationalism, which included a healthy respect for the qualities of both Russian and Western cultural and political development. His frequent references to the brotherhood of man and his description of himself as a 'citizen of the world' are sometimes cited as evidence of cosmopolitanism, yet the *Letters* were replete with Russian national feeling. Though rankled by overheard conversations between two Germans who, 'out of boredom, began attacking the Russian nation,' Karamzin's nationalism was still always tempered by a faith in the European Enlightenment. Like Novikov and Boltin before him, and moderate Westernizers of the nineteenth century, Karamzin applauded Peter I for strengthening Russia and also for introducing Western ideas and techniques to his homeland.[57] This type of nationalism, which aimed for Russian greatness rather than uniqueness, remained a basic theme of Karamzin's writings.

His own tales in the journal indicate his interest in Russian history far more clearly than the sporadic comments in the *Letters*. For example, Karamzin based the story 'Bird of Paradise' ('Raiskaja ptichka,' 1791)[58] on what he believed to be an ancient Russian ballad. *Liodor* (1792)[59] contained a highly nationalistic and romantic evaluation of the Russian past when, he said, the Russian *dvoriane* had 'more characteristic firmness ... than now, when we pursue the blessings of other countries and abandon everything that God hoped would separate us from peoples of other lands ... they have stopped being themselves.'[60] In that same year, he opened *Natalie, the Boyar's Daughter* (*Natal'ia, Boiarskaja doch'*) with the comment, 'who of us does not love those times when the Russians were Russians, when they dressed up in their own hats ... spoke their own language ... and said what they thought?'[61] Hoping to demonstrate his knowledge of ancient Russia, he actually called the tale a 'history,' but the historical tone of the piece did not go beyond allusions to Tsar Alexei Mikhailovich, a revolt in Moscow, and some historical allusions in Karamzin's footnotes. In one of several asides to readers, he qualified an emotional scene by informing them that 'in such a case, I move away from the historical truth on which my tale is based.'[62] Concluding the story with a reference to some ancient script on a tombstone, he gave a realistic atmosphere to the tale. In reality, he was following the not too uncommon urge to hark back to the good old days.[63] National-historical themes notwithstanding, the tales were dominated by the sentimental, self-righteous moralizing which was typical of many of his fellow writers among the gentry. Still, even if he had not intended the historical aspects of the tales to prevail, it is of some significance that a contemporary reader spoke of him as 'the man who beautified the past centuries by his talents.'[64]

In the second year of its publication, Karamzin placed one purely historical article in the *Moscow Journal* and used it to illustrate a political lesson. In this short note he dealt with a real event, that is, the relationship between James II of England and Louis XIV of France and the influence that association had on William III's ability to hold the crown of England. The story was a unique one for Russia at that time since it pointed out the dangers of one ruler recognizing a claimant to a foreign throne without respecting the wishes of the people in that country. Karamzin insisted that, by recognizing James II's son,

Louis xiv had helped strengthen William and assure the success of 'revolution' in England.[65]

His interest in Russia's past and in the role of monarch and nobility in history was not isolated musing. Most of Europe's thinkers, Russia's included, were turning these matters over at least in their own minds. In Russia the debate had been going on since Catherine's commission of 1767 and had been accelerated by the Charter of the Nobility in 1785. Much of this discussion came to a head in the early nineties in the Boltin-Shcherbatov polemics over Russian history. Boltin, who translated Diderot's *Encyclopédie* for Catherine, had attacked the French historian, LeClerc, in 1789 for the uncomplimentary history he had written of Russia. Boltin then began a series of responses to the *History of Russia* written by Shcherbatov, who had sponsored LeClerc. Both Russians extolled pre-Petrine tradition and compared it favourably with Western development. But Boltin saw the historical necessity of absolute monarchy in Russia and even rationalized Ivan iv's actions against the nobility. Shcherbatov defended the role of the nobility in Russian history. The latter writer insisted in his historical work and in a number of essays that monarch and nobility must act together for the sake of Russian security and greatness. Boltin was convinced that the present-day political system in his nation was the natural and proper consequence of uniquely Russian circumstances. Shcherbatov believed that there had been an unnatural development in his homeland since Peter's time, when the nobility had become servants instead of respected participants in affairs of state. Karamzin, too, was worried in these years about the paradox of Russian history being written mainly by foreigners. In the *Letters* he had spoken of his meeting in 1790 with the French historian Pierre Charles Levesque, who had written an *Histoire de la Russie* in 1783. Complaining that Russia still had no adequately written history of its own, he admitted that Levesque's study, 'despite its faults,' was the best to date. He went on to say that Russian history was every bit as fascinating as that of the West and, if written with 'intelligence, taste, and talent,' would be attractive to Russians and foreigners. Levesque, Karamzin said, could not write of Russians with feeling because he was not Russian. Moreover, he had belittled Peter i by saying that 'il n'a su qu'imiter les autres peuples.'[66]

In the midst of the Shcherbatov-Boltin discussion, the last traces of Karamzin's casualness about social and political matters disappeared. The bloodbath in France during the autumn of 1792, the abolition of monarchy and, the final blow, regicide, ended for a time whatever abstract sympathy he might have had for the Revolution. During the following year, Robespierre undertook a policy of terror and the French queen was beheaded. The entire framework of established order in Europe, and the humanistic trends which Karamzin had so admired, were at the point of dissolution. His response was to turn to nationalism on the one hand and to the easy role of moralizer on the other. He blamed the crisis on a lack of moral strength in European society, and hoped it could be revitalized in Russia by examples from the past or by increased education, his now limited synonym for enlightenment.[67]

In 1793, Karamzin continued those themes begun in *Liodor* and *Natalie*. He wrote a series of poems in which he was openly patriotic and fascinated by ancient Russia. In one he boasted of the Volga, 'where rotting corpses told of the miseries of ancient Russians; but where now one people lives in calmness and, everywhere, honour one Goddess; the Goddess of happiness and glory.' Further, he exclaimed in *To the Fatherland* (*K otechestvu*) that 'death is nothing when fetters and shame threaten your sons.'[68] He also acted to defend the European Enlightenment against charges that it had inspired the villainies then permeating society. Reasoning that no one could prove such an hypothesis 'historically,' he went on to show that the collapse of the Roman Empire had not been, as some Russian conservatives suggested, a result of too much education. The source of all the villainy in Europe was idleness, love for luxury, and the inclination toward violence, all of which could be tempered by proper education.

Coupled with a growing historical consciousness, the sections of *Letters* that appeared in the *Moscow Journal* had also reflected his pessimistic mood about political events in Europe. Karamzin now began to look upon pre-Petrine Russia as Boltin had done, with a far less jaundiced eye than most of his contemporaries, many of whom still felt that Russian history began with Peter I. Late in 1792, the *Letters* also began to express his bitterness at events in France. Letters from Paris revealed a dislike of contemporary French manners and lack of discipline. Attributing to Frenchmen 'flighty' and 'insincere' characteristics, he went on to condemn in very Herderian terms what he felt was their proclivity for mob action: 'there is only one comfort ... that with the fall of nations, all human tribes do not fall; one yields its place to another and if Europe is ruined, then in the middle of Africa or in Canada there will blossom a new political society.' He was especially critical of changes in Paris, which he attributed to a loss of 'traditional values.'[69] Despite professions of boredom with the topic of revolution, Karamzin continued to emphasize the dangers of it, declaring in letters from Paris dated April 1790, but published and probably written in 1792, that most Frenchmen were against the revolution and that 'the people still love the royal family.'[70] In the mid-nineties he had, somehow, to solve the contradiction between his great admiration for enlightenment and his growing suspicion that the French Revolution may have been one of its consequences.

Faced by the same dilemma that had confounded the so-called 'Enlightened Despots,' that of a contradiction between a respect for knowledge and a desire to protect the royal prerogatives, Catherine ii had broken with the practice of enlightenment, if not necessarily with its ideals. Karamzin, however loyal he was to the institutions of the Russian Empire, could not follow his empress in this.[71] When Novikov was arrested in 1792, Karamzin was the only important literary figure in Russia to plead his cause, but the poem 'To Mercy' ('K milosti'), which was ostensibly written in the famous publisher's defence, was more a plea for the whole concept of rational and enlightened monarchy than an attack on Catherine's policy.[72] The central theme of his writings for this whole period was therefore an evaluation of the merits of the European Enlightenment.

Two articles published in his almanac, *Aglaia*, in 1794, 'What Does an Author Need?' ('Chto nuzhno avtoru?') and 'Something about Sciences, Arts and Enlightenment' ('Nechto o naukakh, iskusstvakh i prosveshchenii'), dealt with the problem of enlightenment and with the obligations of writers who, alone, could interpret it for the reading public. Ending the first essay with the statement that 'an evil man cannot be a good author,' Karamzin insisted that a writer of quality must not be a 'useless' one, rather he should work to achieve the 'general welfare.'[73] In the second article, he argued against Rousseau and proclaimed that 'Enlightenment is the palladium of good behav-

iour.'[74] More than any other, this treatise was a defence of knowledge
and moral standards, which, in Karamzin's opinion, were the only
means by which man could fulfill his desire to 'live calmly ... and
pleasantly.' Equating the term 'enlightenment' with 'education,' he
echoed Novikov in the idea that, far from subverting civil order, enlightenment had strengthened Catherine's state.[75] Since this was written after the execution of Louis XVI, it can be taken as a sign of
Karamzin's willingness to protect the principles and institutions of
widespread general education from government reaction.

The article also provided further evidence of Karamzin's trust in
the complementary character of enlightenment and true autocracy.
Claiming that education 'quenches the thirst of rulers and slaves alike
... the enlightened farmer does not envy the fortune of a Satrap,' he
recommended that the monarch use it to mould 'better men and
peaceful citizenry.' Karamzin assigned to literature in general and to
authors in particular the task of teaching men to love their fatherland
and to seek out the 'truth.' He assumed that after accomplishing this
aim men could live safely even in a republican state.[76] A particularly
prolific writer at this time, he seemed to be practising his own
speeches, or at least following Petrov's advice that only literary work
could tide one over difficult times.

On closing the *Moscow Journal*, Karamzin had promised his readers that the *Letters* would be completed in *Aglaia*,[77] but the drastic
turn of events in France forced him to withhold all of what he had
written except a few letters from Paris. Remarking on the 'sad
times'[78] in which he lived, the 'horrible events in Europe,'[79] and some
depressing government sanctions against his own publications, Karamzin began to describe his impressions of Europe in a less direct manner. In the first book of *Aglaia*, he wrote a tale from the point of
view of a Russian traveller who was in England, on the last leg of a
long journey, and who now longed for the solitude and security of
his homeland. In an epitaph to Petrov, who died in 1793, he projected a 'history of [my] thoughts' about the time before he had gone
to Europe.[80] Nevertheless, he did not intend his readers to lose sight
of current events. In 'Athenian Life' ('Afinskaia zhizn',' 1795),[81] he
spoke of classical history but contrasted the intellectual freedom of
ancient Athens with the 'mindless horrors of our enlightened contemporaries.'[82] Though the epithet 'mindless' was obviously aimed at

European Jacobins, it did not mean that Karamzin had committed himself to the camp of reaction. Indeed, the theme of 'Il'ia of Murom' ('Il'ia Muromets') could well be represented as a Don Quixotic rebuke of tyranny.[83]

In 1795, Karamzin published his first serious discussion over the advantages and disadvantages of the European Enlightenment. Written in late 1793, it reflected the anguish of his mental confusion, and, undoubtedly, that of many of his contemporaries. Presented in the form of two letters, 'Melodor to Filalet' and 'Filalet to Melodor,' the discussion posed the essential intellectual question of the time: 'Is it possible,' said Melodor, 'that the human species has advanced ... to the pinnacle of enlightenment ... only to be compelled to fall back ... into the depths of barbarism ... like Sisyphus' stone?' Must man, in his moral growth, follow a cyclical path, 'always interchanging truth and error, virtue and vices?' Karamzin answered his own queries in the words of Filalet: 'Perhaps what seems like some great disorder to mortals is a wonderful harmony to angels ... the destiny of mankind is not eternal delusion ... people will sometime cease to torment themselves and each other.' Falling back on the notion of a higher order of things, outside human comprehension, was perhaps an easy solution to this intellectual dilemma, but the alternative was too frightening. Without some reason to be optimistic about the future, there could hardly be any reason to live at all. Karamzin thus began to reason that a 'Golden Age' lay in the future and not in the past, and blamed his recent confusion on an 'unwarranted worship of the eighteenth century.' As he put it, 'the present evil will serve the future good'; a similar optimism was to sustain him until his death.[84]

Deciding that all was not lost because 'virtue was still a characteristic of mankind,' Karamzin added that some kind of leadership was necessary if human virtue was to be successfully reaffirmed. In 'Athenian Life,' he had praised the instructive role of rhetoricians and poets in ancient Greece, implying that leadership had to emanate from men of letters like himself.[85] A more definitive answer to the Melodor-Filalet dialogue appeared in 'Conversation about Happiness' ('Razgovor o shchastii,' 1797), where he insisted that a man need not resent his lot in life, and blamed contemporary hardships on those who tried to speed up the natural process of things. Once more,

Karamzin used historical characters (Attila the Hun, Alexander the Great) to corroborate his point.

It was in these years that Karamzin, possibly unconsciously, had come to recognize the immensely valuable role that history could play as propaganda. In a 1795 collection of translations called *Miscellany*, he included the essay, 'The Deliberations of a Philosopher, an Historian, and a Citizen' ('Rassuzhdenie filosofa, istorika i grazhdanina'), which A.G. Cross attributes to Karamzin himself. In this piece, Karamzin showed contempt for the philosopher who disassociates himself from the practical world, and praised the historian who looks to the past in order to comprehend the present. In Cross's words, Karamzin saw 'history providing a powerful, corrective moral force: it [the essay] is an anticipation of the burden of the *History of the Russian State*.'

The European crises had forced Karamzin to come to grips with the specific problems of life in Russia. Of many domestic issues, the two most pressing were the fate of serfdom and the question as to what might be the best political form for the Russian state. These matters had become particularly important to those Russian thinkers who were torn between love for their country and an awareness of its inherent weaknesses.

A prevailing idea in Karamzin's writings was an idealization of the character and circumstances of Russian peasantry. He had romanticized the relationship between peasant and landowner in 'A Village Holiday and Wedding' ('Sel'skii prazdnik i svad'ba,' 1791), praised the simple farmer in 'Frol Silin' (1791), and portrayed a hard-working, contented peasant in *Poor Liza* (1792), his most famous tale of the nineties. The same motif was repeated in 'Tender Friendship in the Lower Estate' ('Nezhnost' druzhby v nizkom sostoiannii,' 1793), where Karamzin had a peasant reply affirmatively when her mistress asked whether she was 'completely happy in her circumstances ...'[86] Karamzin was well aware of the vice and drunkenness among Russian peasants, and he assumed that peasants were not emotionally equipped to be free. But he did not see these characteristics as innate ones, for they could be cured by enlightenment.[87]

It was this image that he expanded in 'Something about Learning' and which became the writer's basic contention after the turn of the century. Furthermore, in 'Conversation about Happiness' he intimated that equality was merely an emotional matter and that one need not have political freedom to be happy anyway. In this regard, then, Karamzin was exemplifying the idea of Mme Genlis and of his former Masonic colleagues, that social or political freedoms were of little significance so long as one had the opportunity to be happy. Only in a well-ordered, benevolent society where people need not worry about affairs of state could such conditions exist. Obviously, Karamzin had renounced his cosmopolitan individualism, and now saw himself and others as a subordinate part of a larger community, the state.

This image of society, which Karamzin was to repeat in the introduction to his *History of the Russian State*, was hardly a unique one. In Catherine's time, prescribed texts informed Russian school children that everyone had his or her place in society, that rank did not determine one's happiness and that it was their duty as citizens and Christians to be satisfied with things as they were. Orthodox church leaders had been expounding this view for centuries. Karamzin had taken a great interest in the slow unfolding of Catherine's attempts to introduce a system of public schooling in Russia. Though she had established committees to study the matter as early as 1763, the turning point in Catherine's work on the activation of a school system in Russia came when Iankovich de Mirievo was recommended to her as an adviser on education by Joseph ii of Austria. The arrival of de Mirievo assured the adoption of the Austrian plan for general education, but the Russian tradition of training the soul first, and determining the morality of its youth so that they might take the right attitude into further studies, remained.

De Mirievo's plan was adopted by a commission set up for this end in 1782, and was the basis for a statute on public education issued in 1786. Besides an outline of subjects to be taught, the statute called for a revision of teaching methods. The main change in technique was the abolition of corporal punishment and other brutalities which students had had to face, and the institution of mass, rote learning. Rather than attempt to work with individual students and beat an education into them, teachers now taught the group as a whole, having them read aloud and reading to them. The complete mastering of textbooks was insisted upon, and teachers were told not to go beyond the texts.[88] This situation remained throughout the nineties.

The clearest expression of Karamzin's belief that only 'enlighten-ment' could fill the needs of the future came in a long and often ignored ode to Paul I in 1796. The poem also serves as a good exam-ple of Karamzin's proneness to employ literature as a means to advise rulers. Claiming that it was the duty of a subject to make suggestions to a tsar, and of the tsar to heed the counsel of wise men, he said that 'whomsoever shows the truth to the ruler ... and gives him good advice, is the one whom [the ruler]calls his friend.' Karamzin tried to persuade Paul to support educational reforms. He exclaimed, 'Ex-ult! Our Paul is a lover of science, the guide for art' – a suggestive exaggeration to say the least. Mindful of the repression during the last years of Catherine's reign, Karamzin also urged Paul to consider legal reforms. Even when he attacked Speransky's proposed code of laws a dozen years later, Karamzin still believed that a rational sys-tem of laws would strengthen, not weaken, autocracy.[89]

Pleased with Paul's accession in 1796, Karamzin had written to Dmitriev that there would now 'be changes' and to his brother that the 'tsar wishes to rule with justice.'[90] He rejoiced that the Freema-sons, Trubetskoi, Lopukhin, and above all, Novikov, were once again in the good graces of the monarchy. An article prepared in 1797 for an émigré journal, Le Spectateur du Nord, which contained exerpts from the Letters not yet published in Russia, also demonstrated a new optimism. According to Karamzin, the Spectateur letters were to be the first in the next publication of the Letters, but when they did appear in Russia four years later, they had been changed consid-erably in tone and content. So had Karamzin's feelings about Paul.

In 1797, Karamzin also published a four-volume edition of the Letters in which earlier letters were altered enough to suggest an in-creasingly unfavourable opinion of the French Revolution. The Spec-tateur excerpts, though, actually recognized that the revolution marked a new epoch in history, and not necessarily a bad one. Karam-zin did say, once again, that inconsistency was a characteristic of the French, but at the same time spoke very highly of Rousseau, whom many Russians blamed for the Revolution.[91] The 1801 series of let-ters, which he prepared during the last two years of Paul's reign, rep-resented a totally different point of view. Beginning with the question, 'Shall I speak of the French Revolution?' he answered his own query with the harshest possible denunciation of popular agitation:

Every society which has existed for centuries is sacred to good citizens ...
"Utopia" will always remain the ideal of a good heart or will result from
the imperceptible actions of time, a result of slow, but true, secure suc-
cesses of the mind, enlightenment, education and good morals ... all violent
shocks are ruinous and every rebel prepares his own scaffold ... Careless
minds think that everything is easy; wise men know the danger of any
change and live quietly.

As a final touch, Karamzin added to this creed some extracts from
Rabelais's *Gargantua*, which stressed the self-destructive habits of
ignorant multitudes.[92] In these few short paragraphs, which must
have represented his attitude just before the turn of the century,
Karamzin revealed the political core of his forthcoming *History* and
one of the keys to doctrines of Russian conservative nationalists
throughout much of the nineteenth century.

By the end of the eighteenth century, Karamzin foresaw great
changes in the history of mankind. He had abandoned his escape into
philosophical moralizing and began to take a hard look at the real
world once again. The article in *Spectateur* showed clearly that he
planned to look into history for some explanation of events in
France. He took the opportunity to recommend heroes of ancient
Russia as ideal subject matter for 'chivalrous novels,'[93] an idea around
which he was to write an entire article in 1802. Thus, although he
told Dmitriev that he had no 'farsighted plans,'[94] it seemed that historical writing was already the most natural outlet for the things he
wished to say; from it he could explain the present and direct readers
into actions that would prepare the future. In a letter to Viazemsky
of 1797, Karamzin noted that 'the history of mankind becomes more
interesting century after century ... it seems that important, great
changes are being prepared in the political systems of Europe.' He
hoped to find reasons for contemporary social and political phenomena by turning to 'Hume, Helvétius and Mably.'[95] Repeating ideas
expressed in the *Spectateur*, this letter was even more explicit in suggesting that Karamzin intended to delve into the real events of the
past, rather than into abstract philosophy, for interpreting the present.

Since no one could publish freely in the last years of Paul's reign,
Karamzin's feelings about increasing tyranny at home are available

only in his personal correspondence and, indirectly, in a series of short poems placed in the almanac, *Aonides*.[96] As early as 1794, his translation of *Julius Caesar* had been banned from libraries and by 1797[97] had been completely proscribed. But even though he was one of Russia's leading literati, with a wide, adoring public, Karamzin had not complained too bitterly about censorship until the latter date, when he referred to that institution as a 'black bear' standing in the way of progress.[98] In March 1798, he described elaborate preparations for the publication of the *Pantheon of Foreign Literature* (*Panteon inostrannoi slovestnosti*), in which he hoped to make available to Russian readers all the best ideas of foreign writers. Karamzin clarified his reason for such an enterprise in the study itself when he spoke of enlightenment as a 'moral bridle' that would eventually pave the way for Russian greatness. Until then, 'educated people should be obeyed.' He added that only education separated great people from wild people, and that enlightened people would be more likely to obey laws. In another section of the *Pantheon*, he translated a piece that had the ruler's obligations as a main theme. A monarch can be successful only if he governs with justice and refrains from relying upon force when he wishes his policies to be accepted.[99]

A few months later, Karamzin deplored government action that had forced him to eliminate Demosthenes, Cicero, and Sallust because they were republicans and, by the end of the year, was so frustrated by censorship that he threatened to stop writing. On 12 October, he told Dmitriev that he would 'prefer to give it up altogether than to agree to such an operation' and a year later, moaned 'I wish for only one thing; to die in peace ... My talent is like Siberian fruit, never maturing to wither.' In March 1797, he was still able to say that 'the people dote on the Tsar,' but in the summer of that year, he was sarcastic in a letter to his brother about the ludicrous side of Paul's repression: 'the news here is that we will once again be allowed to wear tails, but round hats remain strictly forbidden.' His sympathy for the new régime had dissipated within a year.

The *Pantheon* finally appeared in 1798, in three volumes. A second edition of 1818 was almost three times as large. Emasculated though it was, the first printing mirrored its author's faith in enlightenment, and subtly illustrated his disgust with the literary and social

tant periodicals in Russia during the first quarter of the nineteenth century, the *Messenger of Europe* was primarily historical and political in tone while under Karamzin's editorship (1802-3). In that way, it provided an almost perfect chronological outline of the final stages in Karamzin's transition from literator to historian and political partisan.

2

The Sage and Political Pundit
1800 - 3

Concerned with the problems of Russian society from the early years of Paul's reign, Karamzin had hinted in November 1797 that he would like to produce something that would assure him permanent fame ('gloire'). It is unlikely that he was already thinking of writing the definitive national history[1] but, in June 1798 two diary entries clearly demonstrate that he was going to delve into Russia's past.[2] The first of these embodied some rambling thoughts about a possible study of the reign of Peter the Great:

> *What was Russia? Justification of his [Peter I's] system. Be silent small minds! Only enlightenment is the means to perfection, to happiness! ... a justification of some cruelties. Customary kindness is not compatible with greatness of spirit. Les grands hommes ne voyent que le tout ... Could we not arouse a love for the Fatherland by representing Peter himself?* (11 June)

Here, in this short paragraph, was the essence of Karamzin's solution to contemporary tensions: reliance upon education, nationalism, and autocracy. Here too was revealed his intention of using events from Russia's past to provide lessons for his countrymen.

The next day he wrote in his diary:

> *If Providence spares me ... I will occupy myself with History, I will begin with Gillies, then read Ferguson, Gibbon, Robertson ... taking notes, and then go to the old authors, especially to Plutarch.* (12 June)

Historical studies, then, was to be his main tool, for, as he said to Viazemsky in the same year, 'people with talent read only two kinds of books, historical and speculative.'[3]

For the entire century, Russian monarchs and educators had been speaking of the need for a popularly available national history, and of the benefits which would accrue to state and citizens from such a project. There is ample evidence to show that education was regarded by rulers and statesmen as a means to create good citizens, and the emphasis was constantly on instruction rather than upon enlightenment.[4] Peter's system was a utilitarian one designed to produce skilled technicians and bureaucrats to serve his new Empire; Catherine looked primarily for loyalty in the graduates of her schools. Throughout the century, history was spoken of as the discipline best suited to provide 'lessons' for contemporary youth. In Peter's time, Prokopovich had used examples from the past to justify monarchy in Russia, and Tatishchev had said that history should be used in such a way that his own contemporaries could be moved to imitate the great men of the national past.[5]

The equation of history with the moulding of good citizens (subjects) was a constant of eighteenth-century Russian educational thinking. At mid-century, Lomonosov tried to turn history into a tool of Russian nationalism, and Catherine, whose *Instructions* of 1767 said that 'the Rules of education are the fundamental institutes which train us to be good citizens,' even tried to write a history of her own. Her *Notes on Russian History* (*Zapiski kasatel'no rossiiskoi istorii*), published first in serial form, 1783-4, were printed in two volumes in 1801. But the first state-approved history book designed specifically for Russia's youth did not appear until 1799, and that was written by the Austrian, de Mirievo from material gathered by a German, J.-G. Stritter.[6] The lack of such books for laymen and young students was so striking that the seventeenth-century *Sinopsis* (1674) and Lomonosov's short chronicle (1760) were still the most widely read surveys of Russian history by the turn of the century.[7]

In September 1798, Karamzin was still thinking about writing a eulogy to Peter and even was considering a study on Lomonosov, but his enthusiasm seemed not to have taken him beyond the realm of whimsy: 'The first demands that I dedicate three months to the study of Russian history and to Goliokov; this is hardly possible!'[8] Nevertheless, by May 1799 he claimed to be reading nothing but philosophy and history, no fiction, and at the end of the century historical themes had become the essence of most of his writing. In notes about the eulogy to Peter and in his discussion of the project with Dmitriev, Karamzin had stressed the educational advantages of using Russian historical personages as sources of inspiration for the present. He saw Peter's reign as proof that none but enlightened rulers could assure Russian greatness. Further, effective leadership came only from men of genius, for only those of such high calibre could have the foresight to know when to act harshly, even when it meant going against the wishes of the people. As Karamzin put it to Dmitriev, 'I would like to show that Peter enlightened Russia by the best means' – in this case, by force.[9]

Republicanism in France and increasing despotism in his own state had led Karamzin to conclude that it was his duty as a patriot to instill in readers a comprehension of what he felt were the special needs of Russia and all his writings after the turn of the century were directed towards that aim. Immediately after Paul's death, Karamzin proclaimed that literature was destined to play a new, enlightening role in Russian society. Now, he said, talented people 'can dedicate themselves to all subjects which are useful'; the freer intellectual climate was such that 'literature should have a greater influence on morality and happiness than ever before.' Freedom of expression was so new to many Russians, he said, that only writers were in a position to sway untainted minds.[10] Karamzin fully intended to take part in, even to dominate, the expected wave of pragmatic literature. He planned to do so in two stages; the first order of business was to 'publish a journal in order to gain enough money to live without need,' and this was fulfilled by the *Messenger of Europe*. Step two was 'to undertake a greater work; on Russian history.'[11] In short, the period 1801 to 1803 signalled the demise of Karamzin the creative writer and the birth of Karamzin the political commentator and historian.

However, Karamzin did not limit his efforts to the periodical. He prepared a number of separate essays and revised several of his earlier works. The most characteristic features of each of them were their educative tone and their reliance upon history as the best means to attract readers. Some of these works had kept him busy during the last months of Paul's reign and his concentration on the past was due in part to his realization that comments on the contemporary scene would not pass the censors. Thus when new parts of the *Letters* were published in 1801 they were laden with allusions to Russian history. The connection between his nationalist political views and his historical observations was evident almost immediately in this, the first full edition. In a letter supposedly sent from Paris, he exlaimed, 'what pleasant memories we owe to history!' and then went on to commend Hannibal's efforts against the 'cruel republicans,' or Romans.[12] The telling feature of this comment is that Karamzin had often recalled his boyhood admiration for the Romans, but now temporarily discarded that esteem in order to direct abuse against the character of all republicans.

The Russianism of his historical interests appeared in a letter from St Denis, in which he spoke of 'Yaroslav's daughter, the beautiful Anna,' who had married Henry I of France. Drawing a sad picture of a young woman who had been sacrificed by marriage for political expediency, Karamzin seemed to be acting on his own suggestion that people from the Russian past could well be made the focal point of fascinating historical stories. In the same edition of the *Letters*, Karamzin often spoke of Peter I, whom he praised as a man of 'goodness, cleverness, and wisdom,' and as a great monarch who was not only the 'father and enlightener of millions of people,' but was also the 'expander of his country.' Simultaneously, he followed Boltin's lead by insisting that earlier Russian princes, like Vladimir, Ivan IV, and Godunov, as well as Peter, 'made up the most important epochs in our history and even in the history of mankind.' It was on this note that he spoke of Levesque and complained that 'until now, we have had no good history of Russia.'[13]

In March 1800, Karamzin wrote Dmitriev that he was 'taking notes for a portrait of Russian authors' and a few months later he mailed the oft-quoted letter in which he claimed to be 'submerged in Russian history; I sleep and I see Nikon with Nestor.'[14] One result of this research was *The Pantheon of Russian Authors* (*Panteon rossiiskikh avtorov*), another of the studies prepared while Paul still lived and published in 1801-2.

Of all the authors included in the *Pantheon*, the single characteristic emphasized most often by Karamzin was their work in, or contribution to, Russian historical studies. After giving special credit to

Nestor, he praised Nikon for collecting those chronicles which 'serve as the basis for our history,' Tatishchev (1686-1750) as the 'zealous lover of the history of the fatherland,' M. Popov for 'loving Russian antiquity,' and both F. Emin and V.K. Trediakovsky for their general efforts on behalf of Russian history. He also mentioned the historical inclinations and contributions of A.S. Matveev, T. Dimitry, and Feofan Prokopovich. The major source for Karamzin's biographical information in the *Pantheon* was Novikov's *Historical Dictionary* (*Opyt istoricheskoe slovaria o rossiiskikh pisateliakh*, 1772),[15] and his interpretations on the whole resembled those of A.L. Schlözer (1735-1809) and G.F. Müller (1705-83). Although he cited Novikov's study only twice, Karamzin repeated chronological errors made by his former colleague which, if nothing else, suggests that his 'submersion' in history had not yet resulted in an effective methodological approach.

Like Schlözer, he praised the *Primary Chronicle* (Nestor) by extolling it as a 'treasure of our history' and by maintaining that it was superior to those of other ancient peoples. But, in contrast to the German scholar, Karamzin rebuked the chroniclers in much the same way Boltin had done, saying that they did not provide the historian with information on 'those things which would be most interesting to us; about morals, customs, peoples ...'[16] He also showed himself to be at odds with Schlözer and his followers in Russia, who prided themselves on their 'scientific' approach to history. Schlözer, who lived in Russia for only a short period during the 1760s, had been vehemently opposed to nationalism in historical writing. He had argued against Lomonosov on these grounds and stressed scientific criticism, dates, names, and statistics. 'A short history of 600 years full of truth,' he said, would be preferable to a 'long one of 3000 years of fables' and his personal dictum was 'Prima lex historiia, NE QUID FALSI DICAT.'[17] His successors in Russia, who styled themselves as the 'Skeptical School' of historians, later included several of Karamzin's most passionate critics, M.T. Kachenovsky, N.S. Artsybashev, and Polevoi. But nationalism was still the order of the day when Karamzin began writing historical accounts. In contrast to Schlözer, Karamzin wrote in 1801 that a history should be well organized and state clear opinions; it should be interesting, with an accent on the glories of the Russian past.[18]

There can be no denying that some of Karamzin's tendency to dabble in Russian history at the turn of the century was due to the fact that he could do little else while Paul reigned. But his intention to continue such studies soon became apparent after Paul was assassinated (March 1801). After a flurry of diplomatic maneuvres which relieved Russians of the onerous, and incongruous, task of fighting both the French and the English, Alexander appeared to have brought peace to his subjects. The Russian Empire had emerged relatively unscathed from the cataclysm of war and revolution that had swept over Europe since 1789.

Secure in his faith in the durability of Russian institutions, but anxious to undertake a program of domestic reform, Alexander lifted the stifling censorship and intellectual isolation imposed on Russia by his father. Native writers, rejoicing in unaccustomed freedoms, responded with a wave of enthusiasm for their new ruler and rushed to help shape the promised better society. Paul's extremes had caused a certain amount of amnesia among Russians who could now remember only the good things of his mother's reign. They recalled that Catherine had tried almost single-handedly to enlighten Russia in the seventies and eighties, and they now hoped to bring her early efforts to fruition.[19] Once again writers immersed themselves and their readers in the reigning west European cultural fashions and all the cross-currents of Western enlightenment were reintroduced to Russia. But now most of the Russian writers were at the same time 'Westernizers' and ardent Russian nationalists. They were more confident of their own merits and more selective in their genuflections to Western cultural trends. Lomonosov, Fonvizin, Novikov, and Radishchev had stood almost alone in this regard in the eighteenth century, but now a wide strata of 'enlighteners' hoped, in an openly pragmatic way, to turn Western ideas to Russian advantage. Karamzin was hardly a newcomer to Russian literary circles, but he was nonetheless a central figure in the new wave of writing. The next two decades were to be, as Belinsky and others said, his 'era' in the history of Russian literature. They were also the years in which he published a body of writing that formed a background for the myriad ideas that fell into the large category of Russian conservatism.

Soon after the succession of Alexander I, Karamzin composed two odes to him and an historical eulogy (*Istoricheskoe pokhval'noe slovo*) to Catherine the Great. Some contemporaries accused him of simply trying to put himself in the good graces of the new monarch, but the goal of these pieces was far more ambitious and utilitarian than even his critics assumed. Karamzin now definitely intended to employ literature as a vehicle for his own politico-historical views and history as proof of their validity.[20]

Seizing upon Alexander's promise to rule in the manner of Catherine II, Karamzin carefully praised that empress for all those things which he hoped would be initiated by the new monarch. The frankly educative character of the panegyrics to Catherine and Alexander was emphasized by some of his later critics who felt that they boded ill for his qualifications as an historian. Particularly harsh was the liberal A.N. Pypin, who accused Karamzin of 'lying' about Catherine's reign. Even his ardent admirer, Pogodin, said that the eulogy was a 'stain' on Karamzin's career.[21] For Karamzin, however, the important thing was the present and the impulse behind these poems was the same as that behind his ode to Paul in 1796. Having asked Paul, with no success, to heed the counsel of critical patriots like himself, Karamzin warned Alexander against flatterers and held up Peter I as a monarch who had loved those who spoke frankly to him. Suggesting that Alexander take advantage of counsel from 'good patriots' ('us'), he proceeded to put forward his own formula for achieving Russian happiness and security.

It was in the first ode to Alexander (1801) that Karamzin stated clearly his belief that freedom could exist only where there were laws to sustain them. 'Justice,' he was to write again in 1803, 'is the spirit of state order,' and he constantly adhered to the idea that people could achieve happiness by knowing and following laws. He insisted, too, that the autocrats must also respect the law and said in the eulogy to Catherine that autocracy would be destroyed if rulers 'respect their own whims more than the laws.' The *Historical Eulogy* (1802) revealed the tendencies of thought that were to dominate Karamzin's later works. Among them were his use of the past to justify autocracy as a political system in the present and his portrayal of the princes as the sole movers of the historical process in Russia. His sweeping statement, 'the spectator of centuries, History, presents to us the wonderful performance of mysterious fate ... but what most captivates the attention of wise onlookers? The phenomenon of great souls, demi-Gods of mankind ... they decide the fate of mankind,'[22] has often been used to demonstrate the extent of his monarchism. But the comment represents Karamzin's desire to direct the new ruler toward better things far better than it does his political beliefs of the time. It was not that he was a craven flatterer himself, rather that he was convinced that only through such flowery language, which was a typically courtly form of address anyway, could he persuade the emperor to make beneficial changes.

As an example to Alexander, Karamzin praised Catherine for expanding the Empire, not because he wanted the new emperor to follow suit, but because her policy had been, 'for the benefit of Russia, for ... security.' Sensing the military threat to Russia which existed in 1800-1, Karamzin was concerned for security and peace. The ruler of Russia, he insisted, must first of all 'think of external security ... security in the almighty! Weak nations tremble; the strong, under the aegis of great leaders, openly delight in political events.'

Karamzin had spoken of security before, but the word meant more to him than merely the matter of military safety. He looked upon it in the Montesquieuan way, which began with the assumption that civil and political liberties were inseparable. Montesquieu had defined political liberty as 'a tranquility of mind arising from the opinion each person has of his safety ...' And earlier, 'liberty is a right of doing whatever the laws permit.' Thus, security, whether a matter of political frontiers or peace of mind, was the gift which only a paternalistic government could bestow on Russians. Karamzin then extolled Catherine for spreading enlightenment, 'passing useful laws, and above all, for determining the form of government in Russia – autocracy.' He went on to define autocracy as the only system in which all citizens can become equal and free. Referring to Catherine's *Instructions* of 1767 and several times to Montesquieu, Karamzin was advocating enlightened monarchy in which the rule of law prevails. He was more straightforward about this need in the poems dedicated to Alexander, where he said, 'with your first words, you promised Catherine's Golden Age,' and requested a legislative order of laws because 'evil is greater than goodness!'[23]

Besides glorifying Catherine's contributions to Russia, Karamzin pointed to her interest in Russian history, once again expressing his own opinion when he claimed that Catherine had insisted that 'his-

tory must beautify former times and extoll them.'[24] In this respect,
Karamzin was certainly far closer to Lomonosov's notion of historical writing than to that of Schlözer.

Another aspect of the *Historical Eulogy* worthy of note is that it
attested to an ideological connection between Boltin and Karamzin,
even though the latter historian was generally critical of Boltin in favour of Shcherbatov. Boltin had stressed the importance of the
'morals, habits, and deeds' of each period of history, insisting that
laws and governmental systems were determined by custom and
therefore mirrored the needs of the nation. Karamzin based his whole
defence of autocracy on the same premise. Boltin also preceded
Karamzin in his demand for slow and gradual change and had praised
Catherine for establishing autocracy and for upholding the system of
serfdom,[25] but it was in the concept of the value and need for a Russian history that Karamzin most resembled Boltin. In reviewing
Shcherbatov's work, Boltin had said that Russia did not have a 'complete, good, history ... not because of insufficient documents, but because of a dearth of skilful artists to assemble these materials, to
purify, connect, and beautify them,'[26] a viewpoint practically para-
phrased by Karamzin in the 1801 edition of the *Letters*.

There was no real differentiation between history and politics in
the *Historical Eulogy*, nor was there in most of Karamzin's writings
before 1803. Nevertheless, he avowed time and again that he was
merely portraying the truths of Russian history. Claiming, in the second of the two odes to Alexander, that he was about to 'enter into
the temple of history, and there ... find your cause,' he added in a
footnote, 'the author is occupied by Russian history.'[27] He reasserted
his claim to be engaged mainly in historical studies the next year,
when he said, 'history interests us more than novels; the mature mind
finds a special charm in truth, which does not exist in fiction. In the
saddest circumstances ... man can still console himself with history.'[28]

In the *Messenger of Europe*, Karamzin brought together all of
those traits which had permeated his previous writings: patriotism,
historicism, and a desire to direct the thinking of his readers. The
three tendencies were now inseparably linked and no longer the isolated and inconsistent feelings that they had been in the past. Nationalism dictated his impulse to preach and made it inevitable that history would be the tool for instruction. Karamzin demonstrated

through the pages of the *Messenger of Europe* that he had become a totally secular and practical man.

The first issue of the journal appeared in January 1802, along with an introductory note from its editor. Outlining his ambitions for the periodical, Karamzin disclosed an inclination to connect literature and history and his desire to employ these arts as a means to advise the government and the public. Alluding to the value of literary activities in the evolution of European states, he contended that, 'in Russia, literature can be even more useful than in other lands,' because of the relative newness of intellectual influences there.[29]

In fact, the unifying theme of the *Messenger of Europe* was Karamzin's conviction that a new age was dawning. The Treaty of Amiens (March 1802), augured well for peaceful diplomacy in Europe, at least for those who were not in the inner circles where the precarious nature of the peace was better known. At home, Alexander restored the rights given to the Russian nobility in 1785 by Catherine, but which had been repealed by Paul. Alexander promised to re-establish the old senate, brought new men into the government, and seemed to recognize the claim by nobility to be entitled to participate in decision-making for the state. The government included a cross-section of reformers and reactionaries. Nicholas Novosiltsev (1761-1836), who was later a friend of Karamzin, was one of Alexander's close associates. M.N. Murav'ev (1757-1807), a former tutor of Alexander who was soon to act on Karamzin's behalf at court, became a deputy minister of education. A new legal system, new schools and universities, and stability on the diplomatic front raised hopes for the Golden Age of the future which Karamzin, at least, had predicted in the nineties.

Of all the historically oriented articles in the *Messenger of Europe* during its first year, the most intelligible expression of Karamzin's attitude towards history was in 'On Events and Characters in Russian History that Could be Used as Objects of Art.' In this essay, he went right back to what he believed to be the origin of Russian history; that is, 'the calling of the Varangian princes into the Slavic lands,' and explained how an 'artist' should dramatize that and other incidents. Ever conscious of the lack of nationally oriented literature, he hoped that historical events could be used to help Russians respect themselves and their traditions. In this he was certainly a product of

Novikov's school. According to Karamzin, writers could serve as the apostles of a new patriotism by taking real heroes from the past and holding them up as examples to Russian youth. This was quite in keeping with his belief that an author had an obligation to create works that 'would not be useless to the Fatherland.'

Demonstrating an approach to historical writing quite different from that of either Müller or Schlözer, he stressed the importance of legends as valuable historical sources and even decided which moral lessons should accrue from specific events. The essay 'On Events and Characters ...' had its counterpart in a study written by V.V. Popugaev (1779-1816) a year before. A linguist and jurist, Popugaev prepared a lengthy and somewhat rambling essay in 1801-2 entitled *On the Well-Being of the National Body (O Blagopoluchii narodnykh tel)*. One section of the essay treated with history as an object of political education. History, he said, is a science 'for the formation of heroes, it is a pantheon of famous men, glorious nations and their virtues, for the benefit of mankind; it preserves great deeds for imitation and emulation ... it must not contain anything that does not serve for the resurrection of the heart or as a stimulus towards virtue ...' In contrast to Karamzin, however, Popugaev was convinced that history 'must show only greatness,' and that despots or tyrants have no place in it. A. Pisarev was another who seized upon Karamzin's idea of turning Russia's past into a source of inspiration for contemporaries among writers and artists. His two-volume *Subjects for Artists, Collected from Russian History* appeared in the capital city in 1807.[30]

In the same vein was the consistent reference in the *Messenger of Europe* to old Russian legends. Karamzin had already spoken in the *Moscow Journal* of searching for materials of this sort and had shown some real knowledge, not just curiosity, about them in the *Spectateur* essay. By 1798, he still had not consolidated his feelings for the ancient songs,[31] so it was in the *Messenger of Europe* and then in the *History* that he made plain the extent of his acquaintance with and regard for Russian oral tradition. In 1818, he made a strong plea to the Russian Academy for their preservation, insisting that ballads from the past mirrored Russian genius. Three years later he remarked to Viazemsky that he hoped to edit a collection of them himself.[32] The great significance of Karamzin's efforts to retain and study this element of Russian heritage is that he successfully combatted the attempts of contemporaries among the Skeptical School to eliminate such sources from historical research. It was partly through Karamzin that Russian scholars began to apply the methods of scientific investigation to the vague and enigmatic relics of their past. In Karamzin's words, 'there is the Archive of Foreign Affairs, but a collection of treaties and diplomatic papers are not enough for an historian. It is necessary to turn to foreigners ... and to legends.'[33]

Karamzin furnished readers with a preview of his whole conception of Russian history in 'About Love for the Fatherland and National Pride' (1802), which contained several interpretations later included in the *History*. In the tradition of Lomonosov, he described the bravery, fame, and 'knightly graciousness' of the ancient Slavs, contending that the Russian nation was famous in its infancy, when it destroyed Roman legions and terrorized Byzantium. In Karamzin's idyllic picture, Russians of the eleventh century had to punish Constantinople for her 'effrontery' and were the equals of any state as far as enlightenment and civilization were concerned.[34] The same supposition that the Slavs broke the armies of the Roman Empire later was outlined feelingly, but with little detail, in the first chapters of the *History* and was an integral part of a patriotic, and unusually militaristic, poem written by Karamzin just before the campaign against Napoleon in 1806.[35]

In the second place, Karamzin was very optimistic about those periods that other historians usually considered to be times of terrible, fruitless waste. Instead of complaining that the Tatar invasion and the Time of Troubles had retarded Russian growth, he was grateful that they prompted the people of Russia to make the 'right' choice of strong, central monarchy. Providing readers with a foretaste of interpretations that were to be made popular by the *History*, Karamzin claimed that the Tatars were overcome as soon as a 'firm and courageous prince' arrived on the scene and, likewise, the Time of Troubles ended only after 'the citizens and landowners demanded a military leader.'[36] Already, Karamzin saw Russian history as a series of crises, all of which had ended for the best. It would not be difficult to apply this interpretation to his own day. Finally, the article gave evidence that Karamzin believed the entire process of Russian history to be a matter of the evolution of state authority. He did not, however, fall completely prey to the Lomonosov type of patriotism and so cautioned readers to know their 'own worth' instead of being blinded by nationalism.

Karamzin's 'Historical Memorials and Notes on the Path to the Troitsky' carried the same kind of theme, but with an interesting added dimension. Here, on speaking of Godunov's probable participation in the death of the tsarevich Dmitry, Karamzin wrote that Boris was such an important monarch that 'Russian patriots wish to doubt his complicity in the matter.' He suggested that historians had no right to ignore such things but that he could, for he was not writing a history: 'God will judge secret villainies, but we must praise the tsars for every thing that they do for the glory and welfare of the Fatherland.'[37] There is no evidence with which to corroborate it, but hindsight and Karamzin's own subsequent tendency to speak out on sensitive subjects make it conceivable that he was making an oblique but strikingly risky reference to the death of Paul i.

An historical tale, spread over the first three issues of the *Messenger of Europe* in 1803 and entitled 'Martha Posadnitsa, or the Destruction of Novgorod,' 'Marfa Posadnitsa, ili pokorenie Novagoroda' can in many ways be seen as a direct predecessor to the *History*. Although Karamzin's claim that 'all the main events [in it] agree with history'[38] was an exaggeration, the tale was based on a real and important event in Russian history, the fifteenth-century conquest of Novgorod by Moscow's Ivan iii. Karamzin began the story with the comment, 'here is one of the most important events in Russian history,' but the account was intended to serve as a medium through which he could make pronouncements on what he judged were the most pressing problems of contemporary Russia. To a certain extent, 'Martha' typified the two main lines of Karamzin's intellectual development to that time. In style, tone, and characterizations it resembled his sentimental pieces of the early nineties, yet it also revealed his new sense of historical inevitability and an almost total dependence upon historical subject matter.

The contemporary connotation of 'Martha,' indeed its continuing relevance to the Russian political scene (it was proscribed in 1826), lay in the fact that the narrative revolved around the problem of determining the proper political form for Muscovy. This was certainly one of the leading topics of the day. Alexander's 'Unofficial Committee' was already reported to be discussing constitutional change and the question of serfdom. The secretive nature of such discussion led to rumour-mongering and tension that was to culminate, after such striking turning points as the fall from grace of Speransky, a constitution for Poland and the Decembrist Revolt, in Nicholas I's reversion to Paul's system of repression.

In 'Martha,' Karamzin made sure that readers caught his meaning by saying that Ivan's family would eventually be replaced by one that would continue to rule 'for the happiness of the people.' He added, in a footnote, that 'the wonderful Romanov family now rules.'[39] Turning to the chronicles for necessary background, Karamzin took from them details on the traditional relationship between Novgorod and Moscow but concluded, as he was to do elsewhere, that the Tatar occupation had made any reversion to earlier political conditions impossible. Although he also depended upon old juridical documents, particularly when he spoke of Yaroslav's concessions to Novgorod, probably the most consistently used sources were Müller's account of Novgorodian history and the sixteenth-century *Kniga stepennaia*. For Karamzin, however, the importance of such historical materials still lay primarily in the aura of authenticity which they would provide for his story. The purpose of the tale was to suggest a political lesson and, indeed, his conclusion appeared in the opening paragraphs when he had Ivan III's emissary say, 'wild people love independence, wise people love order, and there is no order without autocratic power.'[40] Later in the tale, the same spokesman uttered Karamzin's political opinion that only organization could assure justice and security, that, for their own sake, people must be obedient because political freedom was 'often fatal.' This was certainly in keeping with his assertion, made the year before, that it was the duty of writers to accentuate the moral lessons of history.[41]

The whole idea of 'Martha' was consistent with Karamzin's political standpoint as it had developed from the early nineties. Repeating the old idealization of republicanism, he emphasized once again that it could not be maintained in practice. Aware of the contradiction, he defended himself in one of the last issues of the *Messenger of Europe* (1803) while he was editor, where he said, 'the historian must sometimes appear hard-hearted and condemn what is dear to him as a man but what would be harmful for a government, for men are no angels.'[42] The fate of France, the epitome of European civilization and the home of the Philosophes, had proven this necessity to him. The republican experiment had lasted a decade and so had chaos; only Napoleon's firm hand had brought France to its senses once again.

In the case of 'Martha,' Karamzin admitted that Novgorod's demands were technically reasonable, acknowledging that Novgorodians were not Jacobins. But he added that such considerations were irrelevant whenever the 'general welfare' was at stake. To balance the worst implications of his theory, he added that if the new dynasty did not rule for the good of the people, then 'God would punish the perjurors.' This rather obscure allusion to a contractual relationship between tsar and people was the first intimation of what became a unique feature of the *History*, that is, the opinion that the tsar and his subjects had a mutual obligation to act in the interest of all Russia. The autocrat's duty was to take over all 'Russian' lands and to maintain strong central government against internal and external subversion. The people, in order to reap the benefits of a secure state, needed only to follow the example of the Novgorodians, who had agreed that 'the will of the autocrat will be our only law.'[43]

'Martha' represented a synthesis of ideas expressed by Karamzin in 1802. In style and tone, it followed the guidelines of 'On Events and Characters....' Its political thinking smacked of 'Pleasing Prospects, Hopes and Desires for the Present Time,' which had appeared in the July 1802 issue of the *Messenger of Europe*. In the latter article, Karamzin had suggested that the French Revolution demonstrated to all classes that only strong governments could assure progress and prevent tyranny, 'that ancient institutions have magical strength,' and that 'only time and the good will of legitimate governments can repair the imperfections of civil society.' Here he seemed to place most of the onus on governments by demanding that they operate for the good of all and by requiring rulers to 'earn the respect and love' of their subjects.[44]

This idea dominated all of Karamzin's writings after 1803. Along with the *History*, it was basic to the *Memoir about Ancient and Modern Russia* (*Zapiska o drevnei i novoi Rossii*, 1811), where he spoke of a specific agreement that bound the tsar to 'sacrifice part for the whole,'[45] and to an *Albom* compiled in that same year. Prepared as a book of readings for Alexander's favourite sister, Catherine Pavlovna, the *Albom* contained extracts from Bossuet, Rousseau, and many others, all of which were included for their monarchical, patriotic sentiments. Its main theme, like that of the *Memoir*, was that rulers must govern according to the needs of the times, introducing change only when society was ready for it.[46] This sentiment was equally essential to his 'Note about Moscow's Memorials' (1817), where he said that autocracy was founded 'for the good of the people, not for the special use of the autocrat,'[47] and to the 'Opinion of a Russian Citizen' (1819), in which he told the tsar that 'God gave you the kingdom and, with it, the duty to be occupied exclusively with its welfare.'[48]

The fundamental assumptions of Karamzin's conception of Russian history were reiterated in articles published throughout 1803. The first, the necessity for an autocratic, centralized political system in Russia, had been the theme of 'Martha.' The second, the traditional view of the princes as the sole activators of Russian history, was expressed clearly in 'About the Best Way to have Satisfactory Teachers in Russia.' It was given broader meaning in the article 'About the New Methods of National Education in Russia.' Here *1803* Karamzin emphasized that all through Russian history, the gentry (*dvorianstvo*), supported fully and willingly by the people of Russia, 'had never failed in their desire to sacrifice themselves for the general welfare.'[49] Agreeing in this instance with Shcherbatov, Karamzin thereby gave credence to the traditional justification for the landowners' claim to own serfs.

It was in the latter article that Karamzin made a strong plea for more and better education, which he had defined in the *Historical Eulogy* as a twofold procedure: moral education of man and the political education of citizens. He added that love of virtue and work, respect for law and order, and a general sensibility to the needs and welfare of neighbours must be coupled with learning to love the fatherland and its institutions. Just as Novikov had done in the 1780s, he demanded that Russia produce its own teachers and at the same time encourage enlightenment so that autocratic government could function more efficiently. Alexander, Karamzin wrote, planned to bring education to all of his subjects ('there will be a light in shacks as well'). The continued absence of a proper general education, he continued, 'prevents any beneficial action on the part of the govern-

ment ... saps the strength of its wise laws, begets evil doing and un-
fairness....' Karamzin illustrated his point by alluding to a love of
work and stability in parts of Switzerland, England, and Germany,
where 'even the farmers have libraries.' Education, he insisted, should
be Alexander's first priority.[50]

Alexander had undertaken to reform Russia's educational system
from the first months of his reign, but the actual decree of reform
was issued in January 1803. A Ministry of Public Instruction was
established and two new universities were founded (Kharkov and
Kazan) with the expressed aim of centralizing and upgrading educational services in the Empire. Karamzin had long objected to the foreign domination of pedagogy in Russia and in two articles he criticized bitingly the tendency of young Russians to adopt the language
and culture of France. In 'Strangeness' ('Strannost,' 1802), he ridiculed an attempt by a Frenchman to establish a school in Paris for
Russians who wished to learn Russian. 'Thank God! We are no longer
barbarians; we have all the means for enlightenment' in Russia, Karamzin wrote, adding that only in Russia could one become a good
Russian. He had protested earlier against the fact that Germans, in
this case Schlözer and his son, Christian, were professors of history
at the Academy. Karamzin's 'My Confession' ('Moia ispoved,' 1802)
showed him to be in the tradition of Fonvizin, Radishchev, Novikov,
and Pushkin, each of whom prepared satires on the education of Russia's gentry. He complained that a wealthy young Russian often read
only French, ignored his own language, and failed to learn even the
rules of being a 'good man and citizen.'[51]

On reading Alexander's decree on general education, Karamzin
wrote that it was the 'strongest proof of the Monarch's divine goodness.'[52] But in 1811, he was still complaining that there were all too
few real 'lovers of higher wisdom' in Russia and that foreign languages
were the key to success for Russian merchants, professional people,
and scholars.[53] The *Messenger of Europe* contained four essays on the
purposes of Alexander's schooling projects and each of them carried
an idea which Karamzin had put forward at some risk in the last decade of the eighteenth century. Ignorance is more dangerous than enlightenment, he said, and the status quo can only be strengthened
through the dissemination of knowledge by Russian teachers who
were dedicated to the inculcation of a moral and patriotic sense of

duty into young Russians. 'Success in enlightenment,' Karamzin wrote in one of the articles, 'will gradually move people away from violence and blood-letting.' The fact that Peter I and Prokopovich had said practically the same thing in their *Spiritual Regulations* of 1722, in an attempt to allay the suspicion which the Church had for education, is a harsh indictment of the lack of progress in Russia's educational thinking between the death of Peter and the accession of Alexander I. Ideas similar to Karamzin's were taken up by V.V. Izmailov (1733-1830) in his short-lived journal, *The Patriot* (1804).[54]

Just as V.N. Tatishchev had hoped in the first half of the eighteenth century, Karamzin wanted Russia to form its own educational heritage. Education could be used to teach a respect for law and the national institutions and, above all, provide the gentry with tools which would enable them to bring the best of Europe's cultural traditions to the Russian Empire. Karamzin constantly looked to the gentry and nobility to provide Russia with stability and expertise, though he did not share Shcherbatov's feeling that they should govern hand-in-hand with the monarch. Thus he regarded Peter III's legislation of 1762, which freed the *dvorianstvo* from many compulsory state responsibilities and so improved their opportunity to partake in intellectual pursuits, as one of the great events of Russian history.[55] Karamzin remained interested in Russia's educational system, and a number of times visited *pensions* with their general-inspector, A.A. Prokopovich-Antonsky, a longtime friend.

The attitude towards serfdom which had prevailed in *Readings for Children*, was maintained in the *Messenger of Europe*. In 1802, Karamzin wrote that 'slavery' no longer existed in Russia (in the *History* he was to claim that it never had) and that the noblemen who had always recognized their obligations to the peasantry rightfully could ask a 'half day of work a week' in return.[56] One might add that this was a decidedly unrealistic estimate of the average peasant's work load. He tried to explain to serfs, in 'Letter of a Village Inhabitant' ('Pis'mo sel'skogo zhitelia,' 1803), that widespread education must precede any substantial change in their way of life, and that their only hope at present was for 'good masters, and the means for an education.' His reading audience included few, if any, peasants. Pypin later charged that Karamzin had even refused to allow one of his own peasants to marry, so it is hardly surprising that, of all the legislation proposed by Alexander at this time, those that had to do with changing the status of the peasantry were among the few that met with Karamzin's disfavour. His position in this regard was summed up in 'About the Best Way...,' when he remarked, 'poverty is, on the one hand, unfortunate for civil society and, on the other, a cause of good; it forces people to be useful.'[57]

All of the important historical themes that Karamzin felt were keys to Russia's survival in the past and, as such, important considerations for the present, were outlined in the *Messenger of Europe*. He was to expand upon the same situations in later studies, particularly in the *Memoir* and the *History*. The *Messenger of Europe* displayed his vision of the Russian state as a self-contained unit in which each class was dependent upon the other for survival; each had a role to play that must be sustained for the good of all. He supported this contention by a number of references to the self-sacrificing characteristic of nobility and peasantry. The Russians even 'generously suffered all the horrors of the time of Ivan [IV] Vasilevich,' he said in 1802, because they realized the 'necessity of obedience' in order to preserve the independence of their state.[58]

By 1803, he suspected that Russian armies might have to take to the field once again and was aware that his beloved empire might well collapse if national unity was not preserved. Karamzin wanted no part of a war with France and pleaded the cause of neutrality, but he wanted Russia to be prepared for the worst. Security and peace alone would allow the fatherland to achieve greatness, so he used his knowledge of the past, or his interpretation of it, to convey two important lessons to his readers.

The first of these was his belief that Poland was of immense strategic value to Russia and so must be retained at all costs. The Poles, he exclaimed, had always 'hoped to tyrannize Russia.' For this reason he had commended Catherine II, in the *Historical Eulogy*, for ending the threat of 'impertinent and vicious Poland.' His second lesson was demonstrated in his praise for Boris Godunov who, he said, had forced 'European states to respect Russia' without resorting to force of arms. He was to continue warning the ruler against granting too much independence to Poland and praising rulers who contributed to Russian prestige by safe, peaceful diplomacy, rather than those who achieved the same ends only by war.

Karamzin also repeated his desire to impress upon foreigners the fact that his people had a glorious history of their own, admitting at the same time that Russians did not know their own history well enough.[59] In 1803, he published two purely historical essays, both of which had the customary didactic aim. Like 'Martha,' 'About the Moscow Revolt in the Reign of Aleksei Mikhailovich' ('O Moskovskom miatezh...') conveyed the lesson that tsars must always be strong and willing to permit some minor injustices for the good of the whole. In other words, there was a time for liberalism and a time to set all such thoughts aside for the sake of general security. In the study on the Moscow rebellion, he demonstrated his own order of priority among criteria for judging the merits of Russian princes. Virtuous monarchs were important, but only if their goodness did not undermine the strength of the state. Thus, after describing how Aleksei Mikhailovich had been persuaded by the people to surrender to them a ruthless but efficient boyar, Karamzin admonished, 'the mistakes of the tsar's weakness had harmful results: soon a revolution in Novgorod and Pskov showed the necessity of strong, firm measures.'[60]

The second article, entitled 'Ancient Russia' ('Russkaia starina'), was an attempt to arouse Russian patriotism by means of history. Regretting once again that his countrymen knew 'old Russia badly,' he tried to describe the customs and architecture of seventeenth-century Moscow, making an analogy between its buildings and those of ancient Rome. In general, Karamzin attributed pious and charitable characteristics to the ancient Russians and quite successfully countered Schlözer's charge that the history of ancient Russia was 'an atrocious concept.'[61]

By the end of the year, Karamzin had already formulated almost all of his historical views, if somewhat superficially, in the *Messenger of Europe*. He had given his version of many events and people in Russian history, including the arrival of the Varangians, whom he called Normans, the Tatar occupation, and the origins of the Russian language. He had also attacked Montesquieu's concentration on climate as the major factor in historical causality and, in much the same manner as Boltin, had placed more emphasis on the 'circumstances of civil life.'[62]

Over the same period that Karamzin was improving and widening his historical knowledge and applying it to matters of the present, his political outlook became more and more settled until he felt that he had found the formula for Russian security and greatness. His enthusiasm for Alexander never waned but he constantly suggested that the monarch take on only 'good patriots' as advisers. We can be sure that he was offering his own services and advising against secret or vested-interest committees. At this stage in his career, he feared tyranny far more than republicanism, which indicates the extent to which Paul's despotism had threatened Karamzin's way of life. He had implied as much himself in 1801 when, in one of the odes to Alexander, he had said, 'a tyrant frightens my pen, whereas it loves a good monarch.'[63]

Because of Paul, there were many Russians who were inclined to recommend legislation that would at least partially limit the power of the autocrat, but Karamzin hoped to eliminate the danger of extremes by less drastic means – by the institution of rational laws. In the opening number of the *Messenger of Europe*, he praised Frederick the Great for establishing 'wise laws' and commented that 'excellent minds are the true heroes of history.'[64] Yet he was not suggesting a legal system that might limit the powers of the autocrat; rather he looked for a means to minimize lawlessness, to check disorders, and to enable the ruler to bring justice to all his subjects. During the first year of Alexander's reign, Karamzin had said that 'there is freedom where there are laws ... there is slavery where there are no laws...,' but he was careful to add, 'equality is only a dream.' In his view of the relations between state and people, he had changed very little from the days when he had translated excerpts from Mme Genlis for the *Readings for Children*.

Going to the extreme of thanking French revolutionaries for proving that people 'must live quietly and obey readily,'[65] he went on to prophesy world leadership for Russia. Karamzin had come full circle from his earlier demands that his countrymen concentrate on European models and now predicted that both Europeans and Asians were soon to follow the Russian lead. By 1803, in a very Slavophile-like tone, he was complimenting the Muscovites of the past and present for the civilized ways in contrast to over-urbanized western Europeans, and congratulating his government for an expedition to Japan that would carry the benefits 'of civilization [Russian] to wild people.' In contrast to opinions he had expressed while Paul reigned, he now objected to Russians copying Parisian fashions.[66] This is not to say that Karamzin was messianic in the manner of 'Third Rome' devotees, or like late nineteenth-century pan-Russians such as N. Ya. Danilevsky. Although he began setting Russia apart from Europe, he did not do so as an isolationist or as an imperialist; instead he hoped to safeguard his fellow countrymen from what he believed were the self-destructive aspects of west European society. Karamzin was, in essence, advocating Russianism without being anti-European, and his essays both mirrored and helped consolidate the growing phenomenon of Russian national consciousness.

Even before the official signing of the peace at Amiens, Karamzin anticipated a truce in Europe.[67] Convinced that this new and promising situation was a product of Napoleon's control of France, he at first expected it to be a lasting one. According to Karamzin, France was back in the hands of 'decisive, firm autocracy,' and Napoleon had ended 'the monster of revolution,'[68] thereby making it safe for the tsar to enact legislation for reform in Russia. Specifically, Karamzin requested legal reforms and did his best to propagandize Alexander's improvements in the educational system. Yet his confidence in the future was shaken within a year.

Not long after Karamzin had commended Napoleon for bringing peace to Europe and order to France ('he cured people of dangerous giddiness'), he remonstrated with the French leader for creating new republics only so that they could be absorbed by France. He became suspicious, too, when the First Consul took on powers that put him above the laws of France. As the Soviet scholar, Iu. Lotman, has pointed out, Karamzin continued his earlier practice of editing translations from foreign sources so that they might fit his own view of things. Among other things, he printed a speech made by the famous French jurist, Jean Étienne Portalis, but altered the original version considerably. For Karamzin, the most important part of the speech on the new French code of laws could be found in the comment, 'the general good always contradicts the personal good of some,' a point hardly touched upon by the author of the speech.[69]

Worried about developments in Russia, Karamzin now began to caution Alexander I against carrying reform too far. He was delighted to see progress in the educational system, but when Alexander seemed bent on making real constitutional changes, Karamzin changed his tune and rushed to the defence of tradition. A poem published in March 1802, 'Hymn to Fools' ('Gim gluptsam'), communicated to readers a complaint that the tsar was not heeding the advice of Russia's most wise and patriotic people.[70] He had already alluded pessimistically to Alexander's 'Unofficial Committee' of advisers in the previous month and was to do so again near the end of 1803. In contrast to the feelings of many of his contemporaries, Karamzin did not worry that such a committee would give too much power to the monarch at the expense of the nobility. He was afraid that it might lead to oligarchy and that Alexander would feel no need to consult with enlightened men like himself. Just as he had written in the late nineties, Karamzin once again said that there had been no Golden Age in the past. Too much had been expected of the eighteenth century, but if Alexander acted wisely there could be a Golden Age in the near future. The teacher wished to be heard.

Complementing his plea for neutrality and warnings about Poland were incessant demands for more patriotism. In issue number four of the *Messenger of Europe*, he published his most famous essay on nationalism, 'On Love for One's Country and National Pride' ('O liubvi v otechestvu i narodnoi gordosti'). A warning about the perverseness of 'blind' patriotism notwithstanding, Karamzin suggested to his readers that:

> I dare not think that there are too few patriots in our Russia; but it seems to me that we are unnecessarily humble in thinking about our national pride. Humility, however, is harmful in politics. Whoever does not respect himself will certainly not be respected by others.[71]

He again cautioned in the June issue of that year (1802) that 'patriotism must not blind us,' but his request that readers send in patriotic anecdotes for publication and his oft-repeated recommendation that the state act to inculcate patriotism through the schools were more indicative of his real sentiments.

In the *Letters* edition of 1801, Karamzin had expressed an idea that was to become commonly accepted in the nineteenth century, that is, that governmental systems derive from the unique historical needs of individual peoples. In keeping with this belief, he concluded that even an obviously successful constitutional monarchy, like that in

England, should not be used as a model for Russia. With due defer-
ence to Herder, whose works were well known to Karamzin,[72] the
feeling had its Russian roots – the historian Tatishchev had expressed
it clearly and in the same manner in the mid-eighteenth century.
Karamzin made it a rallying cry behind his pleas for more patriotism,
saying, in 1803, that 'every plant [citizen] thrives best in its own climate.'[73] He was accentuating the individuality of each national state,
and the naturalness, indeed rightness, for a citizen to love that state.
Karamzin had recourse to this theme often but his feelings about it
were to be summed up most concisely in a letter of 1818 to P.A. Viazemsky, in which he proclaimed, 'Russia is not England ... autocracy
is its soul.'[74]

Certain that only the extant form of government could operate
effectively in his homeland, Karamzin still did not relinquish his feeling that a republic, under certain conditions, was the ideal state. In
the very first issue of the *Messenger of Europe*, he explained that
France under Napoleon was 'none other than a true monarchy,' and
no longer a republic in practice. He admitted, however, that the idea
of republicanism was already firmly and permanently entrenched in
the hearts of all Frenchmen. But neither France nor the rest of
Europe was ready for this type of government, or so he 'proved' by
illustrating the poor leadership of the revolutionary élite. Later in the
same year, Karamzin suggested that although Swiss people quite naturally hoped for a return to a free republic, they would have to wait
for very strong leadership before achieving their ambition.[75] Moreover,
in one of the last issues in 1802, he said that 'without the highest national virtue, Republics cannot survive' – a conclusion that differed
very little from that which he had reached in the nineties and which
he repeated verbatim in the *History*. He continued: 'this is why mo-
narchic government is much safer and is more hopeful; it does not
demand extraordinary things from its citizens and can lift itself above
the degree of morality over which Republics stumble.'[76]

In Karamzin's opinion, the tenor of government was set by the
way in which it was established. The French Revolution had achieved
political freedom for Frenchmen, but only through the agony of un-
controlled violence and terror, thus assuring a new tyranny like that
maintained by Napoleon and more violence. As part of his evidence
to support this contention, Karamzin published a number of short

studies on the French fiasco of 1802-3 in Santo Domingo. In his opinion, the rebellion of Toussaint L'Ouverture was symptomatic of the troubled times, and of France's future without legitimate government. The United States, too, had gained freedom by means of force, and so had doomed itself to a history of violence and tyranny. He supported this in several essays, the most important of which was 'Society in America' ('Obshchestva v amerika'), an article which he had to withhold during Paul's reign.[77] The English, on the other hand, had achieved their revolution (1688) by peaceful means and had chosen to retain their monarchy.[78] They, like the Russians, had found a suitable political system without using force and so had a fortunate, innate stability. The difficulty with republics in practice, he said, was that they invariably reverted to forms of tyranny;[79] it was therefore not the idea of freedom to which he objected, but the republics' failure to fulfill their promises in this regard.

The advantage of monarchy lay in its indissoluble link with law and order,[80] so it was not hard for him to conclude that Russians were best served by their present governmental form. His entire philosophy on governments was summed up in two oft-quoted paragraphs from the *Letters* published in 1801:

> *Every society which has existed for centuries is sacred to good citizens and, even in the most perfect, one cannot help but marvel at the wonderful harmony, concord and order. "Utopia" will always remain the dream of a good heart, or, if it comes to pass, it will come through the gradual working of time, through the slow but true and safe achievements of the mind, enlightenment, education and good morals. When men realize that virtue is necessary for their own happiness, then the Golden Age will come ... But all violent shocks are ruinous and every rebel prepares his own scaffold ... Simple minds think that everything is simple, but the wise realize the dangers inherent in any change, and live quietly ... O new Republicans with depraved hearts, open Plutarch and learn from Cato ... that anarchy is worse than any government.*

Anxious that Russians learn to appreciate their own political system, their own language, customs, and traditions, Karamzin nevertheless maintained his westernism. In fact, he said in 1803 that one of his reasons for delving further into historical studies was to arouse the 'interest not only of Russians, but of foreigners as well.' Ten years later he still grumbled that there was 'little concern in Europe for Russian history.'[81] He believed that Russia was in the mainstream of European culture and political development and he wanted everyone to recognize it. He pleaded with other Russian writers to look for subject matter in their fatherland's history, but was not satisfied with the results. Finally despairing of the efforts of others, he took matters into his own hands and decided to fill the need himself. His decision, however, was not merely an act of patriotism, nor was it part of a plan to enhance his reputation. It was a moral duty, for he saw himself as the patriot sage who, by dint of his great wisdom, was obligated to provide contemporaries with a key to their ultimate happiness and to the national greatness.

In June 1803, Karamzin wrote to his brother that he intended to work on a 'Russian history, in order to leave a reasonable memorial to myself and to the Fatherland.'[82] A few months later, when he presented a petition to M.N. Murav'ev requesting the position of Official Historiographer, he claimed to have been working on a Russian history for 'some time,' and emphasized that his main assets for such a task were his taste, literary talent, and a desire to write 'only for the glory' of Russia. He was granted the position, with a pension. Naturally, as Paul Miliukov so carefully pointed out, the wording of the application was designed to please Murav'ev and the emperor, but there was a good deal of justification for Karamzin's application. Hitherto a belletrist and editor by profession, he also considered himself an accomplished historian. On the face of it, this might seem ludicrous to latter-day scholars, but in the best tradition of the eighteenth century historical writing was still regarded by many as the domain of men of letters. A great many of his contemporaries agreed with Karamzin's self-appraisal, for he had built up enough of a reputation from his historically oriented essays to be offered posts as professor of history at the new University of Dorpat and Kharkov long before the *History* was published. He was asked to teach literature at the University of Vilna where Novosiltsev was curator.[83] The University of Moscow, where Murav'ev was curator, also invited him to teach Russian history. At least one well-known contemporary, A.I. Turgenev, ranked Karamzin very high among living historians and their predecessors. Turgenev registered astonishment in 1805 at Karamzin's

ability to correct earlier historians and in 1809 told his brother that
'Karamzin is one of the best historians of this century, and of the
past as well, which includes Schlözer, Müller, Robertson and Gibbon.
He can be ranked with them.'[84] That Karamzin considered himself a
better critic of the sources than even Schlözer was apparent as early as
1803, when he criticized Schlözer for merely repeating Tatishchev's
errors about Russia's past. Three years later he wrote to Murav'ev
that he was no longer bothered by the omnipresence of the German
scholar.[85]

Before he began to publish the *Messenger of Europe*, Karamzin so
dominated the literary scene in Russia that Andrei Turgenev complained in 1801 that it was impossible for young writers to gain recognition if they dealt with themes other than those popularized by
Karamzin.[86] By the time that he gave up the editorship of the periodical, Karamzin was easily the most widely read writer in his country
and the leading Russian author for Europeans, too. The fact that no
Russian writer before Karamzin had been translated, or had evoked
any sustained interest in the West whatsoever, made this trend all the
more remarkable. At home, a number of Russia's most influential
literati and dozens of lesser lights already referred to themselves as
'Karamzinians.' At this time, he was regarded as an innovator in Russian literary style and language; his followers in matters of letters
tended to be of liberal inclination and they built up in their own
minds a connection between Karamzin's writing style and the new
age of reform. Karamzin's political and historical outlook did not interest them very much. Not all the young writers flocked to him; besides Andrei Turgenev, both A.S. Kaisarov (1782-1813) and A.F.
Merzliakov (1778-1830) resented his domination, but they were the
exceptions.[87] By the turn of the century many writers regularly met
at Karamzin's home and discussed literary matters. His importance to
Moscow society during these years, as an innovator to some, a coun-
terfoil to St Petersburg pretensions for others, as a representative of
Russian tradition to still others, is shown by the fact that his quarters
were often referred to as the city's 'Parnassus.'

Prior to becoming historiographer, Karamzin had presented all his
historical works in literary media and, by his own admission, intended
them to serve as advice for the monarch and for the public. Even
though he was very ironic about the style of current historical novels

and wrote 'A Knight of Our Time' ('Rytsar' nashego vremeni,' 1802-3) to counter the lack of realism in such works, he never eliminated the literary and didactic aspects of his own efforts. Indeed, Karamzin regarded them as integral parts of all good historical writing. His interpretation of Russian history, and of recent events in European history, had led him to reject oligarchy, republicanism, and despotism as forms of government for Russia, leaving only enlightened monarchy as a suitable alternative. Oligarchy, he said, had always led to civil dispute; despotism too closely resembled the reign of Paul I, and even 'the Turkish government was better than anarchy.'[88]

By the time that Karamzin began to write his masterpiece, his attitude towards both history and literature was essentially utilitarian. It was inevitable, then, that the thematic core of the *History* would be political and that its language would be that of eloquent and persuasive literature. After all, the best way to spread ideas is to make them intelligible and pleasurable to the largest possible audience. Even late in 1803, as the first bloom of optimism about peace began to fade, Karamzin was convinced that the 'first decade of the present century will perhaps be always remembered in history,' and he was determined to be remembered as part of it. The *History* easily fulfilled Karamzin's wish.

3
Historian and Man at Court: Karamzin and Russian Society 1803 - 26

Among the wide cross-section of Russian writers who met regularly at Karamzin's home in Moscow were G.R. Derzhavin, Kheraskov, I.I. Dmitriev, S.L. and V.L. Pushkin. A younger generation gathered there too, including the Turgenev brothers, Voeikov, Zhukovsky, and Viazemsky, on whose father's estate Karamzin lived. Others of Russia's talented youth came to be associated with him over the ensuing decade – Batiushkov, Merzliakov and, until he and Karamzin became estranged over their respective political leanings, A.S. Pushkin.

This was an exhilarating time for Russian intellectuals. The *Messenger of Europe* served as a model for other periodicals, most of which appeared in Moscow. But few of them survived very long: P.I. Makarov's *Moscow Mercury* lasted only one year, 1803, V.V. Izmailov's *Patriot* and M.N. Makarov's *Journal for Sweethearts* only through 1804, and P.I. Golenishchev-Kutuzov's *Friend of Enlightenment* lasted but two years. As Ivan Dmitriev said to D.I. Iazykov in 1804, 'My God! So many journals and how quickly they disappear!'[1] Regardless of their fleeting existence, these and other magazines all contributed to an atmosphere of discussion and openness quite unprecedented in Russian society. The creation in 1801 of the Free Society of the Lovers of Literature, Science and Arts (Vol'noe obshchestvo liubitelei slovesnosti, nauk i khudozhestv, 1801-25) and the Friendly Literary Society (Druzheskoe literaturnoe obshchestvo, 1801-6) provided forums for ever wider debate about literary matters.

None of these groups had a unifying pattern of thought, and the intellectual currents and struggles of Russian society as a whole tended to be represented in each of them.[2] Karamzin was made an honourary member of the first of these associations but took no part in its activities, which went beyond literary and into social and political issues. The latter group had an anti-Karamzin hue since it was dominated by Andrei Turgenev and Kaiserov. But Zhukovsky, a great admirer of Karamzin, was a founder of the society. Because he symbolized reform in literature to some, subversion to others, Karamzin was a consistent and often innocent point of departure for discussion in both groups.

Even among those who met at Karamzin's, a wide variety of political and cultural opinions were represented. Viazemsky and M.A. Dmitriev carried on polemics against each other on matters of literature; Griboedov, who was given a letter of introduction to Karamzin by Viazemsky, argued with both Dmitriev and his sponsor. But they all believed that cultural progress was only possible if there were improvements in the quality and quantity of education in Russia and most insisted that literature should not be a monopoly of the nobility. A few were apolitical, some became devotees of the government, and some flirted with liberalism, but their faith in education remained constant. Even those who were opponents in the literary arena tended to keep in touch with each other between 1810 and 1825, and most eventually adopted the enlightened, moderate form of conservatism that was the essence of Karamzinism in political matters.

To illustrate, one need only recall that A.S. Pushkin and Viazemsky were close to M.F. Orlov and N.I. Turgenev in their zealous liberalism during these early years of the century. Yet both adopted an increasingly conservative viewpoint by the end of the twenties. In 1826, Viazemsky insisted that, in spite of the historian's opinion to the contrary, he was very much like Karamzin in political thinking. Viazemsky said that he had been a liberal of the type that would prefer the constitutional monarchy of the restored Bourbons to the despotism of Napoleon; 'there are different liberalisms, just as there are different cigars.'[3]

Though Karamzin became less and less a mediator of Russian letters and more interested in political matters after the French invasion of 1812, his home remained a meeting place, a permanent salon. Even when he lived in St Petersburg after 1816 his residence continued to attract writers and politicians, and discussions of contemporary literature still held pride of place over political topics.

Throughout this time, Karamzin was a focal point for arguments over literary and, to a lesser extent, political debate. Long before he took it upon himself to prepare a national history, his position as founder and editor of several journals, in which he served as literary critic and model for younger writers, had earned him a few enemies. Most of the early criticism of him had been over his style of writing, but at all times there had been certain political overtones to the discussions. In 1801, diverging attitudes towards Karamzin helped split the Friendly Literary Society.

While he was editor of the *Messenger of Europe*, Karamzin's prose writing had been subjected to harsh criticism from Admiral A.S. Shishkov (1754-1841) in a book entitled *Inquiry into the Old and New Style of the Russian Language* (*Razsuzhdemie o starom i novom sloge rossiiskago iazyka*, 1803).[4] Shishkov was responding to ideas such as those expressed in Karamzin's 'Why is There so Little Literary Talent in Russia?', where he had said that Russians should write the way Europeans write. The Shishkovite-Karamzinian dialogue which followed and in which Karamzin took little part, in many ways resembled the so-called Slavophile-Westernizer discussions of the next generation. It also had a 'fathers and sons,' the old against the new, characteristic which became a feature of Russian cultural development for the rest of the century. Many of Russia's writers were still unaccustomed to sharp criticism in periodical literature, and Karamzin had been largely condescending in his own commentary about the efforts of his fellow literati. He had hoped to build up their confidence, he said, so that they would write well and bring honour to their native land. It is also true that the community of writers in Russia during the last decade of the eighteenth century had been too small for any individual to risk making enemies. It was only after the turn of the century that Russian belletrists were confident enough of their skills and that the government would not interfere, to commit themselves to argument in public.

At first Shishkov's incriminations about language were met with ridicule by most interested Russians, and Karamzin's closest friends were so contemptuous about them that they did not show much concern. Even I.I. Dmitriev worried only that a controversy of this sort might aggravate the long-standing hostility between denizens of Moscow and St Petersburg salons.[5] Nevertheless, the *Inquiry* was the first systematic challenge to Karamzin's supremacy in the world of Russia's prose, so P.I. Makarov took the matter to heart and immediately published the strongest possible denunciation of Shishkov's book. Suggesting that Shishkov was a mere apprentice beside Karamzin, Makarov claimed that the latter writer had already 'made an epoch in the history of Russian language.'[6] As far as literature was concerned, the issue was a broad one which pitted young, reforming poets led by Zhukovsky against older, more conservative authors like Shishkov and Derzhavin. One group insisted on change and relied on French, German, and English literary models, the other demanded a return to an older, more traditional Russian style. For Zhukovsky, Karamzin was already a symbol of progress and of the defence against the anti-enlightenment.

The literary tensions of the day could not be separated from the larger political situation. In fact Shishkov treated the discussion as a political one and he was so distrustful of Karamzin's 'Western' inclinations that they took on an almost subversive character in his mind. Leaning to Westernism at this point, a fact evidenced by the very title of his own journal, Karamzin was an object of suspicion to many of those who were convinced that a distinct Russian civilization was being undermined by persistent cultural inroads from Europe. Yet even S.N. Glinka, the conservative nationalist and editor of *Russian Messenger* (*Russkii vestnik*) who published historical accounts and glorifications of Russia's past, complimented Karamzin in 1808 for his 'patriotic' historical writings. Taking the view that Russia was an integral and important part of European civilization, Makarov, Karamzin, and others were not jealous of Russia's uniqueness to the extent that they shut out the good things from Europe. Hoping that the relative openness of society during Alexander's first years as tsar would last, Shishkov's opponents were trying to maintain the influx of enlightenment into Russia.[7] Makarov's periodical, for example, carried prints of Parisian clothing styles in every issue.

Shishkov did receive support from members of the more conservative element in the capital city, the most prominent being A. Griboedov, but in general his linguistic revivalism was ignored.[8] Already in 1804 I.I. Dmitriev had employed the epithet 'Slavophile' for such people and it may have been because of the influential positions held by some of them that a large number of westernizing periodicals had a very short lifespan in the first decade of the century. The Slavophile-Westernizer overtones of the debate were superficial, the term Slavophile having at that time little more meaning than simply one who was Russian oriented. However, even Shishkov could not escape from Western influences, for his wife tended to flaunt them in his own home.[9] Karamzin, in his turn, was later termed a Slavophile by many, and his wife wrote even Viazemsky only in French.

The argument became a rather formalized one when Shishkov and Kerzhavin founded the Gathering of Lovers of Russian Literature (Beseda liubitelei russkoi slovesnosti) in 1811, an organization with the goal of strengthening Russian patriotism by purging the native language of all foreign-derived words. The actual society represented a number of viewpoints, and Karamzin and Speransky were members, but its dynamism came from a hard core of reactionaries who had been meeting since 1807. At that time, the discussions attracted little attention. However, when Russians were once again girding themselves in 1810 for confrontation with France, the debate turned into a political one. Suddenly Shishkov's hint that gallicism in Russian literature represented seeds of revolution received more support among conservatives, and the fact that Karamzin had been supporting neutrality vis-à-vis Napoleon was given an insidious hue by his opponents. During this same period, the arch-conservative émigré, de Maistre, was becoming a force in Russian society while Alexander's reforming minister, Count M.M. Speransky (1772-1839), was coming under increasing pressure for his supposedly pro-French attitude. Karamzin was caught up in the maelstrom of political animosities of the day.

In July 1810, he was awarded the Order of Vladimir, Third Degree, by Alexander in recognition for his work in Russian literature and history.[10] On hearing of that award, a Shishkovite, P.I. Golenishchev-Kutuzov, appealed to the minister of enlightenment to rescind it, alleging that Karamzin was a 'disseminator of free-thinking and Jacobin poison...,' a preacher of 'Godlessness and anarchy.' The open vilification of Karamzin by Kutuzov, who recommended that his works be burned, apparently stemmed from feelings that had been provoked by the historiographer's fairness to Novgorod in the tale 'Martha.' Their personal animosity went back to 1803, when Karamzin had responded to a Kutuzov criticism of 'Martha' by calling him 'malicious' and equating him with the anti-enlightenment. Although he said nothing publicly and told A.I. Turgenev that he did not want 'vengeance,' Karamzin was upset over the new attack and complained bitterly about it to his friends. But Kutuzov's co-editor of *Friend of Enlightenment*, Prince Dmitry Khvostov, remained a friend and admirer of Karamzin's. While his colleague in journalism was vilifying the historiographer in 1810, Khvostov prepared *Verses to N.M. Karamzin* (*Stikhi N.M. Karamzinu*) which praised the writer to the skies. More than a dozen years later, Karamzin was still reciprocating by writing favourably of Khvostov's piety.[11] What neither Khvostov nor Kutuzov knew, of course, was that in these same years, Karamzin was rewriting some of his earlier works and eliminating some of the gallicisms in them. He was also, as we shall see later, attending a very patriotic salon in Tver and preparing his own conservative treatise, the *Memoir on Ancient and Modern Russia*, which was in part an assault on the changes proposed by Speransky.

Six years later, Karamzin still expected 'new denunciations and lies' from Golenishchev-Kutuzov. As far as he was concerned, the argument over language was of little importance, but the allegations against his loyalty were very disturbing. On the other hand, the historian grew quite friendly with Shishkov after he moved to St Petersburg in 1816. Largely because of a nationalistic manifesto which he published in 1812, Shishkov had become popular as a symbol of Russian patriotism.[12] Shishkov, Karamzin said in 1816, was 'honest and civil, but dull.'[13] When Karamzin made his initial speech to the Russian Academy in 1818, he told Dmitriev that his talk on Russian literature had met with warm approval from his former opponent. At any rate, the disintegration of Shishkov's 'barbaric fortifications against Karamzin,' as one publisher called it in 1811,[14] was inevitable, for Shishkov's ideas on writing had little appeal to writers of his time.

Still, heated remonstrations continued after 1811; D.V. Dashkov against Shishkov; Batiushkov and Voeikov against A.A. Shakhovskoi, who had ridiculed Karamzin first in 1807 and published a poem in which he scoffed at Karamzin again in 1815. By 1825, V.L. Pushkin,

Viazemsky, and Zhukovsky had all condemned Shishkovite linguistics, which Batiushkov characterized as 'mandarinist, slavish, Tatar-slavonic.'[15] The coming together in 1815 of a group of young writers who called themselves Arzamas sealed the fate of Shishkov and the Gathering on the one hand, and assured Karamzin a permanent place among Russia's greatest writers on the other. The Arzamas included in its list of members people who, for a variety of reasons, gained considerable influence in the Russian literary world. S.S. Uvarov, Dashkov, Zhukovsky, Bludov, Batiushkov, Dmitriev, K.N. Batiushkov, A.S. Pushkin, A.P. Voeikov, Viazemsky, A.I. and N.I. Turgenev all represented varying degrees of literary competence or at least were regular contributors to contemporary periodicals. F.F. Vigel' and Capodistrias (1776-1831) were also members. As president of the Academy of Sciences for over thirty years, and minister of education for nearly twenty of those years, Uvarov had a different type of influence. Dashkov and Bludov were both active in government service and, although Karamzin was to complain in 1817 that 'Dashkov is not very kind to me,'[16] both had the historiographer's backing in receiving their positions.

The opinion of some nineteenth-century writers that the sole object of Arzamas was to support Karamzin or to enjoy themselves is an exaggerated one, but the historiographer did feel very paternalistic towards them. He attended a few of their meetings and suggested in 1816 that they represented the 'true Russian academy.' Further, he claimed to know 'none wiser than the Arzamas.'[17] Karamzin spoke of them often in letters to Viazemsky, Dmitriev, and A.I. Turgenev. 'Convey all our friendship ... to the Arzamas leaders, S.S. Uvarov and D.N. Bludov. Let them love me as much as I love them; one could ask no more,' he asked Turgenev in 1816.[18] An interesting sidelight to this era, and to a certain extent a foreshadowing of debate for the rest of the century, was the dialogue between Karamzin and Pushkin. They met first in March 1816, in the company of Zhukovsky, A.I. Turgenev, Viazemsky, and V.L. Pushkin. The younger Pushkin lived in Karamzin's home for a few months that year and later recalled the intellectual stimulation which he gained from his many discussions with the sage. He described the arguments as debates, without rancour and with mutual respect. But the two men were far apart in their attitudes towards the historical process in Russia and on the place of autocracy in Russian society. These were crucial matters indeed, but deliberated upon in a gentlemanly manner – a custom that dissipated rapidly in Russian society with the end of the Arzamas.

It is true that Uvarov claimed that members of the society 'accepted Karamzin as their guide and leader,' and that Viazemsky later claimed that it was founded in response to attacks on Karamzin by Prince A. Shakhovskoi, but the connection between Arzamas and the great man can be misunderstood. In 1816, members of Arzamas gathered to present Karamzin with a special diploma, partly to celebrate the Order of Ste Anna which the historiographer was awarded by the ruler on the completion of the *History*, and simultaneously to show their own delight in his success. Written by Zhukovsky, the diploma began: 'To the best of people ... to the father of our ancestors.' It was signed by Zhukovsky, Bludov, A.I. Turgenev, S.S. Uvarov, S.P. Zhikharev, Vigel, V.L. Pushkin, Viazemsky, Dashkov, and Batiushkov.[20] But the liberals, N.I. Turgenev, M.F. Orlov, and N.M. Murav'ev, became members in 1817 and tried to give the society a political mission. Pushkin attended meetings but withdrew when it failed to satisfy his demands for a more national literature. Turgenev and Orlov were present at a meeting in 1817 when the society referred to Karamzin as 'our historian,'[21] but perhaps they held that opinion only until they read the *History*. Furthermore, Viazemsky was later to complain that the Arzamas did not support Karamzin strongly enough when he was criticized in contemporary journals. A.I. Turgenev, however, felt that Karamzin's admittance to the Academy in 1818 was a triumph for all the Arzamas and for their particular literary and ideological interests.[22]

It was the same Turgenev who, perhaps unconsciously, touched on the essence of the Karamzin-Arzamas association. To a very great extent, the historiographer was far more important to these men as a symbol of a new age than he was as a writer or political thinker. Individuals who made up the Arzamas looked upon themselves as the vanguard of Russian enlightenment. Patriotic and increasingly reactionary literature flooded Russian society between 1810 and 1815. The Arzamas, which was more a vague linking of independent thinkers and writers than a formal body, represented a cross-section of those who hoped to counter this trend and to maintain the freedom of the exciting first decade after Paul's death. Drawn together by this desire, each held his own opinion on Russia's political needs. They all resented the stultification and repression which they sensed in Shishkov's writing, but some, Uvarov being the most striking example, were not loathe to use similar methods when they achieved positions of power themselves. 'Karamzinism,' then, was to be a tool for all of them – they made of him what they wished, at times over the protests of Karamzin himself. Members met in St Petersburg and in Moscow, in small groups and in large groups, all with the aim of keeping Russia in the mainstream of modern thought and literature. Witness Viazemsky's comment to Turgenev in 1816: 'Our Russian life is dead ... I go to refresh myself in the Arzamas and to rest from death.'[23]

The goals which drew so many young men of diverse social and political opinions together are suggested in a Viazemsky memorandum of 1817, in which he pleaded for a new journal with which to continue the Novikov-Karamzin type of journalistic enlightenment. In that note, he said that Russia had had only two journalists in the past, Novikov and Karamzin, and that their tradition was being threatened by reactionary forces. The purpose of the new organ, which never really got off the ground, would be to combat 'prejudice, vices and nonsense,' to counter the Gathering and the Academy, and to propagandize actions that would allow Russia to grow strong and prosperous.[24] His colleagues agreed with him in this but not on the matter of Karamzin. Several of the founders of Arzamas, particularly Dashkov, had been anxious to oppose Shishkov but were not interested in defending Karamzin.[25] For Viazemsky, however, defence of Karamzin was already synonymous with defence of the entire Russian enlightenment. This was the very sentiment that was picked up by Pogodin and others and carried well into the latter half of the nineteenth century.

The Arzamas never fulfilled the promise with which its members equated it. Designed to bridge the gulf between Europe and Russia, to be the cultural catalyst that would result in a strong, modern Russian literature, it went the way of other progressive movements. As Uvarov put it in a letter to Speransky, 'our literature grows worse each day. Politics devours everything.'[26]

The emotional attachment that some of the Arzamas felt for Karamzin was disclosed in a eulogistic poem written about him by Batiushkov in 1818, which compared him to Thucydides, and another by Zhukovsky, who called Karamzin a 'sacred name!' in 1831. As late as 1850, Zhukovsky remarked that his 'love for the memory of Karamzin has not lost its warmth.'[27] Others such as Serbinovich, Dmitriev, and Viazemsky were especially active in publishing rebuttals against Karamzin's detractors, the latter still doing so in the 1870s. Permanently enshrined among the great men of Russian letters, Karamzin was by no means free from reproach for his prose and language. His major opponent on literary things in the 1820s was P.A. Katenin, who blamed Karamzin for the lack of progress in Russian literature. In the thirties, I.I. Dmitriev complained of a 'new anti-Karamzin generation.'[28]

A less lively literary debate, carried on mainly in private letters, centred around Karamzin once again in 1818 when he was nominated to the Academy. Some of his closest admirers had been clamouring for his admission to that prestigious institution for a long time, but Karamzin, who looked upon it as the organ of his opponents, claimed to be disinterested. The 'Russian-Shishkov Academy' was what he had called it in 1816 when Derzhavin urged him to let his name stand.[29] Dmitriev had insisted on his entrance as early as 1804 and was especially bitter when he thought that the incentive behind the Academy's belated action in 1818 was the acclaim given Karamzin's writing in western Europe. When Karamzin's leading opponent on historical matters, M.T. Kachenovsky, was granted membership the next year, even Karamzin felt somewhat affronted. Yet, Dashkov felt that the historiographer's appointment was a mistake. Alleging that Karamzin's contribution to Russian literature was less than that of Gnedich, M.N. Murav'ev, and others, Dashkov insisted that they should have been admitted first.[30]

Karamzin remained somewhat distant from the various literary storms that swirled around him. He was more of a symbol than a participant, a figure whose name could be used by the participants in the interest of progress, tradition, or whatever cause they had in mind. He tended to be far more concerned with day-to-day political matters than with literary ones and, of course, he was busy writing the *History*. The arguments were of little importance to him at a time when European states were being shaken by civil strife once again and when he was aware that his own state now harboured groups that looked for its downfall. Even when Shishkov first pub-

lished the diatribe against him in 1803, the historian gave his attention to other matters. Karamzin was not unique in this attitude, for
a number of Russia's important literati avoided participation in political dispute not so much because they were afraid of angering offi-
cialdom, but because they recognized that it was a waste of time.
Zhukovsky, for example, eliminated most of the political sections
from the *Messenger of Europe* when he became its editor in 1808.
His reasoning that 'politics in a land where general opinion is humbly
submissive to the power of government, is not very attractive to
those ... [who] love peace of mind,'[31] mirrored the sentiments of
many Russian writers before their world became dominated by more
activist forces.

In fact, Karamzin was almost invisible to the Russian reading public between 1803 and 1814. Except for the reprinting of several of
his earlier works, a few poems that were of greater political than literary merit, he remained hard at work on the *History of the Russian
State*. 'History,' he said, 'removes us from our contemporaries.' But
he was aware of the storm which was brewing in Europe. In letters to
his brother and to Turgenev in 1808 and 1809, he was pessimistic
about Russia's remaining safe from Napoleon. And he did not ap-
prove of his country's actions in Finland, though he acknowledged
that the alliance with France was otherwise valuable. 'If the great
Napoleon lives for another ten years or more,' he predicted to his
brother in January 1809, 'it will be a miracle.'[32] Finally, in 1810 and
1811 he was jolted out of political somnolence by the obvious threat
of invasion from France and a corresponding menace of administrative change at home under the leadership of Speransky. In response
to both, he prepared his famous, or infamous, *Memoir on Ancient
and Modern Russia* (1811).

This particular work was not intended for public consumption,
but it became relatively well known and represented the social and
political outlook of the majority of Russian conservatives at the time
of its writing. It reflected the strain on Karamzin of the times, a
period when many Russians could foresee the possible disintegration
of the world which they knew and loved. Karamzin was not alone in
his reservations about the future; the ruler was beset at this time by
petitions, pamphlets, and studies from men who expected the entire
future of Russia to be decided within these few years. They were not

far from being correct. The confusion caused by war with France so soon after peace seemed assured was compounded by the humiliation of defeat and the ensuing political disgrace of Tilsit (1807). Within a few years, rumours of joint French-Polish action for Polish independence raised the hackles of even those few Russians who had favoured the alliance with France. Coupled with hints about a complete restructuring of the Russian state system to the disadvantage of the nobility, these happenings catapulted a variety of conservatives into action. Liberals, too, intended to direct the recent and forthcoming upheavals to their advantage. Karamzin was no exception. Considered from time to time as a leading candidate for such posts as state secretary, minister of education, or president of the Academy, he preferred his duties as imperial historiographer, which he interpreted as an advisory office. The *Memoir* was certainly intended to sway the thinking of the ruler.

Although the spirit of the times shaped the ideas that Karamzin expressed in the *Memoir*, he would not have written it if he had not been urged to do so by Catherine Pavlovna, the emperor's sister. Catherine held politically oriented meetings at her husband's estate in Tver. Opposed to most of the changes towards which her brother was working, she invited to Tver representatives of the most conservative forces in Russia and a small group of anti-Napoleon émigrés, including Joseph de Maistre. Karamzin was asked to some of the sessions, where he read extracts from the early volumes of his still incomplete *History* and found that the gathering received them with a great deal of enthusiasm. It was at Tver, too, that he was first presented to the emperor.[33]

For most participants, the immediate source of anxiety were the constitutional reforms proposed by Speransky, for they could foresee the abrogation of their political and social privileges. Others were afraid of a pro-French intrigue at court. Karamzin, too, contemplated Alexander's experiments with some alarm, but the spectre behind his unease had little to do with personal position. He was concerned more with the threat posed to recently acquired Russian prestige by a Napoleonic army and, horror of horrors, its union with Polish legions from the Grand Duchy of Warsaw.

The parts of the *Memoir* that best revealed Karamzin's sense of his instructional role, and tied him indissolubly with nineteenth-century

Russian conservatism were a brief introduction to Russian history and his critique of Alexander's foreign policy. He began his outline of Russian history with the hypothesis that his country's monarchical tradition originated with a Slavic desire to live in peace. Thus, Scandinavians were quite cordially invited to act as sovereigns in the ninth century on the condition that they put a stop to constant internecine wars among the Slavic tribes. Suggesting that the early 'quarrelling democratic states' had always been poverty stricken, he claimed that Norsemen had turned Slavic military prowess into more profitable channels, that is, a means to glory and booty, plus a united Slavdom. He warned, however, that conquest was only useful to Russians while the state remained strong, centralized, and enlightened.[34] Once warfare became a struggle for power among the princes, unity disappeared and the earliest 'Russian' state collapsed.

To emphasize his point, Karamzin claimed that it was mainly through the agency of cunning, peaceful diplomacy that Moscow had been able to restore Russian prestige, the 'sword' only completing the task. In his words, 'the Moscow princes accomplished this great deed by utilizing a wise political system,' not by military heroics. The greatest merit of such a method of government, autocracy, was that its ablest practitioners 'were always ready for peace, they kept out of the affairs of Europe ... they displayed no yearnings for false or perilous conquests, preferring to preserve rather than to acquire.'[35]

Revealing his anxiety over contemporary issues, Karamzin made his distaste for 'useless' warfare the predominant part of his preaching about foreign policy. He chastised Elizabeth for such wars but lauded Catherine II for triumphs that 'assured the external security of the realm' and for her policy of 'non-interference in wars which were of no concern to Russia.' The historian was remarkably consistent in this idea. Ten years earlier, he had praised the expansionist ambitions of both Peter I and Catherine because the 'benefit of Russia' had been their only goal. Catherine's wars against the Turks and her ruthless actions against the Poles were condoned, indeed commended in the *Memoir*, because in Karamzin's opinion those peoples had never ceased planning the destruction of Russia. 'In politics,' he proclaimed in another place, 'self-preservation is the highest law.' Therefore, Russia had to do anything in her power to prevent the existence of an independent Poland. But, he insisted, 'Europe knows that Catherine, ever ready for war, would never have broken the peace herself.'[36]

Having applauded Catherine for her martial successes, Karamzin used the advantage of hindsight to caution other monarchs against overconfidence: 'Russians began to think that nothing could overcome them – a delusion.'[37] He then blamed Paul for the aimlessness of Russia's policies after Catherine's death and charged him with turning the manly 'spirit of War,' which had characterized earlier Russian armies, into 'martinettism.' The bitter tone used by Karamzin when writing about Paul revealed the extent to which he felt obligated to advise the government, for that ill-fated tsar was still taboo as a subject for conversation in Russian society.

Completing the survey of Russian history, in which he underscored the military policies of former princes, Karamzin went directly to the meat of his advice for Alexander in matters of foreign policy. He said, accordingly, that when France had returned to monarchy under Napoleon, 'Russian diplomacy should have aimed at general peace.' Instead, Alexander had committed Russia to assisting England and Austria 'without any particular advantage to herself.' Outlining a series of errors which he felt had been committed in Russia's relations with Napoleon, Karamzin still did not condemn the war of 1806 for, by that time, 'we had no choice but to defend the security of our possessions, which Napoleon menaced by inciting Poland.' As late as 1811, then, he felt that compromise might save the day for Russia, so Karamzin recommended that Alexander try to conclude peace, 'even at the cost of so-called honour – a luxury only strong states can afford.'[38]

Besides the historical survey and analysis of Alexander's foreign policy, the *Memoir* included sections on Russian political institutions, recent legislation, serfdom, financial policies, and on a project for codifying Russian laws. On the matter of Russian political institutions, which had undergone some changes since 1809, Karamzin cautioned against too much haste and suggested that political changes were shaking the 'foundations of the Empire.' He was particularly upset that the changes were being arranged in secret, and advised simply that Catherine's system be re-established. His greatest worry was the danger of a senate or ministry coming between the emperor and his subjects.

Karamzin had been pleased when Speransky had undertaken needed reform in 1808,[39] but the insecurity of the times prompted him to retract. In fact, there were no major differences between his *Memoir* and earlier items in the *Messenger of Europe* or in the *Eulogy* to Catherine II. It is true that the *Messenger of Europe* had nothing but praise for Alexander's attempts at reform, and that the *Memoir* chastised him on several counts. But Karamzin's overall political viewpoint had changed not at all; in each case he found a rationale for enlightened autocracy and firm, law-abiding government.

Karamzin also came full circle in his opinion of Alexander's general legislation. He even complained about too much waste entailed by the ruler's emphasis on education. In this regard, he seemed to contradict his insistence some years before that Russia expand and modernize its educational system. Yet even then Karamzin had been cautious and had often warned against things being done too hastily. He argued, too, against any project to emancipate the serfs. They could not be given land, he said, for it all 'belongs to the gentry,' and without their own land, the peasantry would be driven to 'drinking and villainy.' Freedom, he insisted, could very well harm, even destroy, the state; 'it is safer to enslave men than to give them freedom prematurely. Freedom demands preparation through moral improvement ... The serfs of humane landlords are content with their lot.'

Karamzin also spoke against fiscal policies of the government, particularly about what he believed was a too heavy reliance upon paper money. His case, however, did not go much deeper than a characteristic phrase, 'great breaks are dangerous.' He was equally upset by the project to codify Russia's laws, which had been outlined by Speransky's commission in 1810. Horrified by its similarity to the Napoleonic Code, Karamzin reversed his earlier pleas to Alexander and now said that, 'an old nation has no need for new laws.'

The *Memoir* concluded with a short series of forthright recommendations. The main one, of course, was that Russia must retain autocracy, in which the sovereign is the source of all authority. 'Autocracy,' he repeated, 'is the Palladium of Russia.' The ruler, in his turn, must find honest and able people for government service, he must learn how to deal with men, and he must make his subjects respect him even if they have to fear him first. The ruler must depend upon the gentry for assistance.

The *Memoir* echoed several of the themes that Karamzin had been preaching since the late nineties, but the idea that went back the furthest was his feeling that vices and excessive luxury would inevitably weaken the state. If any society failed to reach a compromise between the very rich and the very poor, then its fate was sealed. In the *Letters*, he had pointed out the 'outrageous confusion of wealth and poverty' in Paris and painted a bleak picture of a nobility that wallowed in luxury, vices, and idleness. The French nobility and clergy were, in his opinion, 'poor defenders of the throne.' In 1802, he had warned that the American republic was falling victim to the same trend. 'The *spirit of trade* is the main characteristic of America,' he said, 'where everyone strives for acquisitions. Wealth appears in sharp *contrast* with poverty and slavery.' The next year, Karamzin complained that the French republic had fallen prey to the same temptation. The government of France was more interested in the success of the Lyons fabric business than in the welfare of its people. If 'sacrifice is justly called a virtue,' he continued, 'then luxury is truly a vice.'[40]

Although he had praised Catherine II's politics in the *Memoir*, Karamzin decried a decline a morals at court and the gentry's 'excessive emulation of European luxury' while she governed. Russians 'lacked decent upbringing, firm principles, and social morality,' but the damage that this might have caused had at least been forestalled by firm autocratic rule under Alexander. Karamzin was to return to this theme once again, in the *History*, where he claimed that 'ambition and self-interest' had caused the demise of Swiss independence. Progress, then, was closely tied to the growth of moral perfection. Ultimately, only powerful, secure states could assure access to that particular utopia.

The *Memoir* is an extremely important exposition of Karamzin's political outlook but it had little influence upon the Russia of his day. It did not alter Alexander's policies, which changed because of the circumstances of the times. Alexander may not even have read it, although it was given to him by Catherine when he visited Tver in March 1811. Pogodin insisted that he did.[41] Karamzin wrote Dmitriev that he had spoken to Alexander for some time during that March sojourn at Tver: 'and what about? About Autocracy! I did not have the pleasure to agree with some of his thoughts.' A sense of urgency and Pavlovna's protection dictated the frankness of Karamzin's message and may have led him into making assertions that he recognized as oversimplified. But the document does represent a clear expression of some basic ideas that were to remain at the core of nineteenth-century Russian conservatism.

Karamzin was not always so practical about war and society as he was in the *Memoir*. The album of extracts from European writers which he gave to Catherine in the same year had as its keynote an extract from Bossuet to the effect that the rise and fall of states, victories and losses, 'dépend des ordres secrets de la divine Providence.'[42] The album contained extracts from Rousseau as well, specifically those of his words which best lent support to autocracy, and from Pope, Milton, Buffon, Pascal, Montaigne, and others. The items were selected because they carried Karamzin's own attitudes. It was the *Memoir*, however, that most clearly reflected his point of view, and that of the conservative, patriotic establishment in Russia.

Although the essentials of Karamzin's scheme for Russian history were outlined in the *Memoir*, the public had no record of his thought from the last issue of the *Messenger of Europe* in 1803 until the appearance of the *History* fifteen years later. However, the contemporary relevance of the message carried in the *Memoir* serves as a gauge of Karamzin's intention to convey the 'lessons of history' to his readers. A letter to Uvarov in 1813, in which he congratulated the future minister of public instruction for suggesting the use of history as a politically educative tool, indicates the same thing.[43]

It has often been suggested that the *Memoir* was a direct attack upon Speransky, and even that it and Karamzin were largely instrumental in the minister's abrupt dismissal in March 1812. Yet there was not even a direct clash of wills involved, for much of the minister's proposed slate of reforms was not publicly known, nor was the *Memoir*. In fact, Speransky was the victim of more powerful enemies than the historiographer, among them Alexander's mother, and of the increasingly general phenomenon of Russian francophobia. When Speransky fell from grace, Karamzin actually sympathized with him and wrote to his brother that, 'the history of Speransky is a secret for us. The public knows nothing. They think that he was caught in some indiscreet correspondence. He is blamed for everything, now they forget ... [his accomplishments] .'

The two men had friendly correspondence in 1810 and, in 1818, Speransky had only praise for the content and tone of Karamzin's *History*, and named him one of the best scholars in Russia.[44] Later, however, Speransky spoke, not bitterly, of Karamzin's opposition to him and regretted that the difference between them was that Karamzin was ignorant of his real ideas and plans.[45] The two men have been regarded as representatives of opposite tendencies in Russian political thought. Mistaken as this view may be (it arose from exaggerated opinions about the rigidity of both men), it is true that a polarization had set into Russian society midway through Alexander's reign, and most thinkers were categorized into one camp or the other. The same dynamic but reactionary nationalism that drove Speransky out, and with which Karamzin was associated in only an indirect way, led to the Jesuits being forced out of Russia in 1815 and to the departure of de Maistre in 1817. Shishkov's political leanings seemed to have won the day.

The period 1810 to early 1814 was one of immense strain for Karamzin. He wrote very little on his *History*, spending much of his time on the *Memoir* and then languishing in Nizhnii-Novgorod where, although he was surrounded by some of Moscow's best known men of letters, he had not the materials to continue his historical research. Napoleon's invasion, the burning of Moscow (and his library), the lingering sickness of his son Andrew, and his own fear that he might be losing his eye sight, all contributed to his general pessimistic mood. He had real financial worries as well, for he was not receiving his stipend as historiographer, nor were his peasants paying him the customary *obrok*. He did not even know where he was to live after his stay at the residences of S.A. L'vov and I.V. Averkiev in Nizhnii. During this time his letters were filled with allusions to God's hand in earthly affairs, and pleas to his friends that they must rally to the assistance of the government and to the emperor. The enormity of coming post-war reconstruction of Russian affairs was apparent to Karamzin long before Napoleon was defeated. He saw that Russians were going to need more than simply a strong hand at the top. They needed wise and able counselling, they needed faith and patriotism. Inevitably, Karamzin was going to suggest that they would not need constitutional changes in the near future, for, if nothing else, this would hamper the entire rebuilding process. It was in this light that

he had carried on the indirect and often overstated debate with Speransky. All in all, Karamzin's constant support of the existing state
system remained more a matter of practical politics than a commitment to some metaphysical, ideological polity. As he stated it, 'I extoll autocracy, that is, I value the oven during the winter in our
Northern climate.'[46]

Even in the face of extreme anti-Napoleon feeling in Moscow, and
his own patriotism, Karamzin kept a practical attitude towards his
nation's relationship with France. According to Viazemsky, 'Karamzin did not support the War of 1812, either before or after its beginning ... He was of the opinion that some diplomatic concessions must
be made ... his patriotism was not like that of vehement journalists,
rather his had the conservative character of an historian.'[47] While
living in the home of a leading Francophobe and governor general of
Moscow, Count F.V. Rostopchin (1763-1826), in 1812, Karamzin
still argued that war with France was unnecessary. In the company of
the count, Iu. A. Nedelinsky-Meletsky, and A. Ia. Bulgakov he spoke
at length on behalf of peace. He mollified Rostopchin by insisting
that Russia fight while Napoleon was on her soil, and claimed that he
was ready to take up the sword himself. Karamzin was sure that Russia would win on its own territory, for they had patriotic incentive
there, but that Napoleon would have the same advantage in France.
It is possible that this was one of the points that persuaded Rostopchin to advise Alexander not to follow the French armies into
Europe. According to reports from Bludov and Dmitriev, Alexander
wanted to appoint Karamzin as secretary of state in 1812, but the
historian's compromising stance turned the decision in favour of
Shishkov, whose impassioned speech on patriotism in that year won
him acclaim.

Karamzin's awareness of the complexity of the impending threat
to Russia's standing in the world was implicit in a letter he sent to
Dmitriev in 1813: 'Moscow no longer exists – only its ashes remain.
Not only were houses burned. Even the morals of its people were
changed for the worse ... Noticeable bitterness and open insolence,
none of which existed before. The government needs unusually wise
measures. However, this is not my affair, it is God's. He knows everything better than us.'[48] Karamzin still looked upon Moscow as the
heart of Russia and now some of the predilections which he had

posed in the *Memoir* seemed to be coming true. Only extraordinary measures could stop and then repair the damage done to the Russian Empire by the destruction of that city. In contrast to a number of his countrymen, Karamzin did not believe that his nation's problems were over with the defeat of Napoleon in 1814. So he was quite upset when Ivan Dmitriev resigned from his post in the ministry of justice. This was a time for rallying, not for quitting. On mentioning his disappointment to Dmitriev, Karamzin said that 'all the wise and honest people' should join state service.[49]

The victory over Napoleon did bring immediate relief to Karamzin ('Every day, I rejoice and thank God'),[50] and so he rushed to the press a poem dedicated to Alexander, the 'Liberator of Europe.' In explaining the purpose of the poem, he wrote that he had 'lived with you, good Muscovites, for a quarter century and the best times of my life. ... The glory of the Monarch is a national one.' The poem was read to Alexander by Karamzin's long-time friend, Neledinsky-Meletsky, and the empress, to whom the author had sent the work, gave him a gift in return.[51] The poem was so much in contrast to Karamzin's avowed distaste for flattery that he actually expressed his embarrassment about it to Dmitriev. Nevertheless, it doubtless represented the feelings of most Russians. Free of foreign wars, they hoped that Russia could now settle down to a time of reconstruction. But when the emperor requested that the historiographer move to the capital city his eyes were opened to further and, in some ways, more disquieting facets of the national life. He was to observe at close hand the inconsistencies of court life and of decision-making at the centre of the empire.

Karamzin's decade in St Petersburg was one in which he commanded considerable prestige in court circles and in society at large. It was also the first protracted period of his life when he could see for himself the difference between the capital city and Moscow. Like many of his class, he continued to look upon the older city as the focal point of Russian tradition. He was emotionally uncomfortable in St Petersburg and often expressed a longing to return to Moscow where he could contemplate the real Russia without having to pierce the glitter and sham of court life. In fact, his initial months in the capital were so unnerving that he actually contemplated selling the *History* so that he could go home all the sooner. Though this rather peevish thought was not a serious one, he did consider returning to Moscow regardless of the ruler's request that he remain in St Petersburg.

Karamzin's feeling about Moscow as the proper centre of the Russian Empire stemmed from his knowledge of Russian history and from his own exhilarating experience there. In an essay written in 1817 and published in 1820, Karamzin described Moscow as the birthplace of Russian autocracy, 'not just for the special use of the Autocrat, but for the good of the people.' The city was reputed to be republican during the last days of Catherine II, he continued, but this inaccuracy was merely the result of the fact that Muscovites took more liberties with life, not in thought, and participated more in the general events in society than did the citizens of St Petersburg. The northern capital remained for Karamzin the symbol of a cosmopolitanism which detracted to a certain extent from the uniqueness of Russia. The building of St Petersburg, he wrote in 1811, was a 'glaring mistake.' Because of that act by Peter I, Russians 'became citizens of the world but ceased in some respects to be citizens of Russia.' Karamzin also regarded himself, with some justification, as one of Moscow's institutions and may have worried lest he lose some of his following in the capital. Even during the unsettled days of 1813 he turned down an offer by Empress Maria Fedorovna to make apartments available to him in Paul's palace in St Petersburg. 'I am not a courtier,' he replied along with his thanks.[52]

Never an admirer of the Russian bureaucrat, Karamzin now could find real reasons to be discouraged with the quality of ministers and other highly placed people in St Petersburg. He began his stay there with a run-in with Count A.A. Arakcheev (1769-1834), a circumstance that apparently cost him some time in publishing the *History*. Arakcheev, however, was not one of the weak officials in the capital and at least earned Karamzin's respect. His general feeling, though, was amply illustrated by the remarkably rare times that he praised an official and by his constant attempts to persuade trusted friends, Dmitriev, A.I. Turgenev, and Viazemsky, to remain in their administrative posts. This was not because Karamzin hoped for authority at court, but because he believed that the Empire could survive only through the assistance of such men. For that reason, Karamzin continued to support Viazemsky to his utmost while others suspected that the young prince was too liberal in his attitudes. Karamzin's reservations about Russia's ministers lasted until his dying days, for in June 1825, he remarked to Dmitriev that an earlier official (A.A. Bezborodko) had had wisdom, a sense of justice, and a knowledge of Russia. 'He was a good Minister,' said Karamzin, 'we have no such people now.'[53]

However, the historiographer's attitudes towards St Petersburg mellowed somewhat during his decade of residence and he resigned himself to living out his final days there. Perhaps the saving grace for him was his close association with the emperor and empress. His correspondence is replete with comments about dinners and discussions with them; he presented himself to his friends as the wise counsellor for the rulers and in 1825 he even claimed to have known about Constantine's renunciation of his right to the throne two years before. Whether or not Karamzin was aware of this event before Alexander's death is unknown. He may well have been indulging in some sort of after-the-fact wishful thinking, for Karamzin was rather a pompous person and very sensitive about his relationship with the Romanovs. His claim to Dmitriev that he was one of the very few people who had been informed of Alexander's arrangements about succession was probably a product of that sensitivity. He may well have been hurt that he did not know. But the fact that he was close to the ruler cannot be disputed. It was Karamzin who persuaded him to appoint Zhukovsky as the Russian-language tutor to the future Alexander II.[54]

Karamzin's actual influence on the court was really not very great when it came to persuading policy-makers, specifically the emperor. But he was listened to with respect and was in a position to gain favours for friends from Alexander and some of the ministers. Capodistrias and Novosiltsev were always helpful, and he numbered among his close friends Count Rumiantsev, Lopukhin, A.B. Kurakin, and A.K. Razumovsky. But some state officials resented Karamzin's meddling in affairs deemed to be in their domain. He complained, for example, that Prince A.N. Golitsyn (1773-1844), who was minister of public instruction and spiritual affairs, was 'only civil to me, I cannot ask him any favours.' There were several members of the administration and nobles who remained suspicious of Karamzin and who tried to have his *History* sent to the censors. One such was A.F. Labzin, a Freemason, who was made vice-president of the Academy of Arts in 1818.[55]

Although his advice may have had little impact on Alexander's decisions, being able to give it gave great comfort to Karamzin and made him bold enough to write such essays as the 'Opinion of a Russian Citizen,' ('Mnenie russkago grazhdanina,' 1819) which had lasting significance for Russian attitudes towards Poland. In general, Karamzin remained independent of the emperor and openly criticized foreign policy and such domestic practices as censorship and the military colonies. Karamzin never turned from his long-held view that censorship prevented the increase of enlightenment and cultural progress, and so was far more likely to lead to anarchy than was a system which provided for a relatively free press. Some years after Karamzin's death, Gogol' singled him out as the first important conservative writer to insist that an author must not be restrained by a censor: 'None besides Karamzin spoke so boldly and wisely, he did not hide any of his opinions and thoughts, although he did not always agree with the government of that time.'[56]

Russia's immense contribution to the defeat of Napoleon and her subsequent prestige among European countries led many Russians to expect much better things at home. It was not unreasonable to hope for a further slackening of the bonds of serfdom, or to foresee the establishment of freer institutions. After all, Russia apparently was far stronger in 1815 than she had been in 1801, when Alexander had considered such moves seriously. Yet an increasing reaction set in and Arakcheev became the leading minister. The new minister of public instruction in 1816, Golitsyn, also helped assure the primacy of reaction and, to Karamzin's dismay, a mounting tendency towards mysticism appeared at court. The ministry of public instruction, the body so important to Karamzin, was dominated after 1815 by other reactionaries – A.S. Sturdza, M.L. Magnitsky (1778-1855), and D.P. Runich (1778-1860). It was these men who made sure that no liberals would have a voice in Russia's universities. The Arzamas would have little chance against them. When in 1817 Alexander combined Golitsyn's three posts (he was also the administrator of the holy synod and of religious affairs) into one ministry, Karamzin termed it the 'Ministry of the Eclipse.' Unfortunately, but fittingly enough, Golitsyn was replaced in 1824 by Karamzin's one-time nemesis,

Shishkov. The historiographer's only remark about the change in ministers was simply that it made very little difference.

However, Alexander had not given up his interest in constitutions. The first step towards a constitution for Russia was taken when he gave one to Poland in 1815. Karamzin took little notice of it in that year. Even in April 1818, shortly after Alexander had addressed the first Polish Diet, Karamzin spoke of the constitution as merely a novelty. But three weeks later he warned that the 'Warsaw speech' had aroused great ambitions in Russia's youth. He was not particularly worried at that time. At least he claimed that 'while the young rage, we smile...,' and a half-year later told Dmitriev that he wished 'neither a constitution, nor representation, but in feeling I remain a republican and at the same time a true supporter of the Tsar of Russia.' The seeming contradiction, he explained, was illusory, because freedom was something for the inner man and of little importance in political matters.[57]

However, when Alexander asked Novosiltsev to plan a constitution for Russia too, Karamzin, who heard of it from Viazemsky, changed his tune. The Polish constitution called for freedom of the press and equality before the law, rights that Karamzin respected, but the emperor had also implied that he might turn over some 'Russian' lands to Poland. It was at this time that Karamzin appealed to Alexander to rescind the constitution for Poland. His arguments were presented so frankly that Karamzin was convinced that he had forfeited the favour of the monarch. Yet, rational criticism was part of the historian's patriotism. A year earlier, he had demonstrated that he was well aware of the risks that any critic of the régime undertook, no matter his rank. He warned Viazemsky to be careful when he did not agree with hierarchical decisions, but pleaded with him to advise as much as possible: 'always be cautious, this will do no harm. We old men can sometimes allow ourselves well-intentioned *licence*, but you young people must be more prudent ... Do not say all that you think, but speak up!'[58]

Karamzin was acting upon a suggestion contained in the *Memoir*, where he had said that the 'true, virtuous citizens of Russia would presume to stop his hand' if the ruler went beyond his authority and tried to limit the powers of his own office. In practising his own speeches, Karamzin read his 'Opinion of a Russian Citizen' to the emperor and accused Alexander of forgetting the obligation, demanded of him by God, to assure the welfare of his empire. The ruler, as a Christian, should treat his vanguished enemies well, but only in so far as his own nation did not suffer from it. 'Love men, Sire,' said Karamzin, 'but love Russians above all!' Alexander had subjected the Poles, but it was 'Russian power that gained their obedience. It is through the Russians that the Emperor has earned the glory of being the liberator of Europe.' Karamzin's intention, then, was to show Alexander that Russia did not need a constitution as long as ruler and people lived up to their mutual responsibilities. Poland deserved neither political freedoms nor independence, for she had always used them to attack Russia in the past. 'Did you not, like your predecessors, swear to maintain the integrity of the Empire!,' he asked Alexander, and pointed out that some areas of Poland had originally been Russian anyway. In a somewhat contradictory vein he went on to say that 'Poland is a legitimate possession of Russia. There are no ancient land-deeds in politics.'[59]

Waxing particularly eloquent, Karamzin suggested that the immediate consequence of the constitution for Poland would be a loss of prestige for the emperor, a slackening of Russian patriotism, and a sapping of Russian courage. Consequently, the empire would become a community led by men who served their own interests, 'real slaves.' Thus, he saw the matter of a constitution for Poland as a two-sided threat to Russia. Even an autonomous Poland would make the empire vulnerable to foreign invasion. At the same time, the constitutional precedent was an internal threat. Demands for a similar one in Russia would imperil the inner freedoms enjoyed by the emperor's subjects, their ability to think and feel freely without political responsibilities.

Karamzin's fear of the constitution in Poland was not a reactionary one in the traditional sense of the word. For one thing, he was inescapably anti-Polish and, if one accepts the judgements of Nicholas Turgenev and Herzen, it was anti-Polish feeling that Karamzin did most to instill into Russian thinking.[60] Above all, however, he simply did not believe that such devices were an answer for the social and political dilemmas of his time. In his opinion, 'to give Russia a constitution ... is to dress up some respected man in a dunce's cap.'[61] He was convinced that any restraint put on the emperor's decision-making powers would only accelerate chaos, but he was as much against terror from the top as he was against terror from the lower levels of society. The best illustration of this was his attitude towards the murder in 1819 of the reactionary poet, A.F.F. von Kotzebue, a known Russian agent in Germany, by a university student in Mannhein named Karl Sand. The incident infuriated German and Russian conservatives, and provoked a series of harsh anti-student decrees from German governments. Many Russians saw in the incident a vindication of the charges made by Alexander Sturdza, a Russian diplomat in Germany in 1818, who had published a very harsh indictment of university students. (Sadly, but perhaps fittingly, he came back to Russia and joined the ministry of education.) Shortly after the murder, however, Karamzin wrote to Dmitriev about the incident and said that Kotzebue's thinking had been out of date. He warned Viazemsky in another letter not to act irrationally about it: 'Be careful about active participation in the fate of Kotzebue. Some time ago he wrote me a kind letter about my *History*. I wept over his drama, then was brave. Sand rendered a service to Sturdza. Many now say, *Sturdza was right*! – not I. If you live forty more years, many will see and remember what I have said.'[62] He was even less moved by the assassination of the Duc de Berry, Bourbon heir apparent in France, and simply commented, 'What a century!'

After 1819, Karamzin was afraid of internal and external pressures that might at any time pull out the underpinnings of the Russian Empire. He was well aware of the widespread liberal movement inside Russia and abhorred the civil strife that beset most European states. All of this trouble he blamed on the French Revolution and he complained often about its leaders who had 'duped the youth of Europe' for generations to come. Still, he believed that most liberals would not be able to hold on to their following. For that reason he did not think that strong measures against liberalism were necessary. Indeed, it was the dynamism of the right that worried him the most. In the diplomatic arena, it was pressure from Metternich, from men of de Maistre's calibre, and from those who wanted Russia to interfere in the internal affairs of other countries that he felt might lead to the downfall of the Russian Empire. At home, he ridiculed and even reviled some liberals, but he also remained on friendly terms with a number of them. He continued to rail against censorship. He not

only evinced horror at the iniquities of the censorship boards, especially when poems of V.L. Pushkin were held back in 1822, but he
was shocked at the stupidity of many of their administrators. Karamzin would have called for the proscription of subversive material himself, but he was horrified when censors changed words that they
obviously did not understand and threatened the very existence of
Russian enlightenment. In 1824, he complained that the censorship
boards were growing, 'for every part of literature, there will be a special censor. So much for freedom! Our literature flourishes with censors but without authors.'[63]

Although he no longer proposed reforms, he had only contempt
for the activities of Runich, and others who took it upon themselves
to stop 'free thinking' in Russia. Curator of the University of St
Petersburg, Runich had several professors dismissed in 1822. Following the lead of Magnitsky, who had purged the University of Kazan
in 1819, Runich claimed that the professors had been preaching jacobinism and atheism. Karamzin knew that Runich's definition of these
two things included anything that was not absolutely conformist,
and so was very skeptical of the charges. The event, Karamzin said,
'was very important for our future.' He concluded, in a long letter to
Dmitriev, 'reasonable people do not agree with him [Runich]. We
leave everything to Providence and to the ruler to decide ... I try to
be a very calm spectator and, as a prudent man, I add: *all this is between us!*' Apparently, even he no longer dared to speak out against
influential government figures.[64]

The historiographer still believed that enlightenment and moderation, not reaction and suppression, could assure Russian greatness. In
this regard, his opinions were like those of Pushkin and Viazemsky,
both of whom detested despotism. The last-named never gave up his
advocacy of enlightenment and sustained the principles of the Arzamas until his death in 1878. Karamzin, Viazemsky said, understood
that men and nations could only fulfill themselves if they always remained open to change. Karamzin and Russian enlightenment
remained synonymous in his mind. Furthermore, Karamzin admired
those of Alexander's earlier ministers who were of a liberal bent. He
was especially drawn to Capodistrias who, though hardly a liberal in
the western European sense, was an active reformer with a rational,
rather than emotional attitude towards politics. Karamzin regularly

received letters sent by Capodistrias from Corfu and tried hard to persuade Viazemsky to serve with him.[65]

It was in his attitude towards serfdom that Karamzin disclosed the progressive nature of his conservatism. He had idealized that institution in the 1790s and had insisted that peasants be satisfied with their lot in life, but he always sympathized with them in their plight. In 1816, Karamzin agreed that there was some possibility of freeing serfs 'in the future' and in 1818 he told Viazemsky that he was prepared to free his own if such attempts by others proved successful. These feelings were echoed in letters to General A.D. Balashev (1770-1837), the minister of police, in 1822. Although he complained when serfs did not fulfill their obligations to him, Karamzin was usually willing to speak on their behalf. 'I really do not know whether or not true civil freedom should be given to the people,' he wrote Dmitriev in 1819, 'but I do know that the path will be long and arduous.'[66]

Viazemsky was involved actively in projects that could lead to lifting the legislated burdens from the shoulders of the peasantry and, in 1820, told A.I. Turgenev that Karamzin both knew of and approved these activities. Karamzin went so far as to question Alexander's policy of establishing military colonies because he believed that they were to the peasant's disadvantage. In 1825, he travelled to some of these settlements to observe conditions at first hand, but came away feeling much better about them. It is quite likely that Arakcheev, who 'hosted me [Karamzin] with unusual graciousness,' arranged things so that the writer could see only the good side of the colonies. It is probable, too, that Karamzin wanted to find some good in the colonies. Nevertheless, his attitude towards the fate of serfs suggests that he expected even autocracy and serfdom to change as the community adjusted to new conditions or, as he wrote in the final year of his life, 'I am an enemy of revolution, but peaceful evolution is necessary.'[67]

He had no patience with radicals. They were not mere proponents of harmless, intellectual trivia, but were traitors. They were the ones who advocated political freedoms, and so reminded Karamzin too much of the French Jacobins. 'In the old days,' he mused to Viazemsky in 1818, 'freedom lived with the law like a cat with a dog.'[68] Advocates of political liberty, he thought, were most unliberal people, because real freedom could only exist in an ordered, peaceful society.[69] Time and again, Karamzin suggested that rabid proponents of any political philosophy, whether Jacobin or royalist, democrat or republican, were in error because of the exclusiveness of their views.[70] Indeed, in a letter sent to Alexander in 1822, the historiographer had said: 'here liberals, there sycophants; truth and goodness are in the middle.' Towards the end of his life, he entered a short but penetrating essay in his diary entitled, 'Thoughts about True Freedom' ('Mysli ob istinnoi svobode'), in which he said:

> *Aristocrats and sycophants wish the old order, for they benefited from it. Democrats and Liberals wish for a new disorder; for they hope to use it for their personal gain ... there is no good without freedom; but this freedom is not granted by a ruler, nor by a parliament, but each to himself with the help of God.*[71]

On looking at recent events in Europe, Karamzin could become no more a supporter of de Maistre or Metternich than he could of liberal leaders, for they all contributed equally to the reigning tension and chaos. He equated the disorder in Europe to an 'epidemic of sickness ... having different symptoms, liberal and anti-liberal, but equally against reason, calmness, quiet, clarity.' For that reason alone he approved of the Carlsbad Decrees of 1819, and the accession of Charles X in France (1824), hoping that firmness would cure the unrest.[72] In both cases, Karamzin felt that peace might ensue from the establishment of rule by law, but he never approved a form of government that was against the wishes of the governed. In the second issue of the *Messenger of Europe*, in 1802, he had praised Thomas Jefferson for creating that 'rare phenomenon,' a government that was interested solely in the general welfare of the country. Remaining true to this belief even in the chaotic times of 1820, he responded to news that Alexander had offered Russian armies to the embattled Spanish monarchy by suggesting that intervention by foreign armies could not solve the problems of Spain if the people wished a return of their hard-earned constitution of 1812.[73]

Abominating revolutions of all kinds, Karamzin still hoped that Russian armies would not interfere in any way with the post-Congress of Vienna uprisings in the European states. He remarked to Viazemsky in December 1820 that 'constitutionalists' in Naples should be left alone to at least clarify their ideas and registered astonishment at the antics of Metternich who, Karamzin thought, could only be acting for personal gain or glory. When most of the revolutions were overcome by the spring of 1821, he expressed thanks that Russia had not been much involved.[74] The Greek-Turkish conflict was a different matter because Karamzin, like most Russians, had a traditional high regard for the Greeks and hatred for the Turks. Nonetheless, he still insisted that Russia keep out.[75] Karamzin was convinced that any unilateral Russian action against the Turks would result in a European combination against Russia. Although by no means alone in this conviction, Karamzin's political astuteness was remarkable for one who professed to be outside of politics. He was certainly close to the mark when he concluded that Europeans would never allow Russian armies to occupy the Black Sea parts of the Ottoman Empire or the Straits. However, unlike Pogodin, General R.A. Fadaev (1824-83), Nicholas Danilevsky (1822-85), and other militants who had the examples of the Crimean War (1853-6) and then the Congress of Berlin (1878) when it came to the so-called 'Eastern Question,' Karamzin recommended conciliation rather than confrontation with Europe. His point of view on such affairs remained consistently true to his remark of 1821 that, 'where good or evil does not depend on me, there I try to be a calm spectator'; this phrase might well reflect Karamzin's entire world view.[76]

His optimism after Carlsbad and then after the accession of Charles x was reminiscent of his feelings about the coronation of Paul i in 1796. Karamzin was equally incorrect in his prognoses for peace in all cases. The action of the Decembrists in Russia was, of course, the last straw, but the historiographer still was able to show compassion for liberals whom he knew or who belonged to families of friends. He was willing to speak on A.S. Pushkin's behalf in 1820 and 1822, albeit somewhat begrudgingly, and never retracted his admiration for the writer's abilities. Karamzin suggested to the young writer that he return the favour by refraining from insulting the government for a year, so his action was not entirely philanthropic. Although Pushkin later claimed in a letter to Zhukovsky that he had fulfilled his promise to Karamzin, the historiographer did not think so. He approved of the government's decision to send Pushkin away from the capital in 1824. According to Karamzin, the poet had not stopped 'his verbal

nonsense ... and could not even get along with Count [S.R.] Vorontsov [1744-1832], who certainly is no despot.'[77] Karamzin was per-
turbed about A.N. Murav'ev (1792-1863) because of his close attachment to that family and seemed to regret the activities of the son
rather than to be angry about them. Similarly, he remained friendly
towards individuals who had strong liberal notions. One such was N.I.
Turgenev, of whom Karamzin said, 'he is a terrible liberal, but good,
though he often looks at me askance because I am thoroughly non-
liberal.' Likewise, O.P. Kozogalev was credited with 'goodness' in
spite of liberal tendencies, and Karamzin had the highest regard for
the talents and character of Nicholas Bestuzhev, a Decembrist. Never
so anti-liberal that he foreswore his respect for law, Karamzin peti-
tioned Alexander in 1825 to provide the Russian Empire with a fundamental code which would assure the rule of law for every citizen.
He claimed to have gained a pledge to that end from the emperor in
the summer of that year.[78] Whatever the case may be, Alexander's
death and the subsequent succession crisis put a temporary halt to
any such project.

Of all those whom he categorized as liberals, Karamzin remained
closest to Viazemsky, his brother-in-law, whom he often addressed as
'Mr young liberal.' In 1818, in the midst of the liberal reaction against
his *History*, and his own deepening distrust of liberalism in Russia, he
wrote Viazemsky: 'A wise man once said, "I do not like old people
who love freedom. Nor do I like young people who do not love freedom." If this is a true saying, then you must love me, and I you.'
Even Karamzin's wife Catherine, whom he also spoke of as a liberal
and who always remained friendly to Pushkin, lectured her brother
for his 'political malaise, or liberalism.'[79] Neither, of course, considered Viazemsky to be radical; he struck them more as an impetuous
youth. Liberals, in their turn, tended to assume the worst from
Karamzin, and the myth grew up later that he had been instrumental
in gaining a harsh indictment against the Decembrist leaders. Although there is no evidence to support this charge, L.N. Tolstoi recalled that the story was still being circulated in the mid-fifties.[80]

In his last years, Karamzin worked on the volume of his *History*
that dealt with the Time of Troubles. The increasing savagery and
confusion in Greece and the strident demands for change in Russia
prompted him to draw analogies between his own time and that un-

fortunate era of Russian history. His letters gave the impression that he believed that only Alexander's personal strength was keeping the state intact. Still disturbed by the growing predominance of mysticism among the highest officials, he exhorted his friends to seek salvation in the realities of Russian tradition, patriotism, and enlightenment, rather than in abstractions. Alexander's death was a great blow to Karamzin and the ensuing upheaval seemed to augur the end of his world. But Nicholas's handling of the Decembrist uprising, which Karamzin saw as the culmination of Napoleon's challenge to law and order, saved the day. 'During the alarm of December 14,' he wrote A.I. Turgenev, 'I was at court with my daughter. We went out onto the St Isaac's Square and saw the Emperor on a horse among the troops. He was completely calm and composed ... the new Tsar is very firm and wise.'[81]

Just as he had done all his life, Karamzin found hope in the worst of situations. 'We Russians are no better than others,' he had said with some shame and added that he was prepared 'to die for Holy Rus'.' The 'criminals and slanderers' were stopped this time and Karamzin rejoiced ('I see a light, as if celestial'), but Russians must not let down their guard again. They must help their own cause by becoming and remaining conscious of themselves as Russians: 'For Russians with a soul, only Russia is unique, only Russia truly exists, everything else exists only in relation to it.'[82]

In the first months of Nicholas's reign, Karamzin noted with approval that the Russian Empire had not really been shaken by the Decembrist incident. At least he continued to lend his support to some of the lesser participants. Moreover, he was aware that the government could carry its victory too far. Karamzin was all too familiar with repression, and so once again, in spite of advanced age and poor health, he offered his services to the emperor.

He helped Nicholas prepare several short papers for government service, but because of illness soon asked to be relieved of all such duties. He also requested funds, complaining that he had received no salary from Alexander and that his peasants did not pay their dues (*obrok*) well enough. Nicholas praised him and financed him, and gave him permission to follow a doctor's suggestion that he move to Florence. But Karamzin never left Russia. On 22 May 1826, he died.

In his last few years, Karamzin had been a witness to, rather than a participant in the changing literary scene in Russia. An important innovator for Russian letters in his youth, his ideas remained the same during the last quarter century of his life. Inevitably, then, he had come to represent the 'old tendencies' in Russian letters by the 1820s. Almost in spite of him, there grew up around him an aura of sanctity. A number of young intellectuals, many of whom only began their writing careers in the 1820s (eg, the 'Lovers of Wisdom' group), made Karamzin a symbol of their own ideals. And so his name remained at the forefront of intellectual and political arguments for decades to come. Some Russians, however, were convinced that his prestige remained an obstacle to progress in Russian literature. Katenin said in 1823 that only when Karamzin died would there be forward movement ('a great revolution') in Russian literature. To the politically inclined, he represented either Russian enlightenment, humanity, and political stability, or the 'Asiatic Despotism' of tsarism.

The entire first quarter of the nineteenth century was termed the 'Karamzinian' era by the radical critic, Belinsky, and the assumption that Karamzin held a leading position in the field of literature was not seriously challenged in that century. In 1849, the Slavophile, important critic, and professor of Russian literature, P.A. Pletnev, said that 'Karamzin embraces the entire history of Russian literature,' and, in 1866, Ia. Grot commented that 'close knowledge of Karamzin will always be an essential element of Russian education.' Further, Viazemsky's suggestion in 1870 that Karamzin had made literature a 'vital part of society' was already a common feeling in the thirties when admirers tended to evaluate contemporaries according to the degree to which they echoed the thoughts of the historiographer.[83] Viazemsky, for example, accorded Zhukovsky his highest praise by remarking that 'he [Zhukovsky] is a true student of Karamzin.'[84] Long after his death, the Karamzinian tradition in Russian society was maintained through the agency of a salon presided over by his widow and eldest daughter, and attended by literary people, statesmen, diplomats, and friends of the late Karamzin. One frequent visitor was the future Slavophile, A.S. Khomiakov, another was Pushkin, who was drawn back to the great man's family and memory. The essence of the tradition sustained by Karamzin's followers is perhaps impossible to define, though for most it meant simply the spirit of

Russian enlightenment. For some, like Shevryev and Tiutchev, he symbolized Russian nationalism.[85]

Viazemsky compared Karamzin's death in 1826 to the passing of Napoleon from contemporary history and of Byron from the world of letters, and he regretted that there was now a gaping vacuum in Russian life that could never be filled. V.G. Belinsky, however, believed that Karamzin's heritage remained, and described it in a vague but somehow meaningful way when he called the *History* a 'landmark' in Russian literature because it kept alive for many generations a sense of Russianism, a 'spirit.'[86]

KARAMZIN'S POLITICAL AND HISTORICAL HERITAGE

4
The *History:* Textbook for Emperors and Citizens

It was not until he had completed a decade of labour on the *History* that Karamzin admitted to Dmitriev that he was writing in order to leave a guide for all actions taken by future emperors of Russia.[1] That he believed Russian rulers and people were in need of such guidance had been made plain long before, in 1803, when he had insisted that 'the historian ... must condemn ... what would be harmful for governments.'[2] Karamzin was like most of the European historians of his time when he insisted that it was his duty to make moral judgements about the past. He did not say so often, but once in the *History* he allowed that although 'history does not decide questions,' the historian must make useful comments in his 'evaluations of characters and events.'[3]

Never reticent about his adherence to the philosophy of eighteenth-century European historiography, Karamzin's practices were especially close to those of British historians. As early as 1790 he had suggested that anyone who wished to read history should turn to Hume and had praised Gillies in the *Moscow Journal* the next year.[4] Whether or not he read the work of Robertson at that time is unknown, but the Scottish historian's study on Emperor Charles v had been used as an educational tool in the Russian court since the 1770s. Certainly, Robertson's introductory comment that 'History claims it as her prerogative to offer instructions to kings as well as to their people' would have fitted perfectly into Karamzin's own foreword to readers.[5] In the *Letters* edition of 1801, he said that history should be written 'as Hume did in his *History of England*,'[6] a work which so impressed Karamzin that he always ranked it above all others, including his own.

The Russian historian's confidence in his British counterparts was no accident. Karamzin had underlined the literary aspects and instructional potential of historical writing and, while his own views developed independently of theirs, the great popularity of Hume and Gibbon served to confirm his ideas on how best to present history.[7] He observed that the main merit of Hume's history was that 'everyone' in Britain had read it. Long after he had begun his own history, Karamzin made notations inferring that he still regarded Hume as the ideal model for historians. During the enforced lull in his work, while Napoleon occupied Moscow, he claimed to have spent his time reading Hume, 'about the origins of ideas!' Even in the foreword to the *History*, Karamzin said that Hume would have been 'the most perfect among modern historians' if he had not tried to be so impartial.[8]

As we have seen, the political stimuli behind Karamzin's move into historical writing were the military and intellectual uncertainties of the French revolutionary era which, he said, posed a serious threat to the security and welfare of all Russians. At least that is what one can gather from observations like that which he made to his brother in 1817: 'the deceased French Revolution remains as a locust and nasty insects crawl out from it.'[9] Hence, the immediate goal of the *History* was to neutralize the social effects of the Revolution on his homeland. Motivated above all by patriotism, Karamzin endeavoured to persuade the emperor to act solely for the happiness of Russians and, simultaneously, to convince Russians that they must accept the existing autocratic system. Attesting to this raison d'être in the foreword, which he began writing in 1804,[10] Karamzin said that a national history was essential because 'it is necessary to know that, from time immemorial, rebellious passions have shaken civil societies' and that those same societies had always been preserved only after the entrenchment of strict order. Politically eclectic, Karamzin saw no contradiction in his aim, for he assumed that Russia's autocratic government was synonymous with both security and the general welfare.

Long before the *History* came to light, Karamzin had insisted that he was compelled, as a patriot and as Imperial Historiographer, to advise the monarchy. Quite generous with his wisdom, Karamzin did not limit his instructions to rulers. He declared in the foreword that 'rulers and legislators act according to the instructions of history ... but the ordinary citizen must also read history. It reconciles him to the imperfections of the visible order of things.'[11] This comment had its precedent in a book review prepared by Karamzin for the *Messenger of Europe* in 1802 when, while discussing a study on the French Revolution, he had italicized a claim that all writers cited in the book had demanded that politicians 'read history!'[12] For Karamzin, then, history had to serve as an 'example for the future.'[13] The extent of his belief in the practical ends of historical writing was revealed even more by a pre-1803 note in his diary: 'what the Bible is for Christians, History is for nations.'[14]

Karamzin's image of himself as a wise and patriotic advisor to the throne was undoubtedly a sincere one. Hoping to retain his independence, he refused to take on any other official duties, although he was offered many, on the grounds that another position might sully his reputation for impartiality. K.S. Serbinovich reported that Karamzin had admitted in 1825 that he would have been 'either a poor governor or a poor historian.'[15] However, it was in the years of disruption and indecision between 1816 and 1819 that he worked hardest to maintain the dignity of his office. Worried about the unfavourable things in his volume on Ivan IV's despotism, he wrote Turgenev in 1816:

> *I hope that there will be nothing against truth, the tsar or morality in my books; but it is possible that the censors will not allow me, for example, to speak freely about the cruelties of Tsar Ivan Vasilevich. In that case, what would history be?*[16]

The fact that he went ahead and published this volume in 1821, in spite of the renewed spate of revolutions in Europe, suggests that Karamzin placed his role as sage above anything else. He even ignored a direct request from Maria Fedorovna (24 August 1814) not to include Ivan IV in the *History*. That volume turned out to be his most educative one. The famous collector, N.P. Rumiantsev (1754-1826), had called on Karamzin to produce just such a book:

> *Ach! If, Karamzin, in your history*
> *You disgrace tyrants who brought dishonour*
> *To the purple:*
> *You will seem as a second Tacitus to the world.*
> *And will be a straightforward tutor to the Tsars.*[17]

That is exactly what Karamzin intended to be.

The great writer rarely spoke of contemporary affairs in the *History*, and so his misgivings about matters of the present were revealed mainly through the nature of his general scheme for Russian history. Nevertheless, his frank treatment of Ivan IV's sordid reign could only mean that he had in mind Russia's future as much as its past. Before describing the terrors of *oprichnina* and cognate events, he warned that 'evil passions rage in centuries of civil enlightenment as well' and so that readers could not miss his meaning, he added in a footnote, 'see the history of the French Revolution!'[18] As a matter of fact, on the very first pages of the *History*, Karamzin made known his intention to compare the 'distant past to the present.'

The starting point for Karamzin's division of Russian history into distinct eras was the assumption that a unified and strong state was the ultimate goal of all peoples. It followed, then, that the degree to which such a polity was attained reflected the greatness of the people represented by it. In order to best serve a plan based on this world view, the *History* seemingly was an examination of the progressive evolution of a primitive society to a sophisticated autocratic one, represented in a pendulum-like pattern of times of strength, decline, and then resurgence to a stronger, more highly developed form. In this way, the plan of the *History* resembled those outlined in earlier pragmatic studies, the *Stepennaia kniga* and the *Sinopsis*, and in the dialectical views suggested in 1766 by Lomonosov, who had written: 'Each unfortunate period [of Russian history] was followed by a prosperity far greater than before, from each time of decline there was a higher revival.'[19]

More precisely, the manner in which the *History* was planned resembled a philosophy of historical progress that Karamzin himself had outlined in 1793: 'the centuries serve as a kind of staircase to rationality, on which reason reaches perfection, sometimes slowly.'[20]

Like most of his predecessors, Karamzin began Russian history in 862, when the Varangian princes were supposed to have arrived, and continued the first stage until the death of Vladimir I in 1015. Emphasizing the accession of Rurik, whom he called 'the first autocrat of Russia,' Karamzin intimated that his scheme was to be dominated by the evolution of autocracy. In his view, the new state soon became highly centralized and reached a level of greatness because of the 'fortunate introduction of Monarchical power.' It started to decline only when Vladimir, following the 'unfortunate custom of the times,' made the great 'political mistake' of dividing the country among his sons.[21]

The second era, from 1015 to the first appearance of the Tatars in 1224, had two distinct stages. The first was marked by the rule of a strong monarch, Yaroslav I, who recreated a powerful autocratic state. On the death of that prince in 1054, however, all traces of the ancient autocracy disappeared. Although Karamzin implied a total disintegration of the state on the very instant of Yaroslav's death in the remark, 'ancient Russia was buried with Yaroslav,'[22] he later pointed to the destruction of Kiev in 1169 as the final blow in the collapse of pre-Muscovite Russia. This event was so important to Karamzin's scheme that he ended volume two with the sacking of Kiev, the 'Mother of Russian towns,'[23] thus splitting the time of Andrei Bogoliubsky's predominance into two distinct parts.

The next era encompassed the time from the Tatar invasion to the reign of Ivan III. In describing the deeds of Ivan Kalita, Dmitry Donskoi, and Vasily II, he drew a picture of an evolutionary progress towards Ivan III's autocratic state. While writing about these events, the historian began to trace what he deemed to be the keys to the success of autocracy in Russia; the gradual consolidation of power in the hands of Muscovite princes and the slow territorial aggrandizement of that state.

Karamzin felt that the synthesis of earlier tendencies came under Ivan III, whom he saw as the 'first true Autocrat of Russia.'[24] He did not attempt an explanation of his use of the designation 'autocrat' for earlier princes, so it is safe to assume that he saw differences between them only in the degree of authority which they held. Thus, the highlight of his fourth bloc of historical growth, 1462 to 1533, which covered the reigns of Ivan III and Vasily III, was the finalization of autocracy as the most suitable political form for Russia, a process consummated by the subjection of Novgorod to Moscow, the overthrow of Tatar domination, and by the end of the appanage (*udel*) system.

The fifth (1533-98) was dominated by the rule of Ivan IV. This stage served as an antithesis to the preceding one, and illustrated the difference between autocracy and tyranny. Karamzin described the degeneration of autocracy into oligarchy when a tsar was weak-willed and, at the same time, the equally unfortunate tendency towards despotism when the ruler was strong but unenlightened. Adhering closely to his scheme, Karamzin followed Shcherbatov's example by placing the early, more moderate years of Ivan's reign and the later, despotic ones in separate volumes.[25]

Karamzin died before the *History* was completed but he worked out enough of his final era to show an ever progressive pattern of growth, in which the state constantly emerged triumphant and stronger from dangerous situations. The last stage of his scheme began with the chaotic Time of Troubles and, presumably, would have ended with the re-establishment of firm autocracy in the person of the Romanov tsars. Major shifts in the degree and location of central authority dictated Karamzin's periodization. For that reason, the *History* was often described as a fragmented survey, with too little connection between epochs. In reality, he developed two somewhat opposing pictures of the evolution of Russian state and society. At first glance, the work gives an impression of sharp changes in governmental forms and very little evidence of historical progress. But a closer look reveals the gradual flowering of a modern state, with each stage in its history serving as a precedent for the next. The former tendency resulted from the author's desire to present a particularly political point of view, the latter tendency was a product of his vast knowledge of Russian history.

The alleged invitation to Varangian princes by the Novgorodians in the ninth century, which Karamzin thought was one of the most important single events of Russian history, set the stage for the fundamental political lesson of the work. That lesson had two sides. The first was the most obvious, that is, that autocracy was the natural and most suitable system of government for Russia. The second, which usually receives far less attention, was the idea that the people of Russia had been instrumental in the selection of their political system.

The merits of monarchy and popular appreciation of it were given equal space in Karamzin's interpretation of the origins of his homeland's state system. In his words, the Slavs 'recalled three Varangian brothers in 862 from the *Russian tribe*, who became the first rulers of our ancient fatherland and from whom we gained the name, *Russians*. This important event served as the basis of the *History* and greatness of Russia....' A few chapters later, he said that the 'beginning of Russian history shows an astonishing and unparalleled circumstance, almost unprecedented in the Chronicles. The Slavs voluntarily destroy their ancient popular government and request sovereigns from the Varangians ... everywhere else the sword of strong men, or the cunning of ambitious men brought in absolute power ... in Russia it was sanctioned by the general consent of the citizens.'[26] The Varangians '*did not conquer* our homeland, rather they were chosen by the Slavs to govern the state.'[27] Needless to say, it was these sentiments that were later picked out by the pan-Slavists and Slavophiles as the most significant part of the *History*.

Throughout the *History*, Karamzin analysed different forms of government as they were tested under Russian circumstances and found all except autocracy to be unsuitable for his fatherland. Autocracy, he said, was 'one of the greatest political creations,'[28] and had been the means for Russian survival in the face of seemingly insurmountable odds. This theme provided him with criteria for stressing some events while ignoring others, and for judging individual monarchs and long-term phenomena. He was convinced that the principle of autocracy was responsible for the fact that, of all the Slavic tribes, only the Russian one 'astonishes the world with its greatness.'[29]

Republicanism, he said, had proven unsatisfactory very early in Russian history. In ancient times, 'each family was a small, independent republic,' but changing conditions had forced them to revise their political habits. Even the wildest peoples, Karamzin explained, 'had to elect mediators between the people and the law' because of man's collective need for security.[30]

Later he turned to the history of Novgorod to fortify his contentions. Echoing his own sentimental tendencies of the 1790s, the historian conceded that it was 'characteristic of the human heart to wish well to Republics, founded on the fundamental rights of freedom of which the heart is fond. The dangers of it ... captivate the young and inexperienced.' He went on to point out that the rights of a few would have to be sacrificed whenever they interfered with the 'independence and greatness' of the whole. For illustration Karamzin drew a sharp line of division between supporters of ancient Novgorod freedoms and those citizens who wished to submit to Ivan III of Moscow:

> *For several days the people listened to arguments between friends of liberty and friends of peaceful citizenship: the first could promise them only a glorious death among the horrors of starvation and vain bloodletting; the other, life, security, calmness, and intact estates: and these finally won....* [31]

Here, then, was the primary justification for autocracy and the main complaint against republicanism: one provided security and strength, the other only weakness and disorder.

But autocracy was not simply a guarantor of national security; it was the only source of 'true' freedom. As Karamzin put it, 'there is no freedom where there is no strength to defend it.' Indeed, he felt that political freedom was the anathema that might destroy Russia; it was an idea that was 'always dear to a people, but unsafe' because it was inevitably the ambition of 'thoughtless people.'[32] Insisting that a republic could exist as long as its citizens remained virtuous, he implied that such political systems were untenable in the modern world. Among the weaknesses of institutions run by citizens was their inclination to go to war or to change opinions for minor reasons. 'The chronicles of republics,' he said, 'usually show us strong effects of human passions, gusts of generosity and often touching triumphs of virtue, among riots and disorder, which are also characteristic of people's governments.'[33] He went on to suggest that republics were more likely to become despotic than were autocracies, for, in a reference to the final destruction of Novgorod's independence, 'the fall of people's states is usually foreshadowed by impudence, abuse of power and the misuse of laws.'[34] He had already said as much in references to France on the pages of the *Moscow Journal* and the *Messenger of Europe*.

After the breakdown of republicanism in most Slavic areas, the various tribes had turned to aristocratic forms of government in which leaders could retain their positions only by dint of their superiority. Granting that 'it became customary for some to govern and for others to obey,' he indicated that such a system, while initially satisfactory, lacked the permanence and strength essential for national survival in later periods. Interestingly, Catherine II used the same phrase in her *Nakaz* (*Instructions*, 1767), where she had said that society requires that there be 'some to govern and some to obey.'[35]

Karamzin did not condemn the aristocracy as a class, rather he often praised individual nobles and the class at large for sacrifices to the Russian community. He believed, however, that an aristocratic form of government inevitably would collapse. The rule of Boyars, Karamzin wrote in connection with the early years of Tatar government, 'produced only *Boyar insurrections*. The Boyar Council sometimes imbued the sovereign with wisdom, but often was disturbed with passions. The Boyars frequently fostered the internecine wars among the Russian princes.' He could hardly be said to be following Shcherbatov's line here. Montesquieu, too, had written that aristocratic governments had difficulty in restraining themselves.[36] Karamzin concluded that members of that class should practise leadership only under the guidance of an autocrat, for 'a Council without a ruler is like a body without a head.'[37] It might lead to oligarchy and it was for this reason that he did not regret the dissolution of both the 'stormy assemblies of the people and the slow duma of the aristocracy' during the long era of Tatar domination in Russia. In his view, an oligarchy was the worst of all possible governments.[38]

From the first step towards autocracy, the establishment of order in the person of the Varangian princes, Karamzin stressed the legal and popular origins of monarchy in Russia. The power held by the Varangians was not unlimited. The Novgorodians, who had invited them, also insisted that they had to rule according to law.[39] This was to the advantage of everyone, but could have deleterious consequences when the law stood in the way of firm, centralized government. In the Kievan state, for example, the people had retained many of their traditional freedoms and so were in a position to subvert the authority of the government. Moreover, the Great Prince had not had complete control over the lesser princes. Indeed, the *veche* and the appanage system were 'to blame for all the unhappiness in Russia.'[40]

Karamzin's faith in centralization, which had been absent during the Kievan era, as the panacea for many of Russia's problems compelled him to give special attention to strong rulers. He noted that when monarchs were strong and able to wield authority over other princes, the people obeyed them unconditionally, and the state was invincible in the face of its enemies. But when the state was divided, the people lost respect for central authority and for the princes themselves.[41] 'If Russia had been a united state,' he said, 'then it would ... probably have been saved from the yoke of the Tatars.'[42]

This emphasis was the main reason why Karamzin incorporated into his presentation the traditional notion that the Kievan system was revived in the Muscovite state of the fifteenth century. He assumed that there was an element of sovereignty extant throughout Russian history. For this end, even the shifting of the centre of authority away from Kiev by Bogoliubsky in 1169 was described by Karamzin as a defensive effort designed to preserve the continuity of single rule.[43]

Closely connected to the theme of centralization was the assumption that Moscow was the rightful centre for all those territories that eventually became part of the Russian Empire. In the century and a half that encompassed the reigns of Ivan Kalita and Ivan III, the main object of the historian's discussion was the 'rise of Moscow, which from the time of the Ivans became the true capital of Russia.' Karamzin concentrated on those monarchs who helped Moscow gain its position of prominence and especially praised those who made alliances with the Tatars so that they might build Muscovite power. During that time military prestige was placed temporarily in the background, and he judged princes and events according to their contribution to the evolution of autocracy. The most concise picture of his attitude towards the value of individual princes occurred in his summation of the fourteenth-century princes who preceded Dmitry Donskoi: 'Ivan Kalita and Simeon Gordyi began the revitalization of single rule; Ivan Ivanovich and Dmitry of Suzdal abandoned that success and again allowed private lords the opportunity to be independent from the throne of the Great Prince.'[44]

However, the first step towards 'true autocracy' was traced to Donskoi, whose victory at Kulikovo (1380) Karamzin said, 'served as a basis for the successes of Ivan III, whom fate appointed to complete the deeds of his ancestors, less fortunate but equally great.'[45]

That victory over the Tatars was very important in establishing the leadership of Moscow, and although it prompted devastating retaliation, Donskoi was able to maintain the city's prestige. Characterizing Donskoi as a direct political descendant of Yaroslav the Great, Monomakh, and Alexsander Nevsky, Karamzin portrayed a succession of great monarchs who by means of their knowledge of the 'science of government' all played a part in the evolution of autocracy in Russia. Karamzin also took the opportunity offered by the uncertainty which followed Kulikovo to blame republicanism for the suffering endured by Muscovites at the hands of vengeful Tatars: 'the people did not listen to the boyars or to the Metropolitan and, recalling the ancient right of Russian citizens to decide their own fate, heeded the toll of the Kolokol and met in a *veche*....'[46] Criticizing the populace for wasting their time in 'stormy arguments,' the historian went on to describe the massacre and destruction wrought in Moscow by Tatars.

Referring to the last years of Vasily I and the early years of his son as the 'most unfortunate epoch of our history in the fifteenth century,' Karamzin maintained the organic theme by finding beneficial results from the civil war between Vasily II and his uncle, Yuri. Subordinating his own nationalism and belief in tradition to what he felt were the best interests of Russia, Karamzin gave tacit approval to a 'cunning' speech from Vasily's spokesman, who allowed that 'ancient Russian customs' were invalid even before the Khans reigned supreme. In Karamzin's opinion, this speech persuaded the Tatar overlords to decide in favour of Vasily.

The eventual recognition of Vasily as the 'legal ruler' by most Russians was pictured as a major step toward autocracy since it set a precedent for sons to inherit the title from their fathers. To Karamzin this 'new system of inheritance' seemed 'most advantageous for general security,' a claim supported by his assertion that all Muscovites left their city to join Vasily. Making use of this incident to suggest an affinity of the Russian people for strong, autocratic rule,[48] Karamzin contradicted his earlier contention that succession by brothers was a natural one resulting from Slavic respect for their elders.

The so-called improvement in the ruling system, which for Karamzin was merely another step towards autocracy, reflected one side of his scheme. Praising Vasily for 'preparing the way for the success of his followers,' and claiming that Ivan III's greatness was 'due to the good beginnings of Kalita and Donskoi,'[49] he again gave the impression that the Russian political system was the product of a gradual and natural evolution. Later, however, he began his volume on Ivan III as if he were dealing with a completely new era in which all the contributions of past princes counted for nothing.

In order to soften the apparent abruptness of the changes wrought by Ivan III, Karamzin inserted a long chapter on the general conditions in Russia from the invasion of the Tatars to Ivan's time. Significantly, he used this section to associate the Tatar period with his scheme. In his opinion, it was primarily due to Tatar rule that Russian nationalism was stimulated enough to allow for the leadership of Moscow and ultimately the achievement of autocracy. The concept that autocracy and Russian nationalism were inseparable phenomena remained an invariable component of the *History*.

Attributing the success of the Tatars to a lack of autocracy in Russia, Karamzin adjusted his information on them to fit his scheme, a practice that led to serious contradictions. To cite only one example: he decried the lapse of the Russian people into barbarism and depravity but then insisted that they had never lost their 'morality, love for virtue and for the fatherland' and concluded that there were 'undoubtedly beneficial results' from that unhappy period.

Karamzin treated the Tatar epoch as an advantageous one for Russia because it was only through alien domination that Russians could be made to see the absolute necessity of autocracy and, at the same time, be provided with the means to attain it. The major obstacles to autocracy had been the ancient right of the people to participate in government and the strength of the *boyar* class. In order to best present his hypothesis that the people chose autocracy for themselves, Karamzin had to blame the disappearance of such privileges on a non-Russian force. Thus, it was a consequence of Tatar rule that the *veche* system and the influence of the *boyars* declined until there was no longer in Russia 'any legal way to oppose the prince.' Since such institutions 'were natural only in small states' anyway, he contended that just as 'Rome was saved by a Dictator,' Russia was saved by autocracy.

Further accenting the role played in the evolution of Muscovite power by the Tatars, Karamzin toned down the plaudits previously handed to Kalita and Donskoi, who he now said 'achieved almost nothing except glory.' So, in spite of his own insistence that an historian 'must not search for proof that everything happens for the best,' Karamzin turned the whole period of Tatar sway into one of long-term benefit for Russia. He ended the section with the remark, 'Moscow owes its greatness to the Khans.'[50]

Once autocracy was assured and power firmly in the hands of Muscovite princes, the final stage of political evolution was forthcoming, that is, world-wide power for Muscovy. The readers' attention was directed toward 'the deeds of tsars who gained independence and greatness' for Russians.[51] Characterizing all Russian history before Ivan III as a time of chaos and weakness, Karamzin gave prominence to the growing prestige of Russia among European nations. It was at this point that evolutionary trends seemed to be forgotten and the achievement of autocracy was represented as an accomplishment of Ivan alone. According to the *History*, Ivan was given a free hand by God 'to decide the fate of peoples,'[52] whereas all other rulers had been responsible for their own actions, the results of which 'depended upon God.'[53] On this premise, Karamzin was able to excuse all of Ivan's reprehensible actions on the ground that they benefited the autocratic edifice.

He used the wars that broke out between Moscow and Novgorod to prove that it was the newly established autocracy that brought the modern age to Russia. Admitting that the Novgorodians had had freedom in the past and that their attempts to revive them were legitimate, Karamzin also insisted that it was now the *veche* itself which was ignoring the basic rights of the town's citizens.[54] The prince at Moscow was therefore under an obligation to prevent that institution from endangering the rest of Russia. So that the position of Moscow might appear in a favourable light, the writer had the wiser and more moderate citizens of Novgorod speak of the propriety of Ivan's position and stress the descent of Ivan from Rurik, whom the Novgorodians themselves had brought to Russia. Ivan finally decided upon war only after consulting with many important people in Moscow, thereby acting in a far more rational manner than the people's government of Novgorod.

Karamzin justified the final abolition of Novgorodian freedoms by a brief account of the threat they posed to the general security of the rest of Russia. Novgorodian leaders 'had neither the love nor the confidence of the citizens; [the people] thought only of their own interests so that, even when in danger of losing all their former privileges, most Novgorodians looked upon Ivan as their defender ... a true monarch.' It was only after the instability and the emotionalism of the *veche* and its susceptibility to demagoguery turned the citizens against Moscow that war broke out again. Ivan's victory, in turn, was greeted by a general sense of relief, for 'the people recognized that the times had changed, that heaven protected Ivan and gave him courage....' In this way, Karamzin illustrated his conviction that the Russians wanted autocracy. It brought peace during troubled times and by maintaining unity and strength saved Russia from further foreign invasions.[55]

Karamzin turned next to the 'even greater' accomplishment of Ivan III, 'the triumphant creation of the independence of our state, combined with the final collapse of the Great or Golden Horde.' Crediting autocracy with the 'final' victory over the Tatars, he even made an analogy between Ivan and Moses, who had freed the Israelites from the Egyptian pharaohs.[56]

In summing up Ivan's reign, Karamzin fitted it into the general context of European development. Ivan, he said, lived in and contributed to a new enlightened epoch for all mankind. It was here that he reverted to his view of Russian history as an evolutionary process. After writing an entire volume to show Ivan III as the sole instigator of Russia's sudden elevation to the rank of a European power, he then admitted that Kalita, Vasily II, and others 'prepared much for the autocracy and our internal power,' and went on to state explicitly that Ivan had merely completed autocracy and initiated other trends that were not to reach maturity until the time of Catherine II.[57]

As far as Karamzin's scheme was concerned, it would seem that the main purpose for this treatment of Ivan III was to demonstrate how easily Russia could reach a level of greatness in an autocratic state. Vasily III's reign was pictured as 'only a continuation of that of Ivan,'[58] a transitional stage between the true autocracy of Ivan III and the despotism of Ivan IV.[59] Such a position, however, led to further inconsistencies. By pointing out that 'Vasily [III] ... completed ... the great matter of internal single rule,'[60] and by claiming that it was only under him that the appanage system finally ended in Russia Karamzin contradicted his earlier proposition that Ivan III had been the lone architect of autocracy.

Maintaining the structural pattern of the *History*, Karamzin prefaced a new shift in the scheme with a general summary of the conditions in Russia from 1462 to 1533, the period before Ivan IV. In this section he described what he considered to be the most important qualities of Russian monarchy, and crystallized his own image of the true autocrat. He made it explicit that an autocracy was something quite different from tyranny or despotism. Adding the efforts of Vasily III to those of Ivan III in the evolution of such a political form, he stated categorically that 'autocracy is not without laws.'[61] Theoretically an autocratic monarch had unlimited power but was restrained in practice by the very important obligation to rule in the best interests of the people of Russia.

Citing a sixteenth-century European traveller's opinion that slavery was common in Russia, Karamzin stated that this was merely an impression created by the 'unwavering devotion of the Russians to the monarch' and that, in reality, 'the people enjoyed civil freedom in most matters.' In his opinion, autocracy had actually eliminated all elements of slavery in Russian society, replacing them with a system governed by 'morality and ... the best civil ideas.' Any backward facet of Russian life was carefully designated as a residue of Tatar occupation or as the result of the whims of a bad landlord, rather than of the general system of law.[62]

While Karamzin claimed that Ivan III was the greatest of Russian tsars, the fact that he devoted far more space to Ivan IV would indicate that he believed that monarch to be at least equally significant for Russian history. Of the two volumes reserved for Ivan IV, the first covered the period when he ruled in a way that suited Karamzin's image of an authentic autocrat: legally, virtuously, and with the aid of capable advisors. The second, volume nine of the *History*, illustrated the consequences of not ruling in that manner. Such an oversimplified treatment led to further contradictions but did enable Karamzin to present a new and clearer vision of how he felt a ruler should govern.

On his father's death, Ivan was too young to rule. Karamzin used the situation to comment on the innate weaknesses of oligarchy. In spite of the chaos created by a government of the nobility, Karamzin maintained, no man had cause to rebel against the legal ruler. He insisted that the people had rallied to the aid of the state in spite of their distaste for the regency. Thus he set the stage for his later thesis that Russians stoically accepted the rule of a tyrant in order to preserve autocracy.[63] In its first years, Ivan IV's reign was marked by dynamic territorial expansion, but all these successes were attributed to the good counsel of men like the priest Sylvester and A.F. Adashev. In this instance, Karamzin was clearly augmenting a theme from his days as editor of the *Messenger of Europe*; that is, the idea that an autocrat must always rule in conjunction with good advisors. Only then could a ruler 'know the true needs of the people who comprise the state: for an autocrat, from the height of a throne, sees persons and things through the deceiving light of distance.'[64] Relying upon a psychological explanation for the 'end of the most happy days in Russia,' he indicated that there were no flaws in the ruling structure. It was only when Ivan 'was robbed of virtue' by the death of his wife that the government began to disintegrate.[65]

By 'virtue' Karamzin did not mean 'goodness' in the sense in which the word is usually used today. He gave it a far broader connotation, which included temperance in personal appetites and pleasures, courage, justice, and practical wisdom. A sense of prudence in diplomatic and legislative matters was one of the cardinal attributes which Karamzin assigned to 'virtue.' He was one with Machiavelli in that he believed that 'virtue' in a prince might call for ruthless acts in order to maintain the state. But his overall attitude was closer to that of Montesquieu who, in reference to republics, wrote that they need 'political virtue' in order to survive, and defined that to mean love of country and love of equality. Karamzin, who had seen republicanism in action in France, applied the same criterion to monarchies. He assumed that 'virtue' could not be sustained under any other political system, especially in large countries.[66]

Karamzin claimed that despotism was merely a final stage through which the state had to pass before autocracy could be accepted unconditionally by all Russians: 'Along with other hard trials of fate, beside the calamity of the appanage system, beside the Tatar yoke,

Russia had to suffer as well the terror of an Autocrat-Torturer; she endured them with love for autocracy because she believed that God sends plague, earthquakes and tyrants. She did not break the iron sceptre in Ivan's hands and bore with the tormentor for twenty-five years in order to have, in better times, Peter the Great and Catherine the Second.'[67] His unrealistically harsh portrait of Ivan IV encompassed all the self-destructive tendencies conceivable in an autocrat, including failure to consult with his counsellors, lust for power which resulted in needless wars, and failure to rule according to law. More than any other part of the *History*, this section can be construed as didactic commentary on events of Karamzin's own lifetime. He said as much himself:

> *These horrible meteors [Caligula, Nero, Louis XIV, Ivan IV], these will-o-the-wisps of unrestrained passions, illuminate for us, in the space of centuries, a chasm of possible human perversity – we shudder at the thought! The life of a tyrant is a calamity for mankind but his History is always beneficial for sovereigns and people. To inspire aversion to evil is to inspire love towards virtue ... May there be no one like him in the future!*

All through the long period of terror and during the time of *oprichnina*, 'no one opposed him: the will of the tsar was law ... the sufferers were dying on the scaffold with generous humility, like the Greeks at Thermopylae, for their fatherland, for faith and loyalty, without ever a thought of mutiny.'[68] The assumption that the supremacy of the monarchs was never questioned by the people of Russia led to another of the many contradictions incurred by Karamzin's slavish devotion to his interpretation. Later he declared that the stupefying impact of this despotism was so great that 'nothing could astonish Russians: tyranny had dulled the senses,'[69] a comment that would seem to disallow any claim that the people consciously acted, or did not act, in order to preserve autocracy.

After spending an entire volume outlining in detail all the cruelties of Ivan, whom he called a 'beast' and 'frantic blood-sucker,' Karamzin decided to say something nice about him.[70] He commended the ruler for his military conquests, his educational and political legislation, much of which Karamzin considered vital for the re-establishment of an autocratic order in the seventeenth century. On closer examination, it can be seen that he was describing two parallel trends during Ivan's reign. The first development was the breakdown of a particular régime because the tsar lost his sense of morality. The second was the fact that the autocratic state had now reached such a level of permanence that a brief alteration in the character of a legal and strong tsar would not affect its continued evolution.

Illustrating a remarkable change in Karamzin's historico-political thought, this section of the *History* gives the reader the first real manifestation of the author's views on the relationship between a ruler and the state. For Karamzin, the state order was now a permanent one on which the policies of individual princes could have a fleeting impact at best. The notion of the state as an organism apart from the rulers was an important ingredient of Karamzin's scheme, although not readily discernible in the *History*. It is conceivable that the subject might have received further attention if he had not died before the work was completed. However, he did express this view clearly in 1819 when he spoke of God-given laws for the social order and advised Alexander I that the Russian Empire was not his own to do with as he pleased.[71]

At any event, despotism was less dangerous than weakness and illegitimacy, both of which resulted from the reign of Feodor Ivanovich. Feodor's weakness undermined autocracy while Boris Godunov, who was potentially 'one of the best monarchs in the world' but 'born a subject,'[72] lacked the all-important virtue and legitimacy to sustain it. Godunov became the ruler in practice under Feodor and, according to the *History*, it was mainly during this era rather than under Ivan IV that the state order began to break up.

The election of Godunov to the rank of tsar was, in Karamzin's view, a legal one, but its consequence was the end of the Rurikid dynasty and of the first full cycle in the evolution of Russian autocracy. Admitting that the people of Russia gladly accepted Godunov as their ruler and were optimistic about the future,[73] Karamzin added that Godunov had 'achieved the throne by villainy ... the punishment of God threatened the criminal ruler and the unfortunate reign.'[74] In the *History*, Godunov's régime was treated similarly to that of Ivan IV. Describing the first two years of the reign as 'the best time of the sixteenth century,' Karamzin then alleged that Godunov's character altered for psychological reasons. Growing suspicious of his associates, the ruler began a period of terror and ignored both the law and his best advisors.[75] In this way, Godunov 'prepared Russia for the most terrible phenomenon in its history.'[76] The support given to the various 'false Dmitrys' during the ensuing Time of Troubles was taken by Karamzin to mean that the Russian people yearned for the return of the traditional dynasty, of rulers 'who loved Russia.'[77] In his conclusions, however, Karamzin did say that even an illegal monarch was better than none at all, claiming that Boris's death resulted in lawlessness and chaos in Russia for many years.

The final blow to autocracy in this period was Shuisky's attempt to limit his own power 'to please the Russians.'[78] Such weakness led to further debilitation of the prestige of the monarchy, rebellions in Moscow, new pretenders, and civil war, until 'Russia was a desert; this time it was not Batu but her own barbarians who raged in her womb, astonishing even the most violent foreigner.'[79] Without autocracy Russia had degenerated into a condition much like that which had enabled the Tatars to conquer it in the thirteenth century. Here again, Karamzin was expanding on a theme already outlined in the *Memoir.*

It was at this point that Karamzin drew the attention of readers to the national spirit of the Russian people as the saviour of the state. 'It seemed,' he wrote, 'that Russians no longer had a fatherland, nor did they have a soul or a faith. It appeared that the state, infected by a moral poison, in terrible convulsions, was ended.' Yet Providence saved them from the Poles and brought forth Pozharsky, 'to be the saviour of the homeland.' Slowly the church, the people, the boyars all recognized the need for central government, that Russia was an autocracy, which 'is soulless without an autocrat.'[80] Just as they had chosen monarchy in the ninth century to avert chaos and had tolerated Ivan IV, the people provided the means to preserve Russia from the present danger. Before he died, Karamzin had taken his account down only to 1610, but he did make a comment that enables one to forecast the conclusion to his historical scheme, that is, that the election of the Romonov dynasty in 1613 proved that everyone in Russia had finally come to recognize that autocracy was the only useful form of government for them. Russians, he said, 'did not fear autocracy in general (as we will see in the History of 1613), but only autocracy in the hands of a foreigner....'[81]

Karamzin's scheme, centring as it did around the evolution and necessity of autocracy in Russia, appeared to be very similar to the traditional ideas disseminated by his predecessors. It was his stress on the role of the people as an integral and contributing part of the state that made his scheme original and modern.

He made it clear that autocracy carried with it certain obligations on the part of the ruler to govern in the best interests of the entire nation, and often spoke of the people as the most consistently reliable force in the state during times of emergency.[82] Assigning to them a constructive role in the evolution of the state, Karamzin commented that 'there is no government which does not need the love of the people for its success.'[83] Elsewhere, he stated unequivocally that popular respect for the administration was necessary 'for the good of the state,'[84] and that the 'most precious commodity' of the nation was its people. As a matter of fact, he proclaimed in no uncertain terms that the fate of each prince hinged upon the degree of love or hatred felt for them by the Russian people.[85] Finally, Karamzin gave the impression that popular respect for autocracy could not be undermined fatally by evils such as those of Ivan iv's reign, which the people had tolerated. A greater danger existed when rulers alienated themselves and their office from the citizens of Russia as Godunov had done.[86]

As the politically determined history unfolded, there also emerged an effective characterization of Russian princes which enabled Karamzin to impress upon readers his image of the ideal ruler and of the ideal citizen. In the main, his image-making was intended for the edification of tsars and statesmen because, in spite of references to other, more general factors in the historical process, in practice he seldom wavered from a conviction that the prince was always the most important activator of historical progress. Extreme instances of this belief can be found in a dedication of the *History* to Alexander i, which he concluded by saying, 'the history of a nation belongs to the Tsars,' and in a later comment that 'great states ... are the product of their ruler's genius.'[87] In the sixth volume of the *History*, Karamzin referred to Ivan iii as a 'God on Land,' thereby rephrasing epithets he had used in 1801 for Peter i and Catherine ii, whom he called 'those favourites of Heaven [who] decide the fate of mankind ... and influence millions of people toward some chosen end of Providence.'[88]

In Ivan III Karamzin found the ideal prince. 'With force and cunning,' he wrote, Ivan restored

> *the freedom and security of Russia ... invented the most sensible system of war and peace, based on far-sighted moderation ... he did not want to meddle in European affairs; he accepted alliances, but only when they provided a clear benefit for Russia. He looked for means to accomplish his own plans but did not serve as a tool for anyone ... always acting as a great and cunning monarch who has no passion for politics except for a selfless love for the lasting welfare of his nation. As a result, Russia, as an independent power, majestically raised her head on the boundary of Asia and Europe, tranquil inside and not fearing outside enemies.*[89]

Most of the criticism of Alexander's policies in the *Memoir* were repeated in these few sentences.

In order to demonstrate the validity of his self-appointed role as counsellor to monarchs, Karamzin constantly alluded to the contributions of such advisors in the past. Beginning this trend of thought by pointing out that ancient Slavic peoples respected the advice of their elders in times of emergency, he went on to praise Vladimir I and Ivan Kalita for their ability in choosing counsel. He then attributed much of Dmitry Donskoi's success to older and wiser mentors and gave like credit to men around Ivan IV for that monarch's early accomplishments. It will do no harm here to repeat that, even before the publication of the *Messenger of Europe*, he had warned Paul and Alexander about flatterers and, in the latter case, had held up Peter I as a model prince who was not offended by criticism. Indeed, in the *Memoir* Karamzin had noted that the ability to select advisors according to their particular talents was 'perhaps the most important gift for an autocrat.'[90] Having established that an autocrat required skilled guidance and, in the foreword, that history was the best written aid to a monarch, then who else but an historian could be the most reliable advisor for rulers?

There are many places in the *History* where Karamzin's comments were clearly intended as warnings to his own emperor. He was obviously attempting to persuade Alexander not to follow in the footsteps of his father when he spoke of the implications of Ivan IV's reign. But despotism was not the only evil to be avoided. Excessive kindness, too, was inimical to enlightened, effective autocracy. In this regard, he reproached Vasily Shuisky for being so condescending that complete anarchy was the main consequence of his reign, and applauded Ivan IV's harsh measures against criminality. Karamzin suggested that cruelty might well be better than weakness when 'the security of honest citizens was involved.' At least it was far ahead of the 'modern idea that it is better for ten criminals to remain without punishment than to punish one innocent.'[91] These lessons had been presented even more concisely in the *Memoir*.

A singularly important lesson in the *History* was implicit in Karamzin's constant harping on the question of when, or when not, the Muscovite princes had to make war. Apprehensive over the inconsistent foreign policy of Paul and Alexander, he tried to persuade Alexander to keep out of European wars. The folly of any war that could not result in some immediate and obvious gain for Russia was a recurrent theme in all his writings. Just as he had done in the *Memoir*, Karamzin stressed in the *History* that battle for honour alone was futile and he showed no tolerance for 'useless wars.'[92] He praised those princes who were wise enough to come to terms with the Tatar khans, but made it clear that a time for war would come. Thus in volume five, which was written in 1809, he commended Donskoi for recognizing the time to 'unsheath the sword.'[93] Later he praised Ivan III for keeping out of European wars and for making alliances only when they were clearly to Russia's advantage.[94]

Continuing a theme from the *Messenger of Europe*, Karamzin also referred to Poland in a way that imparted a none-too-subtle message on contemporary affairs. Frequently showing how a strong Poland had endangered Russian sovereignty in the past, and alluding to 'distortions' in Polish historical scholarship, he claimed that the Poles could never be 'real brothers' or 'true allies' to Russians.[95] In keeping with the tenets of his 'Opinion' of 1819, Karamzin suggested that one of the leading factors in the survival of the Russian state in 1612 was the dynamism provided by Russian hatred for Poles.[96] Apparently, Alexander himself chided his historiographer for wrongfully accusing Poland in the *History*, but the historian replied in a somewhat offended tone that he was not speaking of nations but only of certain individuals. He then directed Alexander's attention to a footnote in the eleventh volume where he had cited Polish historians who had referred to some of their own countrymen as 'haughty, greedy, mercenary, thieving' despisers of Russians and 'their faith.'[97]

As far as policy at home was concerned, Karamzin demanded 'strict, vigilant justice' from his princes. To illustrate the need for strictness he described a Muscovite rebellion against Alexei Mikhailovich, and implied that the reason for the disorder was the ruler's failure to keep his own officials under control. Furthermore, Alexei had been too gentle with those of his subjects who did not follow his commands. An earlier revolt, against Bogoliubsky in Suzdal, was used to illustrate popular dissatisfaction because 'the people hate the most virtuous and kind tsar if there are rapacious courts and officials.'[98] In another place he commented that a 'virtuous ruler who acts contrary to the dictates of strength, security and calmness, cannot be judged virtuous.' Self-contradictory as this statement might seem, it had real meaning for Karamzin, who was hoping to sway the thinking of Alexander I. It was the very next year that he cautioned his ruler, in the 'Opinion,' to relegate certain moral principles to the background when the security of Russia was threatened.

At first sight, then, 'morality' and 'virtue' were merely words employed by Karamzin in a casuistic way. He once insisted that both were the basis of all good policies,[99] but then appeared to condone many immoral actions on the ground that they happened to benefit the Russian state. Actually, it was mainly during those times when Muscovy was about to slip into a period of decline that Karamzin found its leaders to be lacking in 'Christian' virtues. Thus, Ivan IV set the stage for the collapse of Muscovy when he began to disregard the basic tenets of morality; the 'traitor,' Prince Kurbsky, had 'no inner sense of virtue'; Godunov only acted to further his personal aggrandizement; and, finally, Shuisky 'did not have the good fortune to believe in virtue.' Summing up his view on the importance of these enigmatic qualities, Karamzin alleged that during the worst period of the Time of Troubles, 'Russia was effectively lost and could only be saved by God and by its own virtue,' by which, as he explained more clearly in the *Memoir*, he meant patriotism.[100] This is not to say that Karamzin believed that the end justified the means, rather, for him, certain ends justified certain means. In all cases he felt that he must make some judgement, so quite often it was a matter of congratulating a prince for choosing the lesser evil.

Pragmatic and secular as he may have been, Karamzin still surrounded his discourse on politics with moral and Christian rationalizations. In the *History*, this was done by constant allusions to the role of 'Providence' in the course of Russian history. God's hand was omnipresent in Karamzin's scheme: 'God gave Russia Ivan III,' 'Providence ... gave Dmitry Donskoi wise teachers and advisors,' and, of course, 'Providence punishes treachery....' However, with or without the help of divine sanction, Karamzin still maintained that it was the duty of the tsar to rule well, and ruthlessly if need be.[101]

In order to effectively spread the so-called lessons of history, Karamzin had to present them in a manner suitable for a large number of readers. Therefore, he had to create a readable and interesting account of Russia's past since only in that way would the work be popular enough to achieve his aim. Hence, style and tenor were every bit as important to the study as the scheme itself. This posed no real difficulty, for he had few equals as far as writing ability was concerned and, at that time in Russian history, nothing had greater appeal to readers than patriotic studies.

Karamzin made no effort to hide his patriotism, seeing it as an integral part of any good historical writing. Thus, when he first began to labour on the *History*, he wrote in his notebook:

I know that our historians must be objective ... but ... I cannot always hide my love for the Fatherland: J'avais besoin de respirer. But I do not turn vices into virtues; I do not say that Russians are better than the French and Germans, I love them more.... [102]

In his request to Murav'ev for help in acquiring the position of Imperial Historiographer, Karamzin associated his own ambitions as an historian with 'the glory of the fatherland and Russian literature.' Some time later he re-expressed this feeling to the Empress Elizabeth: 'I wrote with love for the Fatherland, for the good of the people in a civil society, and for the sacred laws of morality.'[103]

Claiming that patriotism 'enlivens the narrative ... love of country gives [the historian's] brush stroke ardour, power, and appeal,' he justified it as an effective addition to his style of writing. As a matter of fact, Karamzin once apologized for the uninteresting aspects of Russian history after Yaroslav's death, but added that: 'Russia is our

Fatherland, its fate both in glorious and in terrible times is our memorial ... in a word, the history of our ancestors is always interesting to those who desire to have a Fatherland.'[104] He was therefore following the principles which he had laid down for others in articles published in the *Messenger of Europe*. Like the histories of Tacitus, Hume, and Gibbon, the text of the *History* was dominated by the narrative and was presented in a very picturesque literary style. That he had fully intended to write in this manner was made unmistakably clear in the oft-quoted note to A.I. Turgenev in 1814, at which time he said: 'What a pity if we saw history without such interesting reigns [Ivan IV]; then it would be like a peacock without feathers.'[105] In many respects, Karamzin's powers of narration, characterization, and description resembled those of Sir Walter Scott, for whom he had a great admiration. Indeed, Karamzin was given to reading from Scott for Russian literary societies in the 1820s and spoke of him often in letters to friends.[106] However, the similarities between the two were no more than by chance, or at best were products of similar times, for Karamzin's best historical tales were written long before any of the Scot's major works appeared.

Besides appealing to a popular audience, the *History* had also to attract the attention of Russia's small, but influential, class of scholars and pseudo-scholars. Thus Karamzin was faced with the very difficult task of producing a history that was both artistic and truthful. His awareness of recent scholarship, which placed the main emphasis on accuracy, can be traced back as far as 1791. In that year he differentiated between 'History' and 'Poesie,' assigning to the former the duty to 'describe everything that was' and to the latter that of arousing the passions of the reader.[107] He repeated this distinction in the foreword to the *History* (1815):

> *Truth serves as the basis for historical Poesie; but Poesie is not history: the first wishes most of all to raise interest, and for that reason is mixed with fables; the second rejects more witty thoughts and wishes only for the truth.*

In the meantime, however, he wrote in his notebook that history was 'la domaine de la Poesie.'[108]

The dual element of the *History*, expressed in the parallel notions that history had to be interesting and, secondly, to be dedicated 'solely to truth,' was well illustrated in its foreword. Here he gave pre-eminence to the entertainment value of history. The greatest talent for an historian to have, he said, was the ability 'to depict events' and to enliven the narrative. In the same foreword, however, he also insisted that historical writing 'did not tolerate fictions' and that criticism had to be exacting and strict. Summing up his reasons for the two aspects of the *History*, Karamzin claimed that since an historian dare 'not supplement the chronicles,' he must employ his talents to provide 'order, clarity, power, and picturesqueness'[109] so that the final product would be readable. Yet, in 'Martha' he had already advocated adding to the chronicles because they were often 'very stingy in details.' Conscious of the dangers of implementation, he did caution that such additions could only be made by 'a careful mind, gifted with *historical insight*.'[110]

For Karamzin, studying the distant past was partly an aesthetic exercise. An historian had to recreate ancient Russia with inadequate materials but, since the past could never be totally reconstructed, it could be made fascinating and reasonably truthful at the same time. To a man of imagination, the vagaries of antiquity offered an opportunity to simulate truth. The 'illusion' of truth, he had explained in 1797, 'is a creation of art.'[111] Less fanciful in the foreword to the *History*, he kept on the same track by suggesting that although an historian cannot 'produce gold out of copper,' he can at least refine it.

The fusion of truth and artistry remained one of Karamzin's objectives throughout the text of the *History*, although emphasis on the former was far more evident in his early days of historical writing than later. In 1803, he commented: 'the wise historian [has an] obligation: to discuss and to distinguish tales from the truth.' Two years later, he said that 'probability is not a proof of truth,' a sentiment repeated almost exactly in the first volume of the *History* where he allowed that 'the historian must not suggest probability for truth.'[112] There were other instances where Karamzin kept a sharp distinction between history and literature, but the last came in 1808 when he told his brother that 'history is not a novel, lies can be beautiful while truth, in its simple attire, pleases only some minds.' In the same year, Karamzin asked the state secretary, Novosiltsev, to take the place of the deceased Murav'ev as his patron at court. In a letter to this effect, he stressed far different things than he had in his request for the position of historiographer from Murav'ev some years before; he now claimed that his main intent was 'strict historical truth, thoroughness, and clarity.'[113]

As the *History* progressed, Karamzin's differentiation between truth and conjecture became less well defined. Indeed, he gradually developed a belief in their complementary character. In 1803, he had been most outspoken in his attack on historians who 'repeat the chronicles without criticism,'[114] and in the *History* he rejected one of Schlözer's interpretations with the comment, 'when truth itself is presented to the eyes of the historian, there is no need for strange hypotheses.' However, when Karamzin wished to present an hypotheses himself, invariably he added some minor qualification designed to give his own interpretation the attributes of objective history. In one place, he admitted that 'stories are not history,' but then went on to include tales about Vladimir I and implied that they must be true since they were so like commonly accepted ones about Charlemagne. Likewise, Karamzin said that 'history is not eulogy,' and pointed out a few minor defects in Ivan III's character so as to moderate what obviously had been a eulogy to that monarch. Further, he stated emphatically that 'history does not tolerate optimism,' but then outlined an extremely optimistic view of the Tatar presence in Russia.[115] Karamzin was not going to allow the principles of scholarship to interfere with his general interpretation of Russian history.

In spite of the literary manner in which the *History* was written, and the subordination of it to a general, didactic scheme, there still can be no doubt that Karamzin remained fully conscious of the scholarly demands of historical studies. Besides his footnotes, which were his most important and authentic concession to new trends, there were other indications that he was in keeping with the times. One of these was his censure of the *Stepennaia kniga* for its exaggerated claims. With respect to that source, he said, 'if we wish to interpret history for the benefit of national vanity, then history loses its truth, its main dignity, and will be a boring novel.'[116]

Another sign that he was not unaware of the needs of contemporary scholarship was evinced in the reasons he gave for not wishing to continue the *History* beyond the seventeenth century. Having acknowledged, in the *Messenger of Europe*, that most modern Russian institutions had their origin in the Middle Ages, it would seem natural that he carry his study up to more contemporary events, thereby completing the evolutionary picture. Granted, his attitude towards history per se may have dissuaded him because later times offered less scope for imaginative writing. However, there were scholarly considerations involved in his decision. During a time of general exultation over the Russian contribution to Napoleon's downfall, Karamzin mentioned that he had contemplated a request to write a history of that period, and had decided not to do so. In reality, he had gone so far as to outline a study of the recent wars with France but had given up the project because, he said, factual requirements of modern history would take far too much of his time: 'one must know more than I do....'[117] Later, he pointed out that the greatest difficulty in writing any recent history was the fact that, since the time of Peter I, political reasons of state had distorted historical records.[118] Needless to say, the chroniclers had been equally bound by political and religious dictates, but this had not hindered Karamzin's use of them.

Even as late as 1825, Karamzin refused to write about the French Revolution because 'contemporaries demand more detail, and history must be exact.' Many years before, he had already indicated to Murav'ev that he had no intention of going beyond the time of the first Romanovs and said the same again in 1823.[119] It is true that, in the ensuing year, he considered adding a brief survey of events leading up to his own time, but this in no way suggested a desire to work seriously on contemporary history. It would probably have involved a reworking of the outline in the *Memoir*. Presumably, for Karamzin, the main lessons of history were better represented by accounts of the distant past than by the more controversial history of modern times. As he said in 1815, 'History, modest and grave, loves the silence of passion and of tombs.'[120]

Karamzin's expressed aim in writing the *History* was more complex and modern than that of his predecessors, most of whom held an exclusively utilitarian concept of history. In contrast to them, Karamzin claimed that he wanted to 'unify what has been handed down to us by centuries, into a clear and coherent system...,' and to describe everything 'that goes into the civil being of man.'[121] This stress on unity, which was remarkably like that of Boltin, was in many ways similar to the ideas of Herder, who looked upon the history of a people as an organic process resulting from the interaction of their particular characteristics.

Karamzin had been interested in Herder's views since the early 1790s, when he had begun to show an increasing concern for the preservation of Russia's national integrity.[122] The innate virtue of the Russian people was a subtle feature of the *History*, and just as important to his scheme as the princes and the tsars. It was the national character that remained a constant in Russian history and which he continually brought to light as the pillar of strength for Russia. In his foreword, Karamzin stated categorically that the progressive evolution of the state reached a climax with the 'triumph of national virtue in the Time of Troubles,'[123] thus repeating sentiments expressed in his most Herderian writing, the *Memoir*.[124] In that work, too, he made several direct references to the influence of the people in Russian history and to the interdependence of all class units in Russia or, as he put it, 'the brotherly, national unity of the state classes.' He also spoke of 'natural evolution,' claimed that 'laws of a nation must be an outgrowth of its own ideas' and, in his concluding remarks, said that 'states, like human beings, have their definite life span.'[125] The part of the *Memoir* that most clearly suggested a connection with Herder's thoughts, however, was Karamzin's attack on Peter I for breaking the organic evolution and unity of the country. Still, the *Memoir* cannot be taken as a sign that Karamzin had adopted Herder's view of the historical process in its entirety, although by 1818 he appeared to come back to it even more strongly when he claimed that not even Peter could change 'the beautiful individuality' of Russians.[126]

Karamzin had a much narrower outlook than had Herder, confining himself almost solely to the political development of one nation. The nationalistic tone of the *Memoir* and its defence of Russian autocracy were prompted more by contemporary political controversy than by an Herderian philosophy. In fact, in 1817, Karamzin himself admitted to having read a small book of Herder's three times but without ever understanding it.[127]

Karamzin's view on historical writing was a synthesis of several major influences. His highly literary presentation, moral judgements, and above all, pragmatism, were the products of eighteenth-century practices, while the emphasis on gradual, organic evolution of political institutions and social relations were of more recent origin. Overshadowing all other considerations, however, was his belief in the instructive nature of literature. The formative factor in Karamzin's ideas on the national historical process had been the course of events in France during his own lifetime. The image, in his mind, of the great French nation fallen to a level of barbarism obligated him, as a sage, to make an effort to forestall similar developments in Russia. The aim of the *History* therefore was to instill in readers his own conviction that, for the time being at least, stability and order were essential for the well-being of all Russians. Whether or not he was successful in this endeavour remains to be seen.

5
The *History* and Russian Society in the Nineteenth Century

As we have seen, the first eight volumes of the *History* were published in February 1818. The initial publication proved such an immense success that the entire edition of 3000 rather expensive copies sold within a month, a remarkable phenomenon for a society that previously had not shown much interest in its own history and where the native language had only recently been accepted as one suitable for scholarly activity. In fact, a second edition was already being printed in July of that same year.

The *History* was the first study of Russia's past which combined thoroughness, scholarship, and a writing style that made it interesting reading. Although the historical sciences had progressed significantly in Russia over the last decades of the eighteenth century, little attention had been paid to the needs of the general public as far as historical texts were concerned. The multi-volume works by Tatishchev and Shcherbatov were pretty onerous reading, and the general texts by Lomonosov, de Mirievo, and the oft-reprinted *Sinopsis* were out of date and too skimpy to attract those who wished to read for pleasure. Studies and texts printed in Russia after the turn of the century, by Catherine II, Schlözer, Stritter, K.F. Kalaidovich, and P.M. Stroev, were either too specialized or too superficial to appeal to a reading public anxious for a substantial and nationalistic résumé of their national past. Karamzin's work more than fulfilled this need.[1] The popularity of the *History* was due also in part to its timeliness, for it

appeared when Russians had finally developed a national consciousness equal to that of patriots in the West. The evolution of nationalism in politics and in the arts had reached a crescendo with the defeat
of Napoleon, an event which seemed to justify the rather self-con-
scious claims of equality put forward by earlier Russian nationalists.

There can be little doubt that no previous historical work reached
the Russian reading public in such a variety of ways. Besides remaining the standard authority on Russian history until the 1850s, themes
and characters from the work were adopted by Russian writers
throughout the century. Prominent men of letters, like M.Iu. Ler-
montov, N.V. Gogol', F.I. Tiutchev, and N.A. Nekrasov made extensive use of the *History* for background material and subject themes
for their own productions.[2] Many well-known writers remembered it
fondly as part of their childhood. I.S. Turgenev spoke of it many
times and Dostoevsky actually boasted that at the age of ten he had
'already read almost all the main episodes from Karamzin's history.'
The more liberally inclined Dmitry Miliutin claimed to have accomplished the same feat. Dostoevsky's friend, Nicholas Strakhov, held
Karamzin in the same nostalgic esteem and wrote that as a boy in the
1840s he 'knew the first volume of the *History* by heart. Karamzin
was to me my contemporary.' The great historian, Solov'ev (1820-
1879), had read and enjoyed it a dozen times by the time he had
reached the age of thirteen. So had V.O. Kliuchevsky (1841-1911).
The *History*, Solov'ev said, aroused in him an 'adolescent patriotism'
and a hatred for Batory and the Poles who had transgressed on 'Russian soil.'[3] Even those who were opposed to Karamzin's political viewpoint, among them the Decembrist poet, K.F. Ryleev (1795-1826),
and Pushkin, consistently used the *History* as a source for their own
works. Moreover, it is to the opinions of Pushkin, or to V.G. Belinsky, that Soviet writers have usually directed their readers when they
wish to say something good about Karamzin. The *History* was also
widely read for relaxation alone and many Russians had feelings
about it that corresponded to those of Leo Tolstoi, who said at mid-
century that Karamzin's 'foreword' 'invokes a world of well-being in
me.'[4]

Some of the work's usefulness for other writers was closely tied to
Karamzin's prestige in the literary world. For example, a contributor
to Pushkin's *Contemporary* (*Sovremennik*) in 1836 deplored the prac-

tice of Russian writers who simply 'open up the history of Karamzin, cut several pages from it, paste them together,' and call the result Russian literature.[5] Because of the pervasive nature of censorship at that time, this observation does not necessarily reflect the quality of Russian authors during the thirties, but it does bespeak Karamzin's presence well enough. In the same year, the Slavophile Prince V.F. Odoevsky complained about the number of historical novels and plays that were based on the *History*.[6]

Its literary worth notwithstanding, it was the *History*'s political tone that assured its fashionableness and the longevity of 'Karamzinian' historical themes in Russian upper society. The *History* became the officially approved reference for history taught in schools and some teachers came to rely on it exclusively. N.A. Dobroliubov (1836-1861), a mid-century radical, once complained that he and fellow students had been 'satiated' with Karamzin,[7] but there is little evidence of other objections. In recalling his youth, D.N. Bludov (1789-1864), spoke of the great pleasure the *History* brought into his studies and commended one of his former teachers at Kazan who 'loved Karamzin to the extent of worship.' And F.I. Buslaev cited from Karamzin in most of the sixty lectures on Russian culture which he delivered to the Tsarevich Nicholas Alexandrovich, 1859-60.[8] The liberal Nicholas Turgenev (1789-1871) admitted that Karamzin's history could have a beneficial effect on the moral and ethical behaviour of Russia's youth. This notion was to become such an accepted part of intellectual tradition, and of the Karamzin legend, that even the unlikely and distant periodical, the American *Atlantic Monthly*, carried an article in 1862 in which Karamzin was referred to as a moulder of modern Russia's 'moral strength.'[9] It was with this very aim in mind that the self-styled Karamzinian, N.D. Ivanchin-Pisarev, published the two-volume *Spirit of Karamzin (Dukh karamzina)* in 1827. Thirty years later an educator, N.A. Miller-Krasovsky, who went so far as to suggest that the sole purpose of pedagogy was to breed patriots and to inculcate the word of God into Russia's youth, recommended Karamzin to his fellow teachers.[10]

Besides reaching scholars and literati, the *History* was equally well distributed to the general public. Karamzin's first major bibliographer, S. Ponomarev, listed books on Olga, Vladimir I, Dimitry Shemiaka, Ivan IV, the Battle of Kulikovo, and the conquest of Siberia, all of which were taken directly from the *History*.[11] Others appeared after Ponomarev's book was printed in 1882, among them histories of the Tatar conquest published in 1889 and 1897,[12] and several studies that appeared after the turn of the century. An abbreviated version of the *History*, which was prepared in 1819 as a text for young students, was reissued unchanged in 1824. This 388-page summary was accompanied by vocabulary, translations, and subtitles, so that it could also serve as an aid to German and French students of the Russian language.[13]

In the 1830s, teachers of Russian history used texts by E. Konstantinov, I. Kaidanov, N.G. Ustrialov, and M.P. Pogodin, all of which were little more than abridgements of the *History*. Ivan Kaidanov was the most prolific of textbook writers in Russia during the first decade and a half of Nicholas's reign. The first edition of his *Outline of the History of the Russian State (Nachertanie istorii gosudarstva Rossiiskago)*, appeared in 1829, and was in its fourth edition by 1834. In a foreword, he said that Karamzin's work had been the model for his own, and each edition was dedicated to the 'unforgettable' Karamzin. With Uvarov at the educational helm after 1833, they had little choice, for the newly appointed minister had recommended as early as 1813 that Karamzin's work be the basis for school texts.[14] However, even later texts by Solov'ev, D.I. Ilovaisky, V.A. Abaza, and K.V. Elpat'evsky continued the tradition.

One of Karamzin's life-long ambitions had been to write for the instruction of Russia's youth, so he would have been delighted to hear that I. Baikov printed a special collection of extracts from the *History* for youngsters in 1830. Five years later, the leading Official Nationality periodical, the *Reader's Library (Biblioteka dlia Chteniia)*, recommended a series of notebooks on Russian history and drawings, the text of which was taken directly from Karamzin. The notebooks, said the reviewer, could serve as a 'pleasant and useful lesson for children.' In 1837, Alexandra Ishimova prepared another history of Russia for children. Presented in the form of separate accounts, she followed Karamzin so closely that she even used the historiographer's words.[15]

At mid-century, P. Stroev followed suit and put together a further collection of historical accounts for children between the ages of seven and twelve.[16] Most of the accounts, which were taken from

Karamzin, were designed to encourage historical reading or, as Uvarov put it, to fill in a vacuum created by the generally dull and monotonous tenor of children's history books. Just as Karamzin had once hoped, Uvarov expected the children to learn how to be good Russians from the historical examples set forth in the book.[17] The ensuing decades saw no let-up in the process. N. Timaev prepared several history texts for school reading between 1858 and 1865. Ishimova added to her collection of simple historical accounts. Both adopted from Karamzin. In 1872, Ya. Tiagunov published a study, the title of which openly acknowledged a source that many others were surreptitiously using: *Holy Rus': Extracts from Karamzin and Others* (St Petersburg 1872, 1875). There were many others.[18]

In the last twenty years of the century, the Society for the Dissemination of Useful Books published a biography of Karamzin and a number of historical tales based on his studies. During the same period, A.S. Suvorin, the conservative editor of *New Times* (*Novoe vremia*), printed a number of extracts from the *History* with the expressed aim of popularizing Russian history.[19] The fact that the *History* went through half of its fourteen editions after 1889, the last appearing in 1903, suggests its continuing importance to state ideologists. The 1892 edition, the one most commonly used now, was a reprint of supplements added to each issue of the monthly journal, *Sever* (*North*) during that year.

The great variety of ways in which the *History* reached readers in both Russia and western Europe might be judged from the number of disciplines affected by it. Ponomarev mentioned two geographical productions based on the *History*, one published in the thirties, another in 1844; there were at least two others.[20] Students at the University of St Petersburg noted that P.A. Pletnev (1792-1865) used at least one citation from Karamzin in each of his lectures and one student recalled that even in the 1880s his professor of Greek had students translate parts of the *History* as their main assignment.[21]

The extent of the influence of the *History* on ideas about Russia held by western Europeans can only be judged properly by a detailed study of nineteenth-century European histories of Russia. It is indicative, however, that it was immediately and generally favourably reviewed in France, England, and Germany. A writer for one of Russia's better known journals, *Atenei*, remarked in 1828 that German novelists were already following the example of Russians by taking themes from the *History* for their own books. D.A.W. Tappe used the *History* to create a German-language textbook of Russian history. His *Russisches historisches Lesebuch aus Karamzins Geschichte Russlands* was published simultaneously in three centres – St Petersburg, Riga, and Leipzig – as early as 1819. According to A.I. Turgenev, Tappe so admired Karamzin that the only portrait in his office was of the historiographer.[22]

Parts of the *History* were translated into French, German, and Italian by 1820. Before another decade had gone by, complete versions were available in those languages and in Polish. It was printed in Greek in the 1850s and sections of it were put into Chinese.[23] Although it was never translated into English, the British *Annual Register* noted that it created a 'lively sensation ... throughout all Europe' and Charles Dickens once spoke of 'Karamzin, Russia's great historian.'[24] A quarter of a century after Karamzin's death, Dobroliubov wrote in a decidedly unhappy tone that Europeans still read only Karamzin for their knowledge of Russian history. Karamzin therefore had finally fulfilled by himself the task which he had set for Russian writers in the 1790s. He provided Europeans with a substitute for Levesque's work on Russia's history, which had remained until that time the best known history of Russia in western Europe. In fact, the Arzamas diploma congratulated Karamzin specifically for displacing the works of Levesque and Leclerc. Even Karl Marx turned to Karamzin in 1866, but in this instance to support a sweeping claim that Russian policy of world domination was unalterable.[25]

Among European countries, the *History* had its greatest reception in France, where it remained the major source on Russian history until the seventies.[26] The French translation was carried out in close consultation with Karamzin who, after finding thirty errors in the first volume, moaned, 'God be with them, my translators.' Later, he admitted that 'the French translation is not bad and is true to a great extent.'[27] Reviews of the translation in the *Revue encyclopédique* (1820, 1822, 1823), the *Bulletin des sciences historiques* (1824), *Moniteur universel* (1820), and the *Journal des débats* (three in 1820) all served to persuade the French reading public that this was the definitive study on Russian history. Karamzin himself was astounded that even the liberal press in France praised his work. After such general approval, the publication in 1835 of a five-volume history of Russia by E. Ennesaux and L.E. Chennechot assured that Karamzin's picture of Russia would reign supreme in France for sometime.[28]

At the time when the *History* was first published, Russians were still congratulating themselves on their part in the defeat of Napoleon. Following the Congress of Vienna, there developed a clash of wills between conservatives and liberals in Russia much like that in the rest of Europe, but a majority of prominent Russians were convinced that their nation had been preserved from disaster by the innate strengths of its established institutions. Therefore, while a similar political debate progressed to the detriment of conservatives in western Europe, the opposite was the case in Russia. Having no institutional or economic base, nor a strong ideological tradition from which to launch an attack on the status quo, Russian liberals were not in a position to generate much dynamic support. The *History* became a centre of attention in this ideological struggle, serving as 'truth' or as official propaganda, depending upon the reader's political viewpoint. Caught up in the intellectual and national controversies then sweeping Russia, the *History* was the object of at least two fairly distinct arguments. The first involved a prolonged dispute over the work's contribution to the evolution of Russian historiography. The second originated in the tendentiousness that resulted from the inclination of readers to interpret themes from the *History* according to their personal conceptions of Russian life. The latter category, which is the most relevant to the present discussion, had many manifestations. Published at a time when censorship was increasingly harsh, the *History* became a tool for both sides in the political arguments that preceded the Decembrist Revolt of 1825. In the ensuing years of repression, it became a symbol of the iniquities in Russian society for some Russians; it delineated the greatness and necessity of the autocratic system for others.

We have seen that Karamzin was no stranger to political or ideological controversy. The Karamzin-Shishkov and Beseda-Arzamas debates, which were ostensibly over literary matters, always had had real political overtones. In the first decade of the nineteenth century, Karamzin had represented a new age to many young writers in Russia and conservatives had attacked him for too much innovation. However, even at that time his political thinking was recognizably with the hierarchy. The next generation continued to admire his writing ability, but increasingly and openly (as far as it was possible) criticized him as part of the established order. The *History* was published as the official interpretation of the national heritage so it was inevitable that it would be read within the context of contemporary political polemics.

A few months before the *History* finally appeared, its author disclosed that he was well aware of the attitude some of his enemies would have: 'Many await my history so that they can attack me.'[29] So the flurry of criticism from liberals which began almost immediately on the publication of the *History* was expected. The degree of liberal anxiety over the influence of the *History* indicated the extent of the hold Karamzin had on the contemporary reading public. The future Decembrists M.F. Orlov and N.M. Murav'ev flew to the attack right away. Orlov, who said that he had 'awaited the *History* like the Israelites awaited the Messiah,' was incensed at Karamzin's apparent reiteration of the old 'Normanist' interpretations. He claimed, inaccurately, that Karamzin had ignored the evolution of Russia before the arrival of the Varangians. Murav'ev, the son of Karamzin's first sponsor at court, charged the historiographer with being uncritical of sources and denigrated the study for being an apology for what he called the 'Asiatic despotism' of contemporary Russia.[30] The same accusations were levelled by another Decembrist, G.S. Baten'kov, who on first reading the *History* said, 'there is not much history in it' because of its concentration on 'heroes' and lack of scholarly criticism.[31]

A friend of the Decembrists, A.A. Pisarev (1780-1848), has been credited with writing *Karamzinian Commandments* (*Zapovedi karamzinistov*, 1818) in which he made fun of those who worshipped the Karamzin image. Among the 'commandments' which Pisarev laid down for Karamzinians were admonishments not to recognize anyone as Karamzin's equal, not to mention his name unless in reverential tones, neither to criticize him nor to compare him to lesser lights. Satirical as this essay may have been, it did suggest both the predominance of Karamzin and the antipathy towards him among liberals.[32] Indeed, the debate had already become so heated by the end of 1818 that Dmitriev observed that: 'The critics are not able to forgive Karamzin for being the Historiographer and, consequently, in their minds, a hireling of the government ... they consider the writer to be their greatest enemy.'[33] Since many of Karamzin's most rabid defenders among the nobility and gentry interpreted the *History* as final proof that autocracy was the mainstay of Russian civilization, it is clear that any attempt to rectify the dichotomy was a utopian one, to say the least.

While the Decembrists grumbled, most readers greeted the *History* with enthusiasm. N.I. Grech (1787-1867), editor of the nationalist journal *Son of the Fatherland* (*Syn otechestva*, 1816-1825), said in the first review of the study that 'the most eloquent praise, the loudest leaflets of journalists, cannot extoll this book well enough.'[34] Grech then began to spread the gospel according to Karamzin by printing extracts from it in his periodical – an important contribution to the Karamzin legend because, at 50 rubles, the *History* was more expensive than many of the gentry could afford.[35] In the same year, M.T. Kachenovsky (1775-1842), who was leader of the 'Skeptical School' of historians and who was to become Karamzin's bitterest opponent, published a notice in which he agreed with the praise set out in *Son of the Fatherland*. However, Kachenovsky, who was by that time editor of the *Messenger of Europe*, foresaw the study becoming an object of emotional wrangling and insisted that it be examined 'impassionately.' A few months later, he again congratulated Karamzin for making Russian history 'better known to many,' but suggested that it was not yet perfect and complained very bitterly about those editors who, while praising the *History* to the skies, had not 'taken the trouble to read the creation.'[36]

Discussion increased in 1819 when *Son of the Fatherland* published a letter from Ivanchin-Pisarev to P.I. Shuvalov in which the writer admitted that he was not among the 'worshippers' of Karamzin. While expressing great admiration for Karamzin the man, the writer, and contributor to Russian national feeling, Pisarev asked that the *History* be read from a less emotional point of view. Like Kachenovsky, Pisarev hoped that the *History* would not be so influential as to prevent further research and hinted that a writer who had been so highly regarded as a romantic and as a story-teller might not be the ideal historian. What seemed to bother Pisarev most was that since the *History* had been prejudged by many as the definitive expression of Russian nationalism, few intended to examine it from the point of view of scholarship.[37]

The same premonition struck Kachenovsky, who published a series of letters in 1819 which dealt with the general aims and views of Karamzin as expressed in the foreword to the *History*. Kachenovsky had great respect for Karamzin's plan to make history better known but did not accept the historiographer's emphasis on imaginative writing, or 'excellent fairy tales.' Proclaiming the Skeptical School creed that 'truth is the main source of satisfaction for readers,'[38] Kachenovsky also rejected Karamzin's tendency to moralize and contradicted him by congratulating Hume for a lack of emotion. Kachenovsky was also wary of Karamzin's insistence that an historian must write from a patriot's point of view and claimed, like Schlözer, that 'objectivity is the first unchanging obligation of a would-be writer.' Indeed, Kachenovsky had been most upset about the historiographer's slur on Schlözer[39] and it was on this point that an unhealable rift was formed among Russian historians, many of whom believed that it was the German scholar who had introduced modern historical practices to their country. Kachenovsky and others prided themselves on being the Russian heirs to a 'scientific' tradition established by Bayer, Müller, Schlözer, Stritter, and their own contemporaries, Krug, Ewers, and Lerburg. They worried that the *History*, with its immense publicity, represented the victory of a different kind of tradition in Russian historiography. They assumed, as many have since, that Karamzin's work was the antithesis of Schlözer's and that it marked the zenith of a popular, non-scholarly kind of historical writing which would prove an insurmountable barrier against the acceptance of their own works. If Paul Miliukov's conclusion, made in 1897, that the 'historiography of the nineteenth century came from Schlözer ... a Karamzin *school* of historiography did not exist,'[40] is true, then Kachenovsky and his confrères need not have worried. But few contemporaries denied Karamzin's great following among scholars, creative writers, and the reading public. Furthermore, among historians of his era, there were few who were more scholarly than Karamzin and very few that were his equal as a critic of sources, but that is a matter for another kind of study.[41]

Kachenovsky professed to be surprised at the intensity and volume of the outburst against him, for he wrote to N.I. Gnedich in the spring of 1820: 'One [former friend] avoids me, another does not recognize me, a third calls me ... insane, and a danger to mankind.'

All this abuse, Kachenovsky moaned, was unfair because all he had hoped to do was to speak the 'unpleasant truth.'[42] To compound his difficulties, critics of Karamzin, whether or not they agreed with Kachenovsky, were all simply lumped into one category by Dmitriev and others, that is, 'the fawns of Kachenovsky.'[43] He probably would not have been so surprised by the reaction of Karamzinians if he had known how A.I. Turgenev and Zhukovsky had broadcast the merits of the *History* even before it was published. Zhukovsky had said in 1816, after listening to Karamzin read from the section on the taking of Kazan, 'there is an especially good trait in my soul which is called Karamzinian, which includes everything in me that is good and best ... he read to us descriptions of the taking of Kazan. What completeness ... this *History* can be called the resurrection of the past centuries of our nation.'[44] In the same year, Karamzin was called 'our immortal Historiographer of the Fatherland' by a lesser poet, A. Illichevsky,[45] and as early as 1809 Turgenev wrote to his brother Nicholas that 'Karamzin is one of the best historians of the century, considering the past as well, which included Schlözer, Müller, Robertson, and Gibbon.'[46] Although Nicholas Turgenev was far less optimistic, and replied that 'Karamzin, so far as I know, hopes to prove that Russia was begun and raised by despotism, what we here call autocracy,' the generally high expectations could not help but predetermine judgements of the work once it was finally made public. Even Kachenovsky opened one of his essays by pointing out that no one had dominated the minds of his contemporaries so much as Karamzin, and that to speak against the historiographer bordered on cultural heresy.[47]

Viazemsky and Bludov had no mercy for Kachenovsky. Bludov spoke scathingly of 'someone named Kachenovsky, someone named Shalikov and others who, with heat and arrogance ... with heavy, thoughtless ignorance, storm over our historiographer.'[48] The main line of defence against Kachenovsky, however, was that taken up by Viazemsky, who wrote Dmitriev in 1818 that 'the frog was born to croak in the marsh and Kachenovsky to write oaths from the Luzhnikov Square ... to me it is indecent to attack Karamzin.' Dmitriev called it 'great spite,' and even S.M. Solov'ev many years later attributed the protest to Karamzin's 'envious scholarly brothers,'[49] but both were over-simplifying a dialogue that arose from feelings that were more complex than mere envy or ignorance. For liberals, the crux of the issue was that Karamzin seemed to personify those things that were adored by his defenders – class, tradition, and support of the status quo. For historians and nationalists, problems arose from Karamzin's interpretation of the ancient sources and the degree to which he accepted foreign influences on the early Slavs. Obviously, the *History* was an object for other than academic discussion.

In 1821, Viazemsky made his feelings public in an unusually abrasive poem written for *Son of the Fatherland*, in which he termed Kachenovsky envious and a 'base enemy of talent.'[50] Somewhat plaintively, Kachenovsky retorted that he admired Karamzin and the *History*, but that he still believed it not to be perfect.[51] It is likely, however, that many of Karamzin's more ardent supporters were not in the least bit interested in whether or not the *History* could be improved upon in the scientific sense – it already said what they wished it to say. Karamzin himself was anxious not to be involved in argument, insisting that he wished 'to live out his life in peace,' but Dmitriev and Viazemsky were equally determined to take strong action and persuaded people like V.L. Pushkin to print repudiations against the critics.[52]

Kachenovsky was not the only scholar who was outspoken against the *History*. An ethnographer, Z. Dolega-Chodakowski, writing under the pseudonym of A.I. Czarnocki, published a critical commentary for the *Messenger of Europe* in the autumn of 1819. Sarcastically naming Karamzin the 'Nevsky Plutarch,' and implying that the historiographer was 'hostile' against Poles, Chodakowski wrote the first detailed examination of the way in which ancient Rus' was presented in the *History*. A Polish national, he asked that the next edition be corrected.[53] Opposed to Karamzin's interpretation of ninth-century Russia, Chodakowski said that the *History* 'exaggerated foreign activities in our land.' He thereby helped to reopen the debate over 'Normanism' that had been activated by Lomonosov's diatribes against G.F. Müller in the mid-eighteenth century. The first respondent to Chodakowski was S.V. Russov, who came to Karamzin's defence in 1820 and again nine years later when he replied to similar charges from N.S. Artsybashev (1773-1841).[54]

Stricture of Karamzin by liberals increased so rapidly in the twenties that the teacher and writer M.A. Dmitriev felt compelled to write a series of articles for *Atenei* in 1829 which had as their sole aim the defence of Karamzin. One of the historian's most consistent admirers, Dmitriev asked, 'who would have thought that he would need defence?' Echoing Dmitriev's question in the same year, Russov registered genuine shock that the work could be denigrated by patriotic Russians.[55] A year before, even the liberally inclined journal, *Northern Flowers* (*Severnye tsvety*), had carried a note to the effect that 'almost no one gives thanks to the man who ... dedicated twelve years of his life to silent and tireless work,' and in 1829 another writer for *Atenei* recalled hearing 'the strange conclusion that Karamzin was endowed only with wisdom but not with genius.'[56] Among writers, the editors of the liberal periodical, *The North Star* (*Poliarnaia zvezda*), A.A. Bestuzhev (1797-1837) and Ryleev, best represented those with mixed feelings about Karamzin's work. Both gave him credit for his artistic skills but neither approved the content of the *History*.

The North Star formed part of the Decembrist tradition but the tone of the periodical was hardly a radical one. Many liberals participated in it, but the journal also carried articles by such conservative, pro-Karamzin people as Viazemsky, Zhukovsky, I.I. Dmitriev, Batiushkov, Grech, and A.P. Voeikov. Viazemsky was of a liberal inclination in those years, but he was more a dilettante than a serious reformer. Were it not for Thaddens Bulgarin (1789-1859) and A.A. Shakuovskoi (1777-1846), who were openly and virulently against him, *The North Star* was servile in its position on Karamzin. Its editors and a few more, among them Gnedich, did not openly commit themselves to opposition, not wishing to proclaim their political or literary affinities too loudly.[57]

In the first number in 1823, Bestuzhev praised the style of the *History* but rather pointedly ignored its content with the remark, 'time will judge Karamzin as an historian.' He repeated this performance two years later by reviewing the tenth and eleventh volumes for their literary merits alone. Even Bestuzhev's praise for Karamzin's contribution to Russian literature was offset somewhat by equally kind words for Shishkov and by his commendation for the anti-Karamzin Poles, Lelewel and Bulgarin. Lelewel's critique of the *History*, Bestuzhev said, 'was a pleasant and rare phenomenon in the field of literature.'[58] In 1831, Bestuzhev was much less subtle about Karamzin, calling him an 'eloquent windbag.'[59] On his part, Karamzin complained about the popularity of *The North Star* and was delighted to see Bestuzhev and Ryleev under arrest in January 1826.[60]

As well as the liberals, but for far different reasons, historians other than Kachenovsky were upset by the *History*. N.P. Rumiantsev, who spent many years collecting and editing materials for a history of Russia, felt that it was premature and disappointingly superficial.[61] One of Karamzin's most useful contacts at court, Rumiantsev was still sending the historiographer documents in 1818, after the first eight volumes had been published. But, having been so instrumental in providing Karamzin with sources, he expected a more substantial and scholarly finished product.

The most thorough professional critic of Karamzin was the prolific Polish historian, Joachim Lelewel (1786-1861), who was asked by fellow Poles in St Petersburg to undertake such a task. Lelewel wrote a series of reviews over the period 1822-4 for Bulgarin's *Northern Archive (Severnyi arkhiv)*.[62] Lelewel began with a long commentary on Karamzin's 'foreword' and, in an obvious allusion to the writer's early career, said, 'many writers attempt to be called historians but hardly any of them achieve this aim.' So that readers would not mistake his meaning, Lelewel added, 'Karamzin's opinion on how to write history is quite different from mine.' Continuing his examination, which was limited to the early stages of Russian history and was influenced by the writer's own nationalist and anti-autocratic point of view, Lelewel produced the most scholarly analysis of the *History* written before that by S.M. Solov'ev in the 1850s. The Pole attacked Karamzin for concentrating on autocracy and for sacrificing truth in order to create interest among his readers. His attitude corresponded to that of Murav'ev and Orlov. Karamzin himself referred to Lelewel as 'some kind of Polish student,' but made no effort to refute the charges, rightly assuming that his opponent's nationality would be defence enough.[63] The fact that Lelewel was dismissed in 1824 from his professorship at the University of Vilna may have been due to his general philosophical and political point of view, for those times were hard on non-conformist thinkers. But his attack on Karamzin must have made his position tenuous anyway.

Lelewel's censure of Karamzin's Normanism made his critique popular with some later historians, but in the twenties Serbinovich and others were able to keep the impact of his writing to a minimum by alluding to his 'foreign' prejudices. Bulgarin, who was also Polish by birth, wrote an introduction to Lelewel's series and hinted that Karamzin had not yet been given the advantage of being reviewed by an objective reader or 'true scholar.'[64] Though he moved from liberal to strongly conservative views by the late twenties, Bulgarin never altered his opinion of Karamzin; in turn, the historiographer had little regard for Bulgarin or Lelewel and did not worry over their complaints: 'at least in this matter I am a liberal, I allow them to say and to write what they wish.'[65]

Shortly before Karamzin's death, an article by D. Zubarev in the *Messenger of Europe* foretold the character of much of the future arguments against the *History*. That is, its political and social implications were to be seized upon while its technical merits would be ignored. Zubarev disagreed with Karamzin's picture of civilization in Kievan Rus' in comparison to that of contemporary Europe and said that Karamzin exaggerated the extent of Varangian influence on the early Slavs. Touching upon the volatile subject of Normanism, Zubarev also suggested that Russians had nothing in common with west Europeans until the time of Peter I, thereby opening up one of the many areas for later dialogue between Westernizer and Slavophile.[66] Such inflammatory comments could not help but evoke an immediate response and within weeks N.A. Polevoi had replied to Zubarev, not in defence of Karamzin, but in opposition to the critic's interpretation of Russian history.[67]

There was a lull in the storm when Karamzin died in 1826. Viazemsky's comment that 'he was a kind of life-giving, radiant focus for our circle and of all the Fatherland,' explains the feeling of a huge number of people. Briefly, as Dmitriev pointed out, his passing 're-conciled everyone, even Kachenovsky....'[68] However, the onslaught was renewed with vigour by Kachenovsky and Artsybashev by 1828. Even some of Karamzin's devotees took him to task posthumously for the detail of his historical account. This was the case with M.P. Pogodin who had suggested some years before that Schlözer's treatment of the founding of the Russian state was a sounder one than Karamzin's. Pogodin, who became Russia's leading ideologist of pan-Slavism, kept alive the nationalistic aspect of debate over the *History*. In a short article written in 1823 but not published until 1828, he rejected Karamzin's conclusion that the Varangians ruled the Slavs as benefactors and said that some of the historiographer's 'strained guesses' would not have been necessary if he had taken Nestor more seriously.[69] Developing a nationalist picture of ancient Russia, Pogodin published several short commentaries on the *History* in 1824, two of which questioned Karamzin's slighting of Nestor and one that supported Karamzin against Lelewel. In 1825, Pogodin contested Karamzin's picture of Ivan IV by discrediting Kurbsky as a reliable source and two years later he undertook to revise his predecessor's interpretation of Godunov and the death of Tsarevich Dmitry. Yet Pogodin was confident enough to dedicate and send his master's dissertation to Karamzin, who spoke highly of it.[70]

Kachenovsky and Artsybashev, both of whom tended to overemphasize the rules of criticism laid down by Niebuhr and Schlözer, were most adamant in their claim that Karamzin's work was literature and could not be deemed history. Although the bitter tone in their criticism tended to detract from its value, the tradition that the *History* had no critical merits was carried on by Polevoi and eventually became the accepted opinion of the work on the part of historians. Acknowledging the 'immortal work of Karamzin' in both literature and history, Kachenovsky summarized his feelings in a series of articles published in 1829. Noting the social dangers involved in any criticism of the historiographer, he still cautioned readers against making such a fetish of the *History* that further scholarship might be hindered. He also noted the dependency of Karamzin on Shcherbatov's system and sources, although he did not consider this an undesirable trait. In the second article, Kachenovsky again referred to Karamzin as a writer of 'astonishing artistry' and added that the historiographer was a 'true pragmatist' who could grasp the significance of the past for the present.[71]

All in all, if Karamzin had not symbolized Russian nationalism and enlightenment to so many people and had not been so popular among literati, Kachenovsky would have been a formidable opponent. The younger man held the chair of Russian history at the University of Moscow between 1821 and 1835 and also held the respect of his students. But it was not in the realm of scholarship that the *History* had its greatest influence. Furthermore, Nicholas's government left very few avenues for criticism in Russian life, particularly of things that were generally regarded as part of the official apparatus. Moreover,

Karamzin's defenders were reinforced by those who acted on the *History*'s behalf because they felt that it spoke for the old kind of aristocratic state in contrast to the bureaucratic one that Nicholas was in the process of creating.

In the twenties and early thirties, the criticism levelled by Kachenovsky was not often taken as serious scholarship, nor was that of his contemporary, Artsybashev. The growing malice in Kachenovsky's articles and the venom of Artsybashev's evoked a feeling close to fury on the part of Karamzinians, although the debunkers had one moderate supporter in the person of the historian and archeologist P.M. Stroev. In 1828, Stroev wrote to the editors of the *Moscow Herald* (*Moskovskii vestnik*) to say that if the 'immortal creator' of the *History* had been willing to take the advice of a twenty-two-year old novice (Stroev) in 1818, then he certainly would not have objected to that from professional historians. Stroev's writings were intended mainly as criticism of Polevoi, who published a detailed critique of the *History* that year and who hoped to replace Karamzin as the leading light of Russia's historians. However, when Pogodin and Viazemsky followed suit, Stroev found himself in an unenviable position as everyone's conscience. He attacked the extremes of all sides, Artsybashev's hysteria, Polevoi's petulance, and Viazemsky's sarcasms. Even his plea for moderation aroused the anger of Russov, who immediately placed a rebuttal in *Son of the Fatherland*.[72]

Artsybashev, who was as much an opponent of Kachenovsky as he was of Karamzin, had written two articles in 1821 on the character of Ivan IV and that monarch's contribution to Russian history. Following ideas espoused by Boltin in the 1790s and preceding Pogodin by a few years, he insisted that Ivan's cruelties were hardly unique for that period of time. Like Boltin, he suggested that the tsar's actions were justified because the boyars' conduct was detrimental to the state. In a later study, he again followed Boltin's lead by publishing a critique of the French historian of Russia, LeClerc. Prolific in his condemnation of Karamzin, Artsybashev printed his harshest exposition in the *Moscow Herald* in 1828, to which Pogodin added a note to say that he agreed with much of what the writer had said, but that he had no liking for his spiteful tone.[73]

In general, Artsybashev's criticism had so much the appearance of personal vendetta that his reviews only exacerbated the dialogue. The merits of many of his complaints were invalidated by the pettiness of others and by contradictions so carefully pinpointed by Karamzin's guardian angel, Russov. Ivan Kireevsky took up Karamzin's defence also, and made it an integral part of his well-known essay, 'Survey of Russian Literature in 1829.' He soundly chastised the critics as either petty (Artsybashev), pointless (Polevoi), or slanderous (Bulgarin). Viazemsky, too, sent a satirical poem to the *Moscow Telegraph*, in which he praised Karamzin at Artsybashev's expense.[74] Viazemsky and Kireevsky were also active in defending Karamzin in Moscow's numerous salons. Not deterred by vilification, Artsybashev persevered well into the thirties, making his arguments against Karamzin an integral part of his multi-volume *Tales about Russia* (*Povestvovanie o Rossoi*, 1838), and adding to his charges an attack on Karamzin's picture of Godunov's part in the death of Tsarevich Dimitry.[75]

The same theme had been taken up by Bulgarin, whose criticisms were too superficial to be taken very seriously.[76] A year after he had defended Karamzin, Polevoi decided to enter the fray on the side of the historiographer's critics. His main contention was that Karamzin's entire intellectual framework for judging Russia's past was obsolete. Individuals who participated in the polemics for and against the *History* were divided into camps represented by periodicals. Since Pogodin, Polevoi, and Bulgarin served as editors for a large number of them, the discussion on the intrinsic value of the *History* continued long after its actual detail was outmoded.[77]

The 1840s saw the first historical essays by S.M. Solov'ev, K.D. Kavelin, and Kireevsky. The so-called 'State School' of historians began with the appearance of Solov'ev's master's dissertation on the relationship between early Novgorodian and Muscovite princes (1845). It was given further impetus by Kavelin's article, 'Views on the Juridical Character of Ancient Russia,' which was printed in the *Contemporary* in 1847. Kireevsky had already printed the Slavophile version of the same era in Pogodin's *Muscovite* (1845). Thus, historians revived the old Normanist dispute and added to it the increasingly bitter controversy between Slavophile and Westernizer. In fact, Pogodin did his best to prevent the acceptance of Solov'ev's dissertation, for it challenged the Slavophile interpretation. In turn, Kavelin supported it and persuaded T.N. Granovsky in 1844 to offer the Chair of Russian history at the University of Moscow to the nearly unknown

Solov'ev, rather than to Pogodin.[78] After this era, it was only the ideological implications of Karamzin's works that received attention.

Nevertheless, the stream of arguments against Karamzin from historians did little to diminish the fashionableness of the *History*. It still served as a backdrop for widespread conversation in salons and in periodicals on the role of the state in Russian historical growth, on Normanism, and even on the means of achieving Russian greatness; all topics that were at the very base of dialogue between proponents of Westernizing and Slavophile tendencies of thought after the thirties and forties.

The rapid development of intellectual conflict, the widely divergent reactions to Russia's expanding contact with Western ideas and society, and a growing impulse to reexamine the class structure of Russia assured that the *History* would remain a focal point for political controversy. Only in literary circles did judgement remain consistently favourable but even in the matter of historical prose writing, Karamzin's predominance was undermined by Pushkin and by M.N. Zagoskin. Recent studies have given a place of importance in the evolution of Russian prose to Karamzin's opponent, Bulgarin, who published *Ivan Vyzhigin* in 1829.[79] It was also in the area of letters, rather than in historical studies, that his ideas were consciously propagated by admirers after his death. A typical medium for activity of this sort was a salon conducted by Karamzin's widow and his eldest daughter. The influence of this and other similar groups was particularly extensive in the 1830s and 1840s, yet in them the *History* was regarded mainly as a vehicle for Karamzin's literary talents. Indeed, his daughter, Sofia, once admitted that she had no intention of even reading it because she detested 'the history of Russia, with all those Yaropolks and Sviatopolks....'[80]

The predominantly political nature of responses to the *History* already was apparent when the ninth volume appeared in 1821. Containing a very strong condemnation of Ivan IV's despotism, the volume was taken by many conservatives and liberals alike as criticism of the form of government extant in Russia. Among conservatives, the most extreme example of a new attitude was a comment attributed to Prince Constantine, the emperor's brother, who apparently maintained in 1826 that 'the book is filled with Jacobin teachings.' Karamzin, at least, was not aware of the prince's change of heart for, in June 1821, he had sent a copy to Constantine and had received a note of congratulations and thanks in reply. The prince told Karamzin that he had read it all and was very pleased to have it.[81] At the same time, several Decembrists began to look upon Karamzin as more of a kindred spirit and their greatest poet, Ryleev, said, 'I do not know what is more astonishing, the tyranny of Ivan or the talent of our Tacitus.'[82]

It was at this juncture in time, too, that Pushkin completely reassessed his opinion of Karamzin. In contrast to Dmitriev, who believed that the *History* 'proved by scholarship and eloquence that wise autocracy saved, strengthened and resurrected Russia,' Pushkin had greeted it in 1818 with a short poem which, rather sardonically, had reflected the feelings of most liberal thinkers:

In his History, eloquence and simplicity
Prove to us without any bias
The necessity of autocracy
And the charm of the knout.

On reading the ninth volume, however, Pushkin insisted that Karamzin had been objective after all and, defending him against 'young Jacobin' critics, maintained that the *History* was 'not only a creation of a great writer, but also an accomplishment of an honest man.'[83]

It is hardly surprising that conservatives were enraged at Karamzin's picture of Ivan IV. By the early twenties, mysticism had become the general philosophical tone at court and a political atmosphere already existed that would make Nicholas I's Official Nationality a natural outgrowth of Alexander's reign. The vibrancy and exhilaration of the early part of Alexander's time were now gone. Russians of the right felt so insecure that they believed that any criticism of monarchy, even of a sixteenth-century one, should be left unspoken whether true or not. As one later observer, the metropolitan Filaret, put it, 'a well-described virtue attracts people to goodness but it is not useful to expose and magnify forms of evil....'[84]

Karamzin had expected the ninth volume to create a storm, but perhaps had been lulled into complacency when his readings from it were very well received at the Academy in January 1820. In fact, after reading 'about the beginning of tyranny, about the loyalty and heroism of the Russians who were tortured by the tyrant,' he received resounding applause. The president of the Academy, Shishkov, suggested that the members award Karamzin with a gold medal. One witness said that the historiographer probably received the greatest round of applause since the founding of the Academy.[85] Even the foreign press was surprised at his openness in speaking in 1824 of the tyranny of early tsars. A reviewer for the *Bulletin des sciences historiques* praised Karamzin for pointing to the 'longue série de massacres et de cruautés,' usually ignored in other Russian studies, and for describing them 'avec une généreuse indignation.'[86]

Much of the praise for the *History* was prompted by its being the epitome of a contemporary upsurge in Russian nationalism. Pushkin had subscribed to the myth that Karamzin was his fatherland's 'first historian,' and had said that through Karamzin, 'ancient Russia has been discovered ... as Columbus discovered America.' Similarly, Count F.A. Tolstoi was reported to have said that, owing to the *History*, 'I know what my fatherland is.' N.I. Turgenev said the same thing. Many Russians came to feel that abuse of Karamzin, whether for scientific, academic, or personal reasons, amounted to an attack upon their nationality. A typical result of this criterion for judgement was the outburst of indignation over Pogodin's mild rebuke of Karamzin's conjecture on the origin of the Russian state. Kireevsky scolded Pogodin for his 'disrespect,' though mildly, and charged Artsybashev with 'losing all sense of decency.' Viazemsky, not surprisingly, called Pogodin's action 'indecent' and wrote him to that effect. A year later, M.A. Dmitriev said: 'I demand for Karamzin the *strictest criticism*, but *opposition* to him I will never recognize as worthy of respect.[87]

The passion of Karamzin's defence in 1828-9 reveals the essence of Karamzinism at that time. He was now forever an icon to the moderate conservatives who had seen their educational ideals crushed after 1825. Harsh despotism and a rigid, semi-literate bureaucracy were greater blows to those who wanted enlightened rule than it was to the radicals, who could still hope for revolution. Thus the responses to Pogodin, Artsybashev, and others had less to do with Karamzin than they did with the protection of an ideal. Viazemsky never ceased equating Karamzin with the best achievements of Russian enlightenment. A similar posture was taken by the Slavophile prince Odoevsky in the thirties and by Gogol' in 1847. Pogodin expressed the feelings of most of the Karamzinians when he said that the great man was the 'guardian angel of our enlightenment.'

After the twenties, it became increasingly difficult to find an unprejudiced view of the *History*. The fact that Karamzin had been allowed to publish without submitting to the censors, in spite of voluble protest from some of the nobility, made it inconceivable to critics that it could have been written independently of court pressures. A close personal friendship with the royal family and his title were stigmata in the minds of liberals and radicals although this same association prompted defence even from some who had no liking for Karamzin. On the accession of Nicholas I, who seemed less interested in the *History* than either of his brothers, Karamzin admitted that his 'connection to the throne' was gone. It is true that he had been very friendly with Nicholas a decade earlier and that the new emperor asked for his assistance with a few important state papers,[88] but these instances were rare and the historian preferred not to act in such a capacity. However, to many Russians the relationship seemed stronger than before and social critics like Herzen were convinced that Alexander and Nicholas followed Karamzin's advice. This illusion was largely a result of the adoption of Official Nationality. Many tenets of the creed were similar to ideas expressed in the *Memoir*, so that an outward resemblance between Nicholas's practices and Karamzin's speeches tended to confirm a growing conviction that Karamzin had no other aim than to provide justification for unlimited autocracy and serfdom.

Karamzin did keep company with individual advocates of Official Nationality, among them Uvarov, the formulator of the doctrine. As minister of education, he was able to put pressure on those who committed the 'sacrilegious' act of reproving Karamzin.[89] Nevertheless, it was primarily because of Pogodin, who told his students at the University of Moscow to 'study, study Karamzin!'[90] and who disseminated the official version of Russianism in his journal, *The Muscovite* (*Moskvitianin*), that the *History* became an historical wellspring for Official Nationality. Some Soviet scholars have gone so far as to suggest a link between Karamzin and the militant pan-Russianist, Nicholas Danilevsky (1822-85). To be sure, Karamzin emphasized the uniqueness of the Great Russians among Slavs, but he was more pacifist than militarist and there was a more mutual respect between him and the prominent Czech Slavicist, Joseph Dobrovsky, than there was between the Czech and Pogodin. Karamzin was also on good terms with the Serbian linguist and pan-Slav, Vuk Karadžic, with whom he once dined in Moscow.[91]

The source of most of the difficulties which arise when writers try to categorize Karamzin's political thinking, or anyone else's for that matter, is the complexity of intellectual currents in Russia during the 1820s and 1830s. German idealistic philosophy was just beginning to take hold in Russia during the twenties, at a time when Western idealism was reaching a climax of sorts. In 1823, Pogodin was associated with N.I. Nadezhdin, Odoevsky, and D.V. Venevitinov, who were laying the groundwork for a peculiarly Russian romantic nationalism. He and the messianic nationalists of the last third of the century, Danilevsky and Dostoevsky, were to find great comfort in many of Karamzin's writings, but they would not have found in him a kindred soul. As far as Official Nationality was concerned, Karamzin would not have held to its supporters' efforts to unite society, state, and religion. He would not have approved of their religiosity, nor of their contempt for mankind, nor, particularly, of their disregard for the Russian peasant as an individual.[92]

The *History* was often lumped together with Slavophile literature by their critics, but Karamzin, who was on close terms with I.F. Samarin, would never have supported their more abstract ideas. Yet aspects of his study paralleled Slavophile thinking. Like some of them he exaggerated the native qualities of ancient Slavs, stressed the role of the Orthodox Church in Russian history, and extolled the national character of Russians. To a certain extent, Karamzin gave credence to the Third Rome doctrine by intimating that Byzantium had abdicated her leadership of the Eastern Christian Church at the Council of Florence (1438-9), so that there 'remained no other Orthodox Kingdom besides Russia.' He implied too that Byzantium, by its heresy, had brought about her own destruction at the hands of the Turks. In this way, he seemed to sustain ideological claims made by the Russian Orthodox Church. Nevertheless, in contrast to most Slavophiles, he always insisted in the *History* that Russia was an integral and mutually dependent part of Europe.[93] It was not rare to see Karamzin misquoted by opponents of Slavophilism who wished to stigmatize them with some sort of antiquarianism. But in some cases,

Karamzin was misused quite purposely. Buslaev, for example, quoted the *History* wrongly, or at least out of context, when he told the Tsarevich Nicholas in 1860 that the idea that 'Moscow is the Third Rome, and there will be no fourth one...,' was stated as fact in the *History*.[94]

In public life as well, Karamzin recognized the assimilation of Russian and European societies and told the assembled members of the Academy in 1818 that 'we do not wish to copy foreigners, but we write as they write; we live as they live; we read what they read; we have the same educated minds and tastes.' Prefacing this remark with 'the connection between the minds of ancient and modern Russia is broken forever,' Karamzin could not have insulted budding Slavophilism more directly.[95] Slavophiles' ambivalence towards freedom, which led them to support benevolent autocracy and to reject constitutions, and their confidence in Russia's future, resembled attitudes held by Karamzin, but theirs were a product of far different times. Living under Nicholas I rather than Alexander I, in a society pestered by radicals who were far more activist than the Decembrists had been, and in a state whose international power seemed to be on the wane rather than in ascendancy, the Slavophiles could find what they wished in Karamzin's body of writing, but the interpretation was inevitably their own.

Among Slavophiles, Ivan Kireevsky (1806-56) was the most constant defender of Karamzin. He, his brother, and his sister had read the *History* for two hours after dinner three times a week as part of their early education at home. Kireevsky's famous essay, 'Survey of Russian Literature in 1829', was a passionate tribute to the *History*, whose critics, he said, were merely petty or 'know-nothings.'

Other Slavophiles had mixed feelings about Karamzin and the *History*, in spite of assertions made by Belinsky and M.O. Koialovich that the historian was the founder of Slavophilism. Like Kireevsky, K.S. Aksakov and Pletnev treated the *History* as a 'sacred' part of Russia's intellectual heritage.[96] A.I. Koshelev was a moderate admirer of Karamzin. But A.S. Khomiakov was less convinced of the *History*'s relevance. Among the Slavophile historians, only K.S. Aksakov, who also read Karamzin as a youth, adopted an historical scheme that resembled that of the *History*, in which the periodization followed shifts in political power and where the invitation to Rurik marked the origin of the Russian state and history. Karamzin's stress on the voluntary nature of the invitation to the Varangians as the basis for the Russian state was also taken up by Aksakov. Just as Karamzin and Pogodin had done, Aksakov insisted that the Russian community had been founded and had evolved by peaceful means as opposed to the acts of violence which gave birth to states in western Europe. Like Karamzin, Aksakov overplayed the 'unanimous' request for autocracy by Russians in 1613 but, in general, he underscored Orthodoxy whereas the *History* was essentially secular in emphasis.[97]

The leading historian among Slavophiles and an opponent of the Hegelian concept of history, Khomiakov was far less idealistic about the character of the early Slavic peoples than either Aksakov or Karamzin. On the one hand, Khomiakov's pragmatic view of events from Russia's past, which included the optimistic feeling that Tatar subordination of the principalities forced Russians to recognize the necessity of centralization, resembled Karamzin's.[98] In their belief that political centralization was the key to Russian survival to the extent that force was forgivable if it had that end, Khomiakov and Aksakov both endorsed Karamzin. Khomiakov also acknowledged Karamzin's great contribution to Russian national self-consciousness but said that the *History* 'belonged to art and not to science.' Later, he commented that even though the *History* 'acquainted Russians with the past fate of their fatherland,' it showed signs of 'alienation from the true life of the Russian people.'[99]

It is undoubtedly true that the romantic side of the *History* made it a lasting inspiration for many of the Slavophiles, as it was for any Russian nationalist. But then so were the works of S.T. Aksakov, who had been one of the supporters of Shishkov against Karamzin and a defender of Kachenovsky from Viazemsky.[100] It is also true that the Karamzinian salon, which met under the auspices of the historian's widow in the thirties, had a decidedly Slavophile flavour. Since Khomiakov was among its regular visitors that inclination was unavoidable and, indeed, Koshelev claimed that it increased in the forties.[101] Still, it would be a mistake to assign Karamzin to the ranks of Slavophilism, for, as he said once himself, 'my life is bent to the West.' Nor, of course, was he a committed Westernizer, for anyone who accepted only those European ideas that confirmed the concept of enlightened despotism could hardly be in the same camp as the Decembrist, N. Ogarev, or Belinsky. Moderate in most things, Karamzin was closer to the political conservatism of the sometime Westernizer, Chaadayev, who asked only that carefully selected European ideals be practised in Russia. Like Chaadayev, Karamzin was opposed to blind nationalism and unreasoning patriotism.

Karamzin's tone was closer to the pragmatic one of Official Nationality historians than to the Slavophiles. His scheme for Russian history was like theirs in that it proved the necessity of autocracy for Russia. He had often demonstrated his faith in tsarist paternalism, a system in which the ruler acts in the interests of all his subjects, whether peasant or nobility. In the Official Nationality manner, he was fully aware that other political systems might prove more suitable in non-Russian states. But he never would have accepted their adulation of Peter I. [102] Further, the limited usefulness of any attempt to assign Karamzin to one specific ideology was illustrated well enough by the actions of Bulgarin, who employed his journal, *The Northern Archive*, to promote Official Nationality on the one hand and to attack Karamzin on the other. Karamzin was often praised by the conservative contributors to *The Reader's Library*, but he was by no means a centre of attention for the journal in the way that he had been for some earlier ones. Indeed, the editor, Osip Senkovsky, remained noncommittal even when reviewing S. Skromnenko's (S.M. Stroev) 'Manifesto' of 1834 against the entire scheme for Russian history as it was espoused by Karamzin. [103] One thing that is certain, however, is that the most moderate critic of Karamzin had to withstand the brunt of governmental displeasure or possible social ostracization.

The variety and emotional nature of reactions to the *History* in Russian society was partly a result of an intellectually chaotic atmosphere in Russia, one that prompted A.V. Nikitenko to ask, after observing one of the many debates over Karamzin, 'when will we ... [Russians] be able to argue about ideas, and not about people and interests?' [104] Karamzin himself had pretty mixed political and social notions. The stifling nature of Paul's reign, as we have seen, had prompted him to equate Jacobinism with despotism, and although he was generally in the ranks of the conservatives, his repeated warnings about the misuse of autocratic powers earned him the contempt of ultra-conservatives. Although his *Memoir* was not publicly known during his lifetime, its contents were fairly widely discussed by the

Russian élite. Reactionary as that document was, men of the Gole-nishchev-Kutuzov calibre must have taken umbrage at Karamzin's statement, 'what the Jacobins had done to the republican system, Paul did to the autocratic one; he made people hate its abuses,' or at his allusion to some 'devilish inspiration' behind the 'awe-inspiring tyranny of Ivan IV.'

As the century progressed, Karamzin's ideas became more en-trenched as part of the ruling ideology, and more and more a target for critics of the government. The government itself was instrumental in this phenomenon, for during Nicholas's reign historical writing was closely supervised by censorship boards. Even supporters of auto-cracy, Polevoi, Ustrialov, Artsybashev, and Solov'ev, were not im-mune from restraints.[105] Among the radical critics of Karamzin was Dobroliubov, who several times chided Pushkin for following Karam-zin's 'awkward idea' about historical events, and Pogodin for accept-ing his scheme. Herzen subscribed to the opinion that Karamzin was one of the greatest of eighteenth-century writers, but said of the *History* that 'the idea of great autocracy is the idea of great slavery. Per-haps he thought that a nation of 60 million people only existed to realize ... absolute slavery?' Describing how his father discarded the *History*, like Sofia, because he felt that something about 'Yaroslavs and Olgas' could not possibly be interesting, Herzen still recognized the historiographer's 'great talent.'[106]

From the first year of its publication, the *History* had been an object of panegyrics, condemnation, and arguments which touched upon such important problems as Normanism, foreign influences on Russia, the writing of history, and the character of the Russian state and people. It provided momentum for discussions between conserva-tives and liberals or between proponents of Slavophile and Western-izer thoughts. By giving eloquent expression to feelings held by most of the gentry on the character of historical process in Russia, the *History* thereby helped Russian thinkers to consolidate their views and their arguments about the role of the state in their native land. In this way, it helped to ensure the continuity of intellectual dialogue even during the enforced tranquility of Nicholas I's reign. To the provincial gentry, the Muscovites, and to most nationalists, however, much of the arguing was pointless, for the *History* had given them an heroic past and, as far as most were concerned, a future as well.

6
Karamzin and 'Statist' Thought in Nineteenth-Century Russian Historical Writing

Even its bitterest critics never denied the importance of the *History* in making the national history better known to Russians, but the extent of its persuasiveness in Russian society is incalculable. It did become the primary vehicle of Russianism for youth, students, and gentry. Since so many Russians made a demi-God of Karamzin, it was no easy task for historians to follow him. Even the great Solov'ev recalled how he was confronted by Bludov, who hinted that a new general Russian history was superfluous.[1] But it was through historians that Karamzin's theses became a permanent part of tsarist ideology.

One of those whom Karamzin stimulated towards further nationalistic studies was Pogodin, whose regard for him verged on hero-worship.[2] One need only glance through Pogodin's correspondence with Viazemsky to see this, but perhaps the most indicative letter is one where he seemed to place his eulogy to Karamzin (1866) ahead of all other of his life tasks. Witness, too, Pogodin's own description of his first meeting with the historiographer: 'I was there, looked to the top floor and my heart stopped; here is where he wrote the Russian history! ... this was Karamzin! I froze for ten minutes....' Rarely moderate anyway, Pogodin was particularly aggressive in broadcasting the merits of Karamzin and admonished the youth of his day to rely upon the great man's writings as a 'pure source of Russian wisdom.'[3]

When he was editor of the *Moscow Herald* (1827-30), Pogodin was much closer to Kachenovsky and the Skeptics than to Karamzin in

his attitude towards the detail of Russian history, but not in its leading principles. In fact, Kachenovsky and his disciple, S.M. Stroev,
constantly were critical of Pogodin, whose devotion to the *History*
was derived from his ideological, rather than scholarly pursuits. In
the thirties, a time of extreme social and political unrest in Europe,
Pogodin had said that 'Russian history can become the guardian and
preserver of social tranquility,' therefore almost paraphrasing the
optimistic sentiments in Karamzin's foreword. Forty years later, the
younger man still cited from Karamzin to the effect that history 'reconciles citizens to the general order of things.'[4] Just as Karamzin
had felt insecure in the face of Napoleonic aggression, Pogodin worried about pressure from Prussia and insisted that only autocracy
could furnish the stable conditions necessary for Russian survival.
Ideologically even more state-oriented than Karamzin had been,
Pogodin assigned a role in history to the Russian people only once,
that is, to call in the Varangians.[5] From that time on, he said, only
rulers were expected to initiate change and Russia's first and last law-
ful revolution came in the form of Peter's reforms. Thus, like Karamzin, he insisted that such a phenomenon as the French Revolution
could not possibly occur in an autocratic Russia.[6]

Pogodin proclaimed: 'East is East and West is West ... seeds of
Western revolution do not exist in Russia, consequently we need not
fear Western revolution.' But, belying his own confidence, he still
cautioned the emperor to make certain that the 'wrong people' were
not allowed too much freedom of action.[7] His attitude towards Poland also corresponded to that of Karamzin. In 1865, he said, 'my
thoughts have passed through all stages – and have come, finally, to
the conclusion that there are historical, geographical, and political
reasons that make necessary Polish union with Russia.' Pogodin's
judgement that Poland must not be allowed its independence was
hardly a new one for him; he had expressed the same opinion in an
essay written during the Polish revolution some thirty years before.
At that time, he had complained about western writers like Guizot,
who had no real understanding of the East and so could not recognize that 'Russia and Poland are united ... according to the natural
order of things ... for their own and the general welfare.'[8]

The Polish question was so central to Pogodin's thinking that he
published an entire volume of his own writings on the matter. Posing

as a friend of the Poles, especially of Lelewel and Mickiewicz, he reasoned that it was best for both Russians and Poles that no separation be allowed. In the fifties, he printed moderate open letters to the Poles, trying to give them cause to stay within the Russian Empire voluntarily. He even claimed to support a certain amount of autonomy for Poland, but constant and, in his opinion, unreasonable rebellion soon hardened him. When he spoke at the grandiose celebration of Karamzin's first jubilee (1866), he evoked enthusiastic response from a huge audience by quoting from and praising the historiographer's 'Opinion' of 1819. According to P.A. Valuev, minister of internal affairs, several members of the royal family attended the memorial service for Karamzin; so did almost all the ministers of the crown and about one thousand other highly ranked people. Pogodin gave the keynote address.[9]

As a leading professor of history at the University of Moscow for fifteen years, and then in the service of the Ministry for Public Instruction, Pogodin was able to wield considerable influence on the historical thinking of his time. But his own lectures, according to his colleague, Shevryev, were all based on Karamzin. Solov'ev, who studied under Pogodin, reported the same thing, but in a much less complimentary tone.

Gradually developing a pan-Slavist idea of Russian history, Pogodin based his entire scheme for the flow of Russian history on premises outlined in an article, 'A Parallel of Russian History with the History of Western European States: Their Origins,' written in 1845. In that study, he claimed as Karamzin had done long before that 'Western European states owe their origin to *conquest*, which also determined their ensuing history right down to the present time ... our state did not begin as the result of conquest, but as the result of an invitation. Here is the source of our difference.'[10] Closer to the Slavophiles than to Karamzin in his Herderian picture of a Russian state evolving as an entity apart from Europe, in the view that 'Providence' played a predominant role in that evolution, and in his suggestion that many seemingly irreconcilable deeds must have had ends determined by God, Pogodin rightly credited Karamzin for at least confirming these ideas as part of Russian historical thought.[11]

The first attempt to undermine the influence of Karamzin in Russian historical writing, by creating an alternative work, was the notably unsuccessful effort of Polevoi (1796-1846). The only Russian historian to compile a national history of any length after Karamzin and before Ustrialov, he tried to combine the scientific attitudes of B.G. Niebuhr, to whom he dedicated his major work, and the more general philosophy of Schelling. Thinking that the evolution of Russian history could only be represented properly if placed within the context of world history, Polevoi therefore made an effort to write without the pragmatic and artistic trappings for which he condemned Karamzin. Not wishing to be caught in the same flood of abuse that had overwhelmed Artsybashev, he spent the first three parts of his short critique on the *History* apologizing for what he was about to say concerning Karamzin. He then went on to claim that the historiographer and his models, Hume and Robertson, were 'of the past generation' and proclaimed that 'now there is only general history in which we see the true disclosures of the past, an explanation of the present and a prophecy for the future.' Elsewhere, Polevoi suggested that Karamzin's work merely completed the pictoral type of Russian history begun by Lomonosov.[12]

By means of his *History of the Russian People* (*Istoriia russkago naroda*, published 1829-33), a title which delighted liberally inclined reviewers, Polevoi hoped to create a new trend for Russian historiography and possibly to break Karamzin's domination of such studies. For one thing, he imitated the German idealists by placing the independent evolution of nations within the context of world history. He refused to accept the view that Russian growth had not always been in a forward direction. Likewise, Polevoi placed particular emphasis on the scientific methods advocated by Kachenovsky and Schlözer, pointing out that an 'historian must ... show us the past as it was.' On these grounds he rejected Karamzin's entire picture of Russian history before Yaroslav I.[13] In his first discussion of Karamzin's work, Polevoi had contradicted the historiographer's opinions on the Varangians, the Finns, the Tatars, and the nature of despotism in Russia. He even proclaimed that the time of Minin in the seventeenth century marked the origins of Russia as a nation.[14]

In spite of Polevoi's ambitions, he could not escape the umbrella of Karamzin's scheme. Most of the important tenets from it were left intact in the new history, so that, in the long run, the work served partially to link Karamzin with later developments in Russian historical writing. Polevoi's insistence upon the organic and continuous evolution of Russia has been cited as a stepping stone from Schlözer and Ewers to the 'statist' concepts of Solov'ev and Kavelin,[15] yet in this idea he was not far from Karamzin. This was especially true when he began to ignore his earlier statement that only general history was valid[16] and when he treated the history of Russia completely independently from that of other states. Polevoi was to say, for example, 'we reject any influence of the West on the Russian lands,' and 'the future destiny of the Russian lands must be completely separate from the destiny of other European states....' In this regard he was closer to Pogodin and the Slavophiles than to Karamzin, but in his actual outline of Russian history the growth of the state remained the sole determinant of periodization, autocracy remained the only means for preserving the state, and 'Providence' tipped the scales for the ultimate success of Moscow.[17]

Treating many specific events differently than Karamzin, Polevoi echoed the *History* in a description of Vladimir I, in his emphasis on Simeon Gordyi and Ivan Kalita as predecessors to Ivan III, and on the significance of Kulikovo. He also concurred with Karamzin in the opinion that only the Tatars prevented Russia from being the equals of western Europe in matters of civil enlightenment. More revealing, however, were his generalizations about Ivan III and Ivan IV, which were almost identical to those of Karamzin. Likewise, Polevoi insisted that the fall of Novgorod and even the 'ferocity' of Ivan IV were justifiable prerequisites to the unification of Russia into a single state system. All in all, the essential difference between his and Karamzin's *History* lay in Polevoi's rather poorly handled attempt to redefine the terms 'Russian state' and 'Russian nation,' and to establish a period in time when the former evolved into the latter. In his opinion, the history of the state ended with independence from the Tatars; after that historians must deal with the beginnings of the Russian nation. Polevoi's treatment of this matter was too obscure to be very successful.

In his general interpretation, Polevoi followed Karamzin often enough. Above all, his feelings about the place of Poland in Russian history echoed that of his predecessor. Like Karamzin's, his 'nation' was surrounded by enemies from its birth in the fifteenth century: 'by Poles, whose faith, language, law and, finally, centuries of hostility, inspired irreconcilable hatred against Russia....'[18] A prolific writer, Polevoi published a number of surveys of Russian history for young readers. His *Russian History for Elementary Students* (4 volumes, 1835-41), which he directed to 'dear young readers,' and his *Survey of Russian History to the Monarchy of Peter the Great* (1846) echoed the official versions to the letter. In the second book he incorporated Uvarov's claim that Russia's saving graces were 'nationality, Orthodoxy, and autocracy' into the introduction and boasted that Russia had escaped the divisive forces of Catholicism, Reformation, and 'violent democrats' which had plagued Europe. In each of these texts, he was guilty of the very academic crimes with which he had charged his contemporary, S.N. Glinka, whose own history of Russia was in its fourth edition by 1829. Glinka's only aim in writing a history, Polevoi had said with contempt, was to make patriots of Russia's youth.[19]

It is conceivable that even a better history than Polevoi's could not have surmounted the aura of sanctity which still surrounded the *History*. At any rate, his work was greeted with scorn by defenders of the official version and his journal, *Moscow Telegraph*, became a target for abuse from editors of other periodicals, one of whom suggested in 1828 that 'Mr Polevoi should read more and write less.' The liberal A.A. Bestuzhev claimed in the 1830s that Polevoi's survey had 'penetrated into the hearts of people,' but he was almost alone in this opinion. At mid-century, Pogodin recalled Polevoi's 'absurd lies' and Viazemsky, who ridiculed Polevoi in the thirties, was still doing so in the sixties.[20] The Slavist N.V. Savel'ev-Rostislavich took enormous personal affront at the slurs on Karamzin, who had sent him a signed copy of the first edition of the *History*. Lashing out at Polevoi and others who dared challenge the great work, Rostislavich called their patriotism to question and announced that there was simply no need to criticize the 'immortal' study.[21] A vehement defence of Karamzin was hardly necessary, for even the anti-Karamzin radicals admitted that Polevoi had done nothing to displace Karamzin's *History* as the final word about Russia's past.

An even closer adoption of Karamzin's conception of Russian history was that of N.G. Ustrialov (1805-70), who was the imperial historiographer from 1858 to 1864. A devotee of Official Nationality, he prepared a textbook that was recommended to Russian schools by

Uvarov. Ustrialov followed Karamzin and Pogodin in their belief that the existing state apparatus was a result of Russian political circumstances and so was a reflection of the particular characteristics and needs of the Russian people. In an introduction to his five-volume *Russian History* (*Russkaia istoriia*, St Petersburg 1837-41), Ustrialov mentioned that Russians were naturally peaceful and, in a manner reminiscent of Karamzin and Pogodin, claimed that this quality kept Russians 'unshaken among the general shocks in the western states during the French Revolution.'[22] He tended to be closer to Pogodin than to Karamzin in his opinion that only rulers had influenced the course of Russian history, and in contrasting Russian to west European development.

The similarity between Karamzin's scheme for Russian history and that of Ustrialov was mirrored quite clearly in a dissertation prepared by the latter writer in 1836 entitled 'About a System of Pragmatic Russian History,' in which he said that 'Karamzin forced us to forget all his predecessors.'[23] In writing that study, Ustrialov expressed an intention to look at history from a different perspective than Karamzin had done. In both the 'System' and his *Russian History*, he planned to outline the evolution of Russian society, rather than merely the lives of rulers and princes. He was no more successful in this attempt than Polevoi had been. Ustrialov criticized Karamzin for not suggesting a continuity between events but in general he merely redefined and made more precise the ideas expressed in the *History*. As a protégé of Uvarov, he could hardly fail to insist that autocracy and Orthodoxy were the 'pillars' of the Russian state system.

Opening his discussion with the Karamzin-like remark that Russians could benefit from their own history more than other peoples could from theirs, Ustrialov went on to describe how a Russian state founded under the leadership of the 'Norman hero, Rurik,' reached its first apex under Yaroslav the Wise and then fell into decline when its unity was dissipated in the eleventh century. All was not lost, however, because the 'idea of the necessity of centralization never disappeared.' During the subjection of all these lands by the Tatars, power gradually fell into the hands of Muscovite princes who, on the accession of the Romanovs, recognized their obligation to force back into the fold not only 'Russian lands' of the north-west, but territory held by Poland, the Livonian Order, and Sweden as well. The union of all such areas was 'inevitable' and, 'according to the natural order of things, even Poland had unavoidably to become part of the Russian state.'[24]

Particularly familiar was Ustrialov's opinion that Russian growth was the 'result mainly ... of the activity of those people with whom fate entrusted the helm of government,' and the view that the Time of Troubles did not alter the 'state organism ... laws or ideas' but resulted in a 'variety of miraculous, almost unbelievable events which eloquently reflected the national character.'[25] Intended as a critical analysis of Karamzin and Polevoi, the 'System' brought an immediate response from the Karamzinians. In 1836 Viazemsky wrote an angry open letter about Ustrialov to Uvarov and was supported in his denunciation by Pushkin.[26] The censors refused to allow Pushkin to publish the letter in *The Contemporary*, so little came of the affair except some bitterness between the combatants. Ustrialov knew of the letter and never forgave Viazemsky for it.[27] Several historians, too, were upset by Ustrialov's work. Nikitenko recalled how Ustrialov's public defence of the thesis attracted literary people like Pletnev and historians from the University of Vilna who objected to his suggestion that Lithuania had always been part of Russia. These circumstances might help explain why Ustrialov was not always very deferential to Karamzin's memory. Dobroliubov reported incidents in the fifties when 'Ustrialov, if drunk ... howls against Karamzin.'[28]

Like Pogodin, Ustrialov argued with much of the detail of Karamzin's *History*. But all three held and spread similar thoughts about the essence of Russian history. Their common ground was best represented in the school textbooks prepared by the two younger historians. Pogodin in 1835 and Ustrialov four years later synthesized their writings into short studies designed for young students of Russian history. Unadorned by serious discussion, these books carried their authors' basic assumptions about their country's past and present. Uvarov and *The Reader's Library* gave them enthusiastic recommendation.[29]

In both texts, there were parts that might have been written by Karamzin himself. In his introduction, Ustrialov said that the study of history alone could reveal to youngsters the moral and religious virtues of their ancestors, that it would help explain the circumstances of present-day Russia. Like so many of his colleagues among historians, Ustrialov was fascinated by the evolution of the state. Russian history, he said, 'is a science which explains the gradual evolution of our fatherland's state life.'[30] Therefore an historian need only examine the careers of famous individuals who contributed to that growth. Pogodin did not attempt any explanation of his work – it was hardly necessary.

Pogodin and Ustrialov began their concise histories of Russia at the year 862. They then proceeded to present an historical outline based on times of weakness and greatness according to the degree of authority held by the monarchy. Moscow, they both said, was from the beginning the 'core' of the Russian state system. Pogodin actually referred to Karamzin several times in his textbook and in his final pages claimed that one of the greatest events in Russian education was the initial publication of the *History*.[31] In both texts, the abrogation of Novgorod's special liberties was justified on the grounds that only in that way could Russia have achieved a powerful, autocratic state.[32] In all cases involving the expansion of Muscovy, the Russian princes were simply 'returning' lands to their proper overlords; similarly, it was always the Poles who had stood in the way of Muscovy's rightful inheritance.

There were many other nineteenth-century historians to whom the *History* was a model for general principles of Russian history, if not for the detail. Among these were K.N. Bestuzhev-Riumin (1829-97), who claimed to be searching for a compromise between opposing 'extreme' views of Karamzin and Solov'ev on events in the Russian past. Another was D.I. Ilovaisky (1832-1920), who hoped to incorporate the 'great work of Karamzin, Solov'ev and ... Bestuzhev-Riumin' into his own studies on Russian history and whom the Marxist historian M.N. Pokrovsky practically equated with Karamzin.[33] Bestuzhev-Riumin, a nationalist historian of Pogodin's ilk, came to appreciate the militant pan-Russianism of N. Ia. Danilevsky and, in his own *Russian History* (*Russkaia istoriia*, St Petersburg, 2 volumes, 1872-85) stressed the need for unity and autocracy in Russia, a theme for which he had praised Karamzin.[34] Never entirely sure which school of thought he should follow and not capable of developing one of his own, Bestuzhev-Riumin complimented Solov'ev and K.D. Kavelin on their extension of J.P.G. Ewer's theory of *rodovoi byt*, which according to the State School historians of the second half of the century was the basic social and political unit from which the Russian state system developed. In his own history, however, Bestuzhev-Riumin agreed with Karamzin on such important matters as the arrival and contribution of the Varangians, the place of the Tatars in Russian evolution, and in the belief that it was Ivan III who contributed most to the centralization of Russian political power. Saying that 'Ivan III created the Muscovite State, completing the business of his predecessors and destroying the autonomy of appanage princes,' he repeated Karamzin's picture almost exactly. Moreover, Bestuzhev-Riumin went further than Pogodin in his description of Karamzin as an excellent critic of the sources and, like other nationalists, regarded the *History* as the best among all Russian books for instilling 'patriotism and love of history.'[35]

Ilovaisky was typical of the pragmatic historians of nineteenth-century Russia. He too believed that 'history is the great teacher and instructor for new generations' and a means 'to help the growth of national self-knowledge.' Insisting that Russian history was limited to the 'factual history of the Russian state,' he articulated a fundamental principle held in common by Karamzin and the later State School historians, namely that an historian should direct his attention only to the evolution of the state structure, since a political edifice results from the needs of its people. He also wrote a textbook on Russian history which went through thirty-six editions between 1860 and 1912.[36]

Besides serving as a model for individual historians in nineteenth-century Russia, the *History* contributed enormously to the crystallization of an historico-political style of thinking common to a prominent group of historians in Russia during the second half of the century. Often referred to as representatives of a State School of historical writers, these scholars tended to disregard Karamzin as an historian, but held many ideas similar to his. The term State School is a loosely defined one and there has been considerable debate as to which historians are encompassed by it.[37] Its members, if that epithet is a valid one, were not agreed on the detail of Russian history, yet they all looked at the historical process from the same viewpoint.

Historical growth, they insisted, was embodied in a political evolution of society from a patriarchal tribal system (*rodovoi byt*) to a modern state system. So they focused their attention almost exclusively on the development of the Russian state apparatus. Thus, in their opinion, an historian need concentrate only on the activities of the heads of government, from ancient princes to latter-day tsars. This kind of thinking, of course, was not unique to 'Statists' but it was due to them that the practice was confirmed in Russia at a time when it was becoming less acceptable to historians in western Europe. Convinced that the historical process was a rational and necessarily evolutionary one, members of the State School, most of whom were liberal and moderate by inclination, so abhorred the surge of radicalism in the Russia of their own day that they came to oppose all abrupt changes in society. Just as Karamzin had done in an earlier revolutionary era, they looked to history for explanations and rationalizations of contemporary events and institutions.[38] No matter how iniquitous or apparently retrogressive a past event seemed, they assumed it to be an unavoidable part of the natural development of Russian history. For this reason, they were often accused of fatalism.[39]

Early representatives of this school of thought included Solov'ev, Kavelin (1818-75), and B.N. Chicherin (1828-1904); later Russian scholars who fall within the same category were the important juridical historians V.I. Sergeevich, A.D. Gradovsky, and F.I. Leontovich. In most studies involving the State School and Russian historiography, the relation of these historians to Karamzin has been given scant attention and some writers, like Miliukov, went to the extreme of claiming that the State School arose as a reaction against him.[40] The Germans, Schlözer and Ewers, are more often than not portrayed as the initiators of State School thinking, and indeed, as the first nineteenth-century historians of Russia. Karamzin generally receives accolades as the synthesizer of trends from the previous century.

Schlözer and Karamzin normally have been regarded as representatives of two different directions in Russian historical writing: Karamzin as the promulgator of the artistic, romantic type of production, Schlözer as the initiator of more scholarly, critical efforts.[41] Although this belief was held by some as early as the 1820s and was widely accepted by the end of the century, it is an exaggeration which arose from a tendency to concentrate on dissimilarities between the two rather than on the several attitudes they had in common.

Doubtless there were major differences between the German and the Russian in their attitudes towards history – Karamzin attested to this when he admitted that, for him, criticism was 'trifling work ... a painful sacrifice,' but he qualified the remark with the meaningful adjective 'necessary.' Though Schlözer was far more interested in the scientific study of the sources than Karamzin was, the latter writer was aware of the need for criticism and was probably far more rational in the application of Schlözer's methods than historians of the Skeptical school. It is perhaps of some significance that Leopold von Ranke spoke well of Karamzin in the sixties.[42]

Karamzin read Schlözer's *Nestor* carefully and, when Schlözer died in 1809, the historiographer seemed sincere when he suggested to Turgenev that the German's death was a setback to his own work. Karamzin disliked Schlözer's style of writing, for, as he put it, 'the lion only recognizes dates ... almost no reflections,' and he felt that the Nestor project 'had little use' because Schlözer's interpretations were poor and the 'old man did not know the language of the chronicles well, nor their content outside of Nestor.' Karamzin and Schlözer actually carried on a mild debate and the German responded, in the first edition of *Nestor*, to the Russian's earlier rebukes.[43] Karamzin's close ties with the leading scholars of his time, with the archivists, Kalaidovich and P.M. Stroev, with members of the Historical Society, A.I. Turgenev, A.S. Lerburg and J.P. Krug; and his thorough knowledge of the work done by Schlözer and Stritter meant that he was as familiar with current trends in the historical sciences as any of his contemporaries. The fact that these men and even some of the Schlözerists in Germany, Gatterer and Heeren, held Karamzin in high regard, is further evidence that he ranked among the best scholars of his day.[44]

Ewers (1781-1830) was the German scholar most often designated as the founder of the State School.[45] The significance of Ewers's research stems almost solely from his formulation of the notion of *rodovoi byt* as the social order from which the Russian state evolved. It was because of this concept that both Kavelin and Solov'ev pointed to him as the initiator of ideas basic to their own studies.[46] In fact, Ewers was given credit by a later member of the State School, F.I. Leontovich, for providing the entire 'historico-juridical direction' to Russian historiography.

A student of Schlözer's, Ewers brought to historical studies an inflexible faith in primary documents and a contempt for the flowery, literary kind of work that had been so large a part of historical writing in the eighteenth century. His first efforts in Russian history appeared a few years before those of Karamzin, but they made very little impression on Russian writers.[47] Moreover, Karamzin's actual manuscripts were finished, and their contents fairly well known, some years ahead of Ewers's publications. The first two volumes of the *History* had been completed by 1805. The third, which carried his description of Russian history up to the mid-thirteenth century, was done by the spring of 1808; within another year he had taken his account to the end of Donskoi's reign. The eighth was ready for printing by 1815.[48] From 1804 until the time of his death Karamzin regularly read from his manuscripts to friends in his own home, to enthusiastic members of salons in Moscow and St Petersburg, to the emperor at Tver in 1811, and to meetings of historians. Thus, years before the *History* was available in bookstalls, devotees of literary and scholarly circles in Russia's two largest cities were familiar with its content and emphasis.

Karamzin and Ewers met for the first time in 1808. They became so friendly that Ewers was granted full access to Karamzin's historical library and collection of manuscripts. He was even given a key to the older man's private study. It is hardly surprising, then, that a close friend of Karamzin, A.I. Turgenev, later claimed somewhat inaccurately that Ewers had been one of the historiographer's students.[49]

In his best-known study, *Das älteste Recht der Russen* (1826), Ewers concentrated on the legal and social structure of ancient Rus', and he had to use Karamzin's research to corroborate his interpretation. As a matter of fact, Karamzin's history was far wider in scope than that of Ewers and contained entire sections on the relationship between the early princes. It was Karamzin, not Ewers, who was the first historian of Russia to purposely centre his attention on original juridical sources.

Ewers's and Karamzin's schemes for Russian history were very much the same, though couched in somewhat different terminology and tone. Both drew a picture of the progressive evolution of a primitive society into a sophisticated monarchical one, represented in a pattern of times of strength and decline, and then resurgence to a more highly developed form. Ewers's plan for Russian history was based on the premise that the natural evolution of a state system made up the entire historical process in Russia. He followed Karamzin's lead by insisting that even the most miserable circumstances in Russia's past had contributed something vital and dynamic to the forward historical growth of the existing state. Ewers also copied Karamzin's division into epochs and cited the *History* many times for interpretations of ancient Russian documents. His image of a highly organized state emerging from a society that originally had no internal cohesion, a procedure which Ewers said was founded 'in human nature,' was practically the same as Karamzin's. Each of them contradicted Schlözer by writing that military leaders had formed defensive leagues and thus political institutions in Russia long before the arrival of Rurik.[50] Karamzin and Ewers assumed that these early associations were bound by patriarchal custom rather than by formal law, and they held in common an assumption that the Varangians stimulated the actual process of state building.

Ewers began his overall scheme by saying that 'originally, each family existed by itself.' For security, these units tended to combine until they formed a patriarchal clan in which nepotism was an initial stepping stone towards monarchy. The essence of this essentially political formula for Russian historical growth lay in his conviction that 'for the foundation and preservation of simple unity, the establishment and observation of strict order is necessary everywhere. The preservation of general law was necessary for the personal benefit of each prominent family....' Often seen as the starting point for State School writers of a later era, these notions on Ewers's part echoed those of Karamzin.[51]

It has often been written that Ewers was the first modern historian of Russia to demonstrate clearly that Rurik was a consolidator of existing social structures, and not the 'founder' of the Russian state. Even more often it has been said that Karamzin succumbed to Schlözer and followed the 'Normanist' interpretation of the origins for Russia. These traditional assumptions are misleading on several counts.

In the foreword to his work, Karamzin began by challenging Schlözer's entire periodization of Russian history and was the first to propose a tripartite division of his nation's past.[52] Somewhat resignedly, however, Karamzin 'guessed' that the actual process of state building had begun in Russia in 862. But in his footnotes he contradicted Schlözer's reasoning on this matter, and in his text he discounted his own starting point by referring to the 'ancient popular governments' which preceded the Varangians by many years. He went on to describe the customs and institutions of that earlier era in considerable detail. Karamzin spoke of the patriarchal nature of the growing communities which, he claimed, were drawn together by a need for security. He traced the metamorphosis of republican forms into oligarchical and then monarchical ones. The Slavs were 'ruled by civil authority' as early as the sixth century, he wrote, and added that Rurik was by no means Russia's first prince. All the premises about Russia's socio-political development so often attributed solely to Ewers were clearly visible in Karamzin's historical writing.

Though the German and his own students were far more thorough than Karamzin in their study of ancient Russian law, Ewers acknowledged that there was very little in the Russian's work that he could fault. Karamzin, in his turn, claimed to respect Ewers and his ideas but, in 1825, suggested that it would be in bad taste to publish some of Ewers's more 'absurd opinions.'[53] Not to be outdone, a group of foreign scholars under Ewers's guidance published a study in 1830 for the purpose of re-examining ancient Russia in general and Karamzin's picture of it in particular. The collection of essays, *Studien zur gründlichen Kenntniss der Vorzeit Russlands*, was ignored in Russia at the time but it contained, among other things, a detailed analysis of Karamzin's use, and sometime abuse, of Nestor, the Primary Chronicle.[54]

All three of the early statists, Solov'ev, Kavelin, and Chicherin, took Karamzin to task for one or more of his interpretations of past events in Russia. Yet disagreement with details from the *History* did not detract from the real continuity between their work in history and his. As Pogodin had done before them, Solov'ev and Kavelin credited Karamzin with initiating their interest in Russian history,[55] but only in a very indirect way did either of them admit that the *History* included ideas similar to their own. The tendency of statists consciously to disassociate Karamzin's scholarship from theirs was partly a result of their justifiable belief that historians of their time had far surpassed their predecessors in mastering the techniques of the profession. The simplicity of Karamzin's study, its eloquence, erudition, and even the nature of its reading audience weakened the *History*'s reputation as history, but its author's influence on most later Russian historians cannot be denied. In carrying forward, in a most persuasive manner, the state-oriented tradition of the chroniclers and of Muscovite writers, Karamzin's contribution to statist thought and writing was considerable. It lay in the important realm of frame of reference, sentiment, or ideology, that is, in matters much less definable, but more durable than scholarship.

Solov'ev accused Karamzin of looking upon historical writing solely as an art,[56] yet in his lengthy analysis of the *History* there emerged a striking resemblance in their views of Russian history. Solov'ev claimed to have adopted from Ewers the notion that the entire historical process in Russia involved a natural progression from a family system of government to a centralized state structure. In Solov'ev's history, the gradual replacement of one type of society by another was not so clearly defined as that described by other statists and, in fact, both Kavelin and Chicherin criticized him for leaping from one stage in history to another without delineating any real basis for change. But his insistence on the organic nature of Russian growth was made plain enough in a foreword to his own *History of Russia (Istoriia Rossii)*,[57] where he said, 'do not divide, do not splinter Russian history into separate parts ... explain every phenomenon by its internal causes.' It was for lack of continuity that Solov'ev rebuked Karamzin,[58] but he admitted at the same time that Karamzin was the first after Boltin to outline the progressive and organic evolution of Russia. Furthermore, he recognized the historiographer's reference to Ivan Kalita's attempt to build autocracy long before Ivan III as a 'great step forward'[59] in Russian historiography.

Solov'ev saw other important principles in Karamzin's work. For one thing, he said that the *History* had provided a way for Russians to know the significance of their present state – that is, that it represented the only independent and powerful nation formed by a Slavic people. Secondly, he attributed to Karamzin the Hegelian notion that the historical life and character of Russia could have meaning only in the evolution of the state, thereby hinting that Karamzin was his predecessor in this idea. Much less consciously Hegelian than his colleagues,[60] Solov'ev was nonetheless like them in attitude and believed that the natural culmination of any historical process was a national state in which all the needs of a people were fulfilled. This is exactly why Karamzin believed a strong state to be essential, that is, to provide for the wants and happiness of all Russian citizens. For Karamzin and Solov'ev, the people were an integral part of the state, not apart from it. Neither assumed that the state was a static edifice, for as the later historian put it, 'as soon as the known form of government does not satisfy most of the needs of national life in a given time, it changes....'[61] Karamzin had always equated time with change. In a manner of thinking so often credited to Hegel and his followers, Karamzin and Solov'ev saw an uninterrupted contest between conflicting forces as the dynamic essence of Russian history. Karamzin had referred constantly to the struggles between advocates of centralization and advocates of division. Solov'ev, in a far more sophisticated way, which befitted the overall progress in the discipline of history since Karamzin's time, defined progress in terms of an encounter between the 'forests' and 'steppes,' inextricably entwined with a struggle between *rodovoi* and state elements.

All historicism aside, it was in the social and political thought that dominated his writings that Solov'ev most resembled Karamzin. Less directly political in approach than Karamzin, he was more inclined to a religious overview of life. In the 1840s, he had tended towards Slavophilism but he eventually turned against adherents of that creed. Among other things, he accused them of being amateurs meddling in historical studies.

Assuming that history was the 'science of national self-consciousness,'[62] Solov'ev lauded Karamzin for contributing to that end. The traditionalist elements of his own work echoed those in Karamzin's; expansion and centralization by Muscovy were prerequisites to the future greatness of the Russian state but military 'conquest played a very minor role' in the gradual integration of large areas of land. Solov'ev retained the old picture of Muscovite princes as 'collectors of the Russian lands,' an achievement for which he praised Ivan III. Of all the specific interpretations in Solov'ev's *History of Russia*, that closest to Karamzin was his picture of the Time of Troubles. Here he eulogized the 'good people' and the 'best citizens' for helping the church to save the state and suggested that anti-Polish feeling was an important unifying factor at that time.[63]

Fear and distrust of Polish motives towards Russia in history were themes even more consistent in Solov'ev than in Karamzin. In a special study on the collapse of the Polish kingdom, Solov'ev nurtured Karamzin's interpretation of Polish-Russian relations. Not only did he make unfavourable comments about the character of Poles and their enmity towards Russians, which he assumed was uncalled for, he also took a very practical attitude towards the policy of Russian suzerainty over that one-time nation. Claiming that 'weak states cannot preserve their independence,'[64] he insisted that Russia must dominate that area lest other European states move in. Added to the political danger of a weakened but independent buffer between Russia and Europe, Solov'ev also conjured up an equally perilous force which he termed 'Catholic fanaticism.' Poland had abandoned its Slavicism by accepting the dictates of the Council of Florence (1438-9), which he considered one of the major crises of European history, and so had no real reason for existence as a separate state. Like Karamzin, Solov'ev insisted that Poland remain subservient to Russia, but his rationale was more religious than political. The successes of Russian defences against Polish aggression in the fifteenth and seventeenth centuries were inevitable, he said, because of the moral superiority of Orthodoxy. Indeed, Solov'ev's sentiments towards Poland were so hostile that, like Karamzin, he praised Catherine for terminating 'Polish history' and he was so convinced that it was Russia's prerogative to control Poland that he accused Austria and Prussia of being 'vultures' when they too absorbed territories once held by the Polish state.[65]

Approving Karamzin's continual emphasis on the role of Moscow and of the Orthodox Church as preservers of Russian unity, Solov'ev also praised the historiographer's version of ancient Russia, which he considered to be 'more true than that of his predecessors.'[66] Going even further, Solov'ev said that the *History* represented the 'first attempt at a many-sided view of Russian society,' commended Karamzin for devoting space to the *Russian Truth* (*Russkaia pravda*), and even lauded his critical ability.[67]

Solov'ev's own history was a great deal more comprehensive than that of Karamzin. But the general plans for the two studies were almost identical; both followed the reigns of the princes and then added separate sections devoted to social conditions. Their periodization (a concept which Solov'ev denied in theory but maintained in practice) was determined by changes in political institutions or, more specifically, by progressive stages of growth towards autocracy in Russia. Karamzin's idea that the citizens of Russia recognized that their own welfare could only be safeguarded by sacrificing 'private interests for the good of the whole' was echoed clearly in Solov'ev's scheme.[68] Both claimed that the Russians requested monarchical rule from the Varangians in the ninth century and autocratic rule from the Romanovs in 1613. The analogy between Solov'ev's and Karamzin's treatment of these events is further demonstrated by the former's opinion that the appeal to the Varangian princes began Russian history, while 'Providence,' a growing 'moral strength,' and the 'best people' played a prominent role in ending the Time of Troubles. In that respect, Solov'ev's comment that the 'dreadful experience of the people of Moscow had taught them what dissension and instability ... meant' could easily have been written by Karamzin.[69]

Uvarov, who continued to regard the *History* as a sacred book of Russian history, recognized the similarity between the two writers. In 1848, he recommended that Solov'ev's essays be published in *The Contemporary*. For the next decade, Solov'ev's historical articles remained a feature of the journal even though the radical, N.A. Nekrasov, had taken it over from Pushkin. One such article dealt with the election of Michael Romanov in 1613 and was very much like Karamzin's description of the same event. Suggesting that the Muscovite state could not possibly survive without a single ruler and that the Troubles did not weaken the 'strong foundations of the state,' Solov'ev insisted that that era was a 'great lesson for the Russian land.' Like Karamzin he took the election of the Romanovs, as autocrats, as a sign that Russians had taken the lesson to heart.[70]

Solov'ev and Kavelin followed Karamzin in attributing at least some significance to the colonizing role of Novgorod in the north and of Moscow in Siberia, and the commercial importance of those areas to the later power of the Russian Empire.[71] It is certainly no coincidence that as early as the 1860s G.Z. Elizeev and K.S. Aksakov, independently of each other, actually considered the work of Solov'ev to be a continuation of that of Karamzin.[72] But, as in the case of Pogodin and Ustrialov, Solov'ev's main contribution to the spreading of Karamzin-like ideas through Russian society came in the form of a school textbook. His short text for Russian history was published first in 1859 and was widely used in schools right down to the Revolution of 1917. In that book, he followed a scheme like Karamzin's and actually devoted a page to the historiographer, in which he described him as the leading literator and historian of Alexander's reign. Disagreeing with much of the detail, and even the nature of the *History* in his larger study, Solov'ev limited himself to a general conception, a collection of principles, in the textbook. Here is where he echoed Karamzin's political thought. Solov'ev's abridgement, in turn, served as a model for other textbook writers, among them K.V. Elpat'evsky, who cited Solov'ev as the expert on Karamzin, and V.A. Abaza, who prepared two texts in the eighties.[73]

Kavelin, too, was critical of Karamzin for failing to stress internal connections between events and deprecated his critical ability. He even praised Kachenovsky for daring to attack Karamzin. However, Kavelin did credit Karamzin for contributions to Russian historiography and allotted to him a place in the elaboration of State School principles. To be sure, Kavelin saw Karamzin's participation as a slight one, but this does not lessen the importance of his acknowledgement of the *History* as at least a vague starting point for his and Solov'ev's historical thought. In a review of one of the writer's historical works, Kavelin said: 'The main merit of Mr Solov'ev exists in the fact that he described as the basic moving factor of our ancient history – *rodovoi* principles. None of his predecessors succeeded so well in this as he,' although several, 'even Karamzin,' touched upon it.[74] Designating the *History* as the first stage in the development of nineteenth-century Russian historical studies, Kavelin categorically rejected the idea that Karamzin was merely the last of the eighteenth-century historians, and said that the *History* contained 'hints' of those thoughts developed by Solov'ev.[75]

In order to illustrate the value of style, Kavelin pointed out that Karamzin had far greater influence on contemporaries than had his more scholarly German colleagues. He attributed this to the fact that Karamzin was Russian and so able to understand Russian ways, and spoke of the *History* as a 'vital revelation of the national soul, its character and its inclinations....' Although Kavelin did not insist that artistic presentation and national feeling were the main ingredients of historical writing, he was one of the first important post-Karamzin historians to see value in such traits, noting that Russian writers were still influenced by the 'charm cast upon us by the *History of the Russian State*.'[76]

A later member of the State School, I.E. Zabelin (1820-1908), concurred with Kavelin on this point. Zabelin praised Karamzin for his ability to blend eloquent description with scholarship. Like Kavelin, too, he felt that Karamzin's work was simply out of date, but competent for its own day. Zabelin had ideas close to those of Solov'ev on the origins of the Russian state system. He followed Pogodin and Karamzin in the assumption that conquest dictated the development of society in the West, in contrast to the more natural origins of social and political institutions in Russia.[77]

Kavelin's historical scheme was outlined clearly in his 'Views on the Juridical Existence of Ancient Russia' (1847), in which he developed a picture of Russian growth much like that of Karamzin. He saw the Varangians as the innovators of the 'first idea of the state on our soil,' and noted that periods of disintegration were an essential feature of Russian growth. He also assigned to the Tatars 'an important negative role in our history,' because they 'destroyed the appanage system at its roots, and recreated political unity, in a word, acted in our interests.' According to Kavelin, Ivan III played a major role in the evolution of the state but much of that prince's accomplishments was 'prepared by his predecessors,' Ivan Kalita and Simeon Gordyi. A recent Soviet article explains that it was this point that made the Statists so different from Karamzin, who, the author says, credited Ivan III alone for the formation of the Russian state. But careful reading of Karamzin reveals an evolutionary picture almost exactly like that of Kavelin and Solov'ev.[78]

Kavelin had criticized Solov'ev for paying too little attention to a transitory stage in the process of change from *rodovoi* to state system, a period which allegedly began in the fourteenth century and was marked by what he called a 'vague, hardly noticeable, thought about statehood.' Karamzin had remarked upon that very development and had, among other things, alluded to the establishment of primogeniture by Dmitry Donskoi as an important stage in the development of the monarchical idea. Both Solov'ev and Kavelin had rejected Karamzin's representation of Ivan IV as being too severe and assigned to that ruler a more important role in the development of the Russian state. Kavelin felt that Karamzin had concentrated far too much on Ivan III, to the exclusion of other princes, and suggested that he had thereby broken the continuity of his story of Russian history. Yet it was precisely the idea of organic, progressive evolution that Karamzin had brought into Russian historical writing. Even in the context of his very biting picture of Ivan IV, Karamzin had still credited that monarch for providing autocracy with a firm legislative foundation.

Solov'ev and Kavelin endorsed Karamzin in seeing the entire Russian historical process mirrored in the evolution of the state. Solov'ev, who claimed that Russian history developed 'according to known laws,'[79] was explicit in this matter, saying that, 'a government in one form or another is the product of the historical life of a certain people and is the best verification of that life.'[80] In his concentration on the actions of the princes and in his claim that an historian had to 'study the activities of ruling people,' Solov'ev followed a practice perfected by Karamzin. In Solov'ev's opinion, 'ruling people' were not only the main initiators of historical growth but in their actions they represented the general wishes of the people. An effective prince had to have strength of will and a desire to rule for the benefit of all Russians.[81] Like Karamzin and Solov'ev, Kavelin also looked upon independent statehood as the ultimate goal of national evolution and claimed that 'the state element activity absorbs and concentrates all Russian national life.' Thus, in his works, the history of Russia and the history of the Russian state were one and the same thing.[82]

To a great extent the analogies between Karamzin, Solov'ev, and Kavelin arose from the social and political attitudes which they held in common, and from their Great Russian patriotism. Solov'ev, who once referred to liberals as the 'ulcer of our landed society' and as 'ignorant and noisy' critics of Karamzin, reiterated the historiographer's political dictum when he said that 'nations do not make leaps in their history,'[83] thus opposing any radical change in the social or political milieu of Russia. Like Karamzin before him, Solov'ev attributed the French Revolution to a 'weak government that could not resist' unwise and rash people, and believed that only under autocracy was true freedom possible. Furthermore, he parroted Karamzin when he insisted that one of the leading stimuli for revolution in

France had been the government's policy to limit literary freedoms. In the manner of other 'liberal' conservatives, he assumed that the state must change sometimes but only when such change suited the needs of most Russians.[84] Though he disapproved of both serfdom and despotism in principle,[85] Solov'ev felt that they had served an essential if not necessarily permanent function in the national history. Needless to say, the historical writing of the Statists served the same purpose in the latter part of the century that Karamzin's had done much earlier. Whether they intended it or not, their works supported the status quo in the face of pressure from liberals and radicals at home, foreign aggressors from abroad.

On the accession of Alexander II in 1855, there was a brief time of laxity in government controls comparable to the early years of Alexander I's reign. Nicholas's time had been so oppressive that even Pogodin, one of the most consistent supporters of Official Nationality, complained in the 1870s about the inequities of censorship in the previous reign. Particularly appalling from his point of view was the fact that even some of Karamzin's writings had been suppressed by the censors in the early fifties.[86] Just as the historiographer had done in the respite which followed Paul's assassination, Kavelin and his colleague, Chicherin, were enthusiastic about the possibility of responsible reforms after Nicholas's demise. Kavelin, who had been campaigning for the abolition of serfdom since the late forties, reached a peak of optimism. Chicherin proclaimed that Russia's future lay with liberalism. But within a short time, both were convinced that proper change could only come from within the bounds of the existing system.[87] Consequently, they outlined political philosophies very much like those of Karamzin and Solov'ev and, like them, expressed their ideas in the form of historical interpretations.

Kavelin's proposition that the 'tsar is the state' and his moderately conservative attitude that less reaction and more education were the best cures for what he termed 'nihilism and materialism,'[88] resembled the notions of his famous predecessor. So did his trust in an enlightened absolutism, which would allow for freedom of expression, and his fear that a growing bureaucracy might separate permanently the tsar from the people. Consistent with Karamzin's politically determined scheme were Kavelin's beliefs that 'the history of Russia shows that any time the boyars are strengthened ... the state is plunged into

difficulty' and that the *veche* system often led to riots.[89] He blamed
Novgorod's dissolution as an independent city on an 'insufficiently
firm state structure.' Personally concerned with the problem of individual freedom, Kavelin, who was liberal enough in his early days to
support Herzen, never relinquished his conviction that people must
be free. But anarchy in Russia during the 1860s persuaded him that
freedom was possible only when administered by a strong state apparatus; indeed, the state could create true freedom only by exercising
its authority. Like Ewers and Karamzin, each of whom had expressed
that very sentiment, Kavelin kept as a constant in his scheme for Russian history the assumption that it was in the nature of man to strive
for order and security. 'This,' he explained, 'is what leads patriarchal
society to a juridical and civil order.'[90]

A Great Russian bias was more openly a part of Solov'ev and
Kavelin's writings than it had been of Karamzin's. Boasting that the
Russians were the only Slavic people to develop a powerful and independent state 'with a decisive influence on the fate of the world,'
Solov'ev repeated a theme that was an integral and important part of
the *History*. Like Montesquieu and other eighteenth-century political
theorists, Solov'ev assumed that climate and geography were decisive
factors in determining the form of a nation state. Thus, the very size
of the 'Russian lands' was a portent of immense power for Slavs, but
'mainly for Russians.'[91] Kavelin, who asserted in one place that 'only
on Great Russian soil was there engendered a strong and lasting state
... Russia is the only free Slavic state,' and that 'the Russian state was
founded by the Great Russian tribes' in another, utilized the same
point to justify both his Great Russianism and his belief in autocracy.[92] Since the state represented the fulfillment of all the aspirations of the people, then the autocratic system need be altered only
on the initiative of the state which, alone, could determine the time
when the nation's needs changed.

In their attitude to the role of great men in the historical process,
Solov'ev and Kavelin had Hegel as their theoretical model and Karamzin as their Russian precursor. Solov'ev believed that 'the great man
is always and everywhere the representative of the people, and satis-
fies the needs of the nation in a certain time ... the activity of the
great man is always the result of all the previous history of a nation.'
The genius in history had been a consistent topic for Karamzin, who

once suggested that great rulers were 'demigods' whose lives made up the history of nations. His commitment to the concept of great, individual agents in the historical process had been clearly demonstrated by the large amount of space devoted to Napoleon in the *Messenger of Europe* while Karamzin was editor.[93] Solov'ev was equally consistent in looking to individuals to find reasons for change but was more careful than Karamzin to point out that any great historical personality 'is the son of his people ... he is the reflector of the national thought.' Therefore, he concluded that Peter the Great, who was a special focal point for State School historians, represented a critical point in the evolution of Russian history but had not changed its natural course. This, too, was a notion conceived by Karamzin as early as 1818 when it was a far less acceptable one. For Solov'ev, Peter was 'the great teacher of the nation' and for Karamzin he was the one who 'educated the Fatherland.'[94] But neither historian accepted the idea that he had altered the natural progress of Russian history or the native qualities of the Russian people.[95]

Solov'ev once complained that Karamzin had assigned too great a position in Russian history to Ivan III but, like many others, he was misled by the sweeping phrases in the historiographer's volume on that monarch and so ignored the evolutionary picture developed in the other volumes. Solov'ev's own statement, 'we know [it] was prepared for him ... we know that Peter the Great did not lead Russia from a non-existence into being, that the so-called reform era was [a] phenomenon of natural growth,'[96] would have been accepted in toto by Karamzin. Solov'ev recognized this himself by accepting Karamzin's own suggestion that Russian history be divided into ancient, middle, and modern eras, which provided for long, transitional periods of growth. Moreover, Solov'ev praised Karamzin for noting the 'organic connection between Ivan III and Peter the Great' and again credited him with being the first after Boltin to examine the preparatory role of Peter's predecessors in the development of modern Russian. This same view was maintained by Kavelin, who said that although 'Peter acted as an educator,' his actions would not have been possible or successful 'without the organic connection of our past with our present.'[97]

There were, of course, many instances where Solov'ev and Kavelin's interpretations of Russian history differed sharply from those of

Karamzin, but the overall attitude of all three writers to the course of Russian history was remarkably alike. Even on the key issue of continuity, Karamzin was not nearly so far apart from the Statist position as the later historians suggested. Only in his exaggerated praise for Ivan III did he appear to introduce a break in the organic development of the Russian state. Since that hiatus was due to the uniquely educative aim of the *History*'s author, it was toned down in succeeding volumes.

For Kavelin, the entire course of Russian history was the gradual realization of the state idea.[98] Similarly, Solov'ev claimed that the main question for the historian was to determine the relationship between the Varangians and those tribes who invited them to Russia, the changes in tribal relations through contact with Varangians and other retinue, and the development of those relationships into a state system. Karamzin did not use the same terminology, nor did he speak specifically of this type of synthesis as the key to understanding Russian history, yet throughout the *History* such relationships and the manifestations of an evolvement from tribal-to-princely-to-state organization played an important part. Like the early members of the State School, he determined these changes and their implications by examining ancient charters and laws that illustrated the connections between the princes.[99] His interest in such matters led him to attribute a far greater role to the Tatars and their *yarlyks* in Russian history than Solov'ev did. In this instance, most members of the State School agreed with Karamzin.[100]

The essential principles of the State School were formulated most clearly by Chicherin, who placed those ideas espoused by his older colleagues on a more legalistic and philosophical plane.[101] In an essay, 'Views on the Juridical Development of the Rural Community in Russia,' and in his, *Regional Institutions in Russia in the XVII Century* (1856), he gave the work done by his predecessors a sound theoretical foundation. The dissertation exacerbated the Slavophile-Westernizer debate at the University of Moscow to the extent that Solov'ev and Kavelin publicly came to his defence against Krylov and Samarin.[102] The leading Hegelian of the State School, Chicherin saw the state as the 'highest form of society, the highest manifestation of nationality [narodnost'] ... which is reflected mainly in a single language, is collected into one body, sustains one fatherland and begins the nation.' Like the others, Chicherin felt that the state represented all the aspirations of the Russian people so that alterations in it would come slowly to meet changes in the needs of a people. Such modifications could come, he assumed, only on the initiative of the state.[103]

Though Chicherin's trust in autocracy wavered towards the end of his career, he remained convinced, in the Hegelian way, that the state itself, no matter its form, had the right to expect obedience.[104] From time to time, he insisted that rampant individualism had to be overcome by dynamic and strong leadership, and that service to the state was the obligation of all citizens, each of whom had to remain in his place in order to perform his service in the best possible way. Opinions like these prompted Herzen to complain that Chicherin had taken up a 'philosophy of slavery.'[105] But the radical was wrong in his judgement of Chicherin, who assumed only that the political organization most likely to originate useful reform was autocracy. Once change set in, then new governing principles might also follow. Similarly, Kavelin suspected that Russia might sometime have to resort to constitutional monarchy when older institutions, especially serfdom, had outlived their usefulness.[106] Karamzin would have agreed.

Chicherin's studies in Russian history, which were almost exclusively limited to juridical and political relations, upheld his previously formed idea that autocracy was necessary for his homeland. Following a pattern set by Karamzin and continued by Solov'ev and Kavelin, he asserted that 'the achievement of a state – is the turning point of Russian history' and claimed that the actions of the princes had been the sole means for progress in Russia.[107]

Some of Chicherin's historical ideas were closer to Karamzin's interpretations than to those of either Solov'ev or Kavelin. For one thing, he attached more significance than his contemporaries did to Russia's size as a determinant for its political structure. In the same way that Karamzin and, to a lesser extent, Solov'ev had done, Chicherin cited Rousseau and Montesquieu to support his opinion that republics are feasible only in small states, while 'larger states are formed and maintained ... by concentrated power, which is the only condition that preserves them from collapse.' Using the example of revolutionary France, he went on to suggest that chaos was as likely to result from reactionary government as it was from failure to retain central authority.

Chicherin had the same utilitarian view as Karamzin on the role of education in Russia, seeing it as a tool for the training of Russian youth in 'the problems of state life and those virtues which are demanded of a citizen.' In his understanding of revolution and its relation to the historical process, he accepted the familiar sentiment: 'history, like people, does not make jumps.'[108] Chicherin tended to translate his beliefs into action and, accompanied by the usually apolitical Solov'ev, went into the streets in a vain attempt in 1861 to persuade students not to riot. Above all, he hoped to protect them from the 'ignorance, stupidity and banality' of such radicals as Chernyshevsky and Dobroliubov, whom he felt were largely responsible for the 'senseless propaganda which was intended to destroy all existing social structures.'[109]

The integration of Chicherin's political views into his historical writing is what made his scheme for Russian history appear to follow a tradition popularized by Karamzin. Believing in the 'necessity of power and order' because only an ordered society protects 'the weak from the strong and makes it possible to develop freedom of thought,'[110] he agreed that the *veche* system was inevitably accompanied by 'bloodshedding riots.' His study of the ancient *veche* institution and the growing restlessness in his own Russia of the sixties combined to convince him that any attempt to weaken the overall power of the state apparatus would result in anarchy or despotism. When it came to writing about Russian history he conformed to the traditional scheme by attributing the first state mechanism to the Varangians. After a long evolutionary process, the state came to its apex under Peter the Great, whom he referred to as an 'educator,'[111] albeit with a more exclusive meaning than like epithets from Karamzin, Solov'ev, or Kavelin.

Both Kavelin and Chicherin journeyed through Europe, but they returned home with somewhat different impressions of the West as a potential model for Russians. Neither, however, assumed that Russia should be, or could be, exactly the same as its neighbours. Kavelin projected Russian leadership of Europe, but admitted to Dostoevsky that 'all nations on earth learn from other ... nations.' Chicherin intimated that no one area was a perfect model for another.[112] In his historical writing, Kavelin, who once rebuked Chicherin for equating Russia and the West, stressed the unique evolution of Russia.[113] So did Chicherin, who underscored the independent development of Russia and minimized European influence in various ways. His definition of the difference between East and West, however, more clearly paralleled that of Karamzin:

> *The great merit of the Russian people, which made Russia one of the leading European powers, was ... their readiness to sacrifice everything for the tsar and the fatherland – directly opposite to the spirit of personal liberties.*[114]

Solov'ev had enunciated the same idea less directly when, in 'Ancient Russia' (1856), he suggested that a society could be assured of survival only after its members learned to recognize their duty to sacrifice the 'interests of part for the interests of the whole.' In the sixties, he blamed Western-type individualism for the collapse of Poland.[115] The Statist emphasis on unity and individual sacrifice was by no means original, for similar thoughts can be traced back to the early years of Musovy, but it was Karamzin who popularized such ideas for the nineteenth century in 'Martha' and who made it a lasting part of historical writing by means of the *History*.

Solov'ev was far more constant than either Karamzin or Chicherin in accentuating distinctions between Russia and western Europe and on this issue was closer to Pogodin, his opponent on most other things. Seeing religion as the main determinant of differences between Russians and west Europeans, Solov'ev still agreed with Karamzin's insistence that Russia was part of Western civilization. He was a 'Normanist' of the Karamzin type and often attacked the Slavophiles because he felt that isolation would prove fatal to his nation's further development. Like Karamzin, Solov'ev said that peoples could not return to past times and so some of the characteristics of west European life and ideas should be adopted and turned to Russian advantage. Again like his famous predecessor, and a growing number of his own contemporaries, Solov'ev felt that west European states, with their traditionally aggressive bent, could not be trusted to keep out of matters vital to Russian security. Indeed, he came close to Danilevsky in his idea that Russia's Western neighbours hoped for the destruction of his homeland. Thus, he expressed dismay but not particular astonishment at the cavalier way in which the European powers would rush to assist pagan Turks against Christian Russians.[116]

Karamzin's historical views were more pragmatic and were more directly a result of contemporary social and political circumstances in Russia than those of State School adherents, whose studies had a much broader philosophical base. Certainly the Hegelian content of the historical writings of Kavelin, Chicherin and, to a lesser extent, Solov'ev, was an important ingredient of their work, but Hegel's main interest lay in the realm of ideas whereas pragmatic, political concerns dominated the efforts of the Russians. Hegel had made many specific judgements about the relationship between state and individual, and on that of both in history, which had their counterparts in the writings of Russia's State School. According to Hegel, for example, the historical process centred on the evolution of the state; only in a state could one have true freedom, and every state mirrored the real needs of the community which it represented. The monarch, who was 'the absolute apex of an organically developed state,' must govern for the benefit of his subjects and under no condition could he revert to despotism, an opinion in which Hegel joined Karamzin. Certainly, the idea that history is a description of the evolution of 'true freedom,' which was central to Hegel's philosophy of history, was part of the outlook of Karamzin and the early Statists.[117]

Faith in the complementary nature of freedom and order was the premise for their acceptance of serfdom as a natural and just part of Russian history. In the past, serfdom enabled Russians to live in relative security because it had freed the gentry to serve the state, but in the nineteenth century it was enough of an anomoly that even Karamzin foresaw its end. One must remember, too, that in Karamzin's time slavery was still the norm in the United States and Adam Smith's writings were just then gaining popularity in Russia. Indeed, serfdom had not disappeared in western Europe. Further, Karamzin could remember tales of Pugachev, and he knew well the role of the mob in the French Revolution. He had seen, too, his own government's reaction to Radishchev, yet his attitude towards serfdom was still not far apart from those of the later writers. Members of the State School agreed that serfdom had been an integral and necessary part of state-building but all insisted that it had little application to their own time. Solov'ev saw the growth of serfdom throughout Russian history as a product of special circumstances, and he insisted that the peasant revolts in Russian history were unjustified. But he predicted that its retention in Russia could result only in revolution. Though more generally conservative than either Kavelin or Chicherin, he admitted that serfdom was a 'blemish' on Russian society. Like Karamzin, he tended to rationalize it as being the result of attempts by the early princes to protect the peasantry[118] and he followed the official scheme by saying that since the gentry had to work for the state then peasants must remain to till the land for the gentry. In his own time, however, serfdom was no longer relevant. Kavelin was more like Karamzin in that he referred to the landowners as protectors of the peasantry, and Chicherin also saw serfdom as an essential innovation for state-building in the sixteenth century, but both had strong reservations about its application to their own times.

For State School historians, the ultimate goal of Russian history had been autocracy, a view prompted largely by apprehension provoked by events in Europe. Kavelin, for example, was virulently anti-French and Chicherin followed suit,[119] but all of them considered Russia to be part of the European state system. Like Karamzin in the early nineteenth century, members of the State School saw many advantages in association with Europe but at the same time they assumed autocracy to be the only suitable form of government for their own country. As Solov'ev put it, 'a government, no matter what its form, represents the people; the nation is personified in it,' and Chicherin said that the state was 'an organic union of peoples which reflects the will of the people.' Karamzin would undoubtedly have concurred.

The genesis of State School political thinking, which helped determine its adherents' interpretation of history, was largely a product of the social upheavals of their time. The philosophical superstructure which enabled them to define their ideas was also partly a product of the contemporary fashionableness of Hegelian notions. But Russian tradition and Nicholas Karamzin's *History* contributed even more to the historical and emotional frame of mind which they took with them into historical studies. Consequently, their interpretation of their nation's past and present, and their prognoses for Russia's future, differed very little from that of Karamzin.

Conclusion

As a practitioner of historical writing, Karamzin brought together the two main tendencies of his predecessors in eighteenth-century Russia: the pragmatic 'lessons of history' approach and the notion that history had to be as masterfully written as the works of a Raphael or of a Michelangelo were painted. By paying heed at the same time to the more modern historical methods being introduced to Russians by European scholars at the turn of the century, he was able to produce a national history that was far superior to any published previously in Russia. But it was not Karamzin's historical method that had the greatest long-term import for his society. It was the Russianism of the *History*, its emphasis on duty, and its inexplicable sense of destiny that made a lasting impression on Russian minds. Russians of many walks of life could identify with the *History* for much of the century, just as the youth of his own time looked to its author as the spokesman of their sensibilities. Above all, the study gave ideological comfort to the provincial nobility and was a starting point for a cross-section of religio-political creeds ranging from those of the most pragmatic of conservatives to those of the most abstract of Slavophiles.

Karamzin's emphasis on the continuity of historical evolution and on the interdependence of all classes in Russia was typical of a growing view that a nation state formed a uniform whole, with systematically arranged parts. This type of thinking became the fountainhead of most political creeds, whether liberal or conservative, in the nineteenth century. For Karamzin, as for the State School historians, the existing state always mirrored the needs and aspirations of its people. Before them, he was the first historian of Russia to attempt a scholarly proof that autocracy was founded in law. His insistence on the historical necessity of autocracy, which he claimed had been established for the good of the people and not for the special use of the autocrat, and his assumption that representative assemblies were naturally unstable, also were beliefs held by later historians.

When the *History* first appeared, political theory in Russia was still relatively unsophisticated. There were no real 'schools' of thought whose members harked to well-defined principles of political evolution, theory, and practice. For that reason, Karamzin's socio-political frame of mind is somewhat elusive and much harder to characterize than his historical thinking. His general philosophy of history had been shaped by the events of the French revolutionary era. Convinced that Russian civilization was in great jeopardy, he turned to historical studies to seek out some immutable truths that could serve as the basis for order and stability in his homeland. Eventually concluding that 'ancient institutions have magical strength' and that the Revolution demonstrated to most people that they must live quietly and obey readily, he made a major contribution to the rapidly expanding body of writing in Europe that sought to justify the status quo.

The final crystallization of Karamzin's political thinking came only after many years of serious, and often anguished selection from a number of related social and political value systems. At times these values appeared contradictory, and at times his choice was determined by some inner, unaccounted-for preference rather than by a rational decision-making process. In applying his ideas to contemporary situations, he was sometimes forced to overrule principle for the sake of expediency. He was hardly unique in that. The two most enlightened rulers of Russia during Karamzin's lifetime, Catherine II and Alexander I, had opened the door to intellectual and political freedoms, only to find themselves faced with revolution. The other two monarchs, Paul and Nicholas I, bolted the door to the same freedoms and their reigns degenerated into tyranny. Therefore, many Russians of the time had to face a dilemma posed to them by their intellectual awareness of the merits of education and of the various 'freedoms,' and a concurrent conviction that a majority of Russians were ill prepared for such things.

The same intellectual currents of thought that had moulded Karamzin's way of thinking had also produced Radishchev and, less directly, the Decembrists. The flow of ideas from western Europe during the 1770s and 1780s did not eliminate xenophobia in Russia; nor did it produce a lasting and widespread westernism that forever reviled Russian tradition. It resulted in a multitude of value systems and attitudes. Karamzin was one of those who was able to make a viable synthesis of native and foreign traditions and innovations. A sentimentalist and optimist to his dying days, he was still astute enough to recognize the flimsiness of his idyllic version of Russia's past and present. He therefore lectured and ultimately pleaded with readers, whether emperor or citizen, to be rational and just, to accept change when it meant improvement for all Russians, to reject it when it meant chaos. Thus, his message to Russian society was above all else a civilizing one.

Karamzin's greatness lay in the fact that he remained an honest and responsible citizen in the face of enormous odds. It was Viazemsky who first termed Karamzin a 'liberal-conservative,' but Koshelev was the first to apply the term to Karamzin with some explanatory comment. The charge that the historiographer was an arch-conservative was simply an 'untrue one,' he said. Instead, the great writer was a 'gradualist.' Koshelev continued: 'the essence of Karamzin's liberalism exists in the recognition of the status quo and its inevitable change by an organic process, undisturbed by any forceful break...'[1] Openly conservative about some things, Karamzin always remained an enemy of tyranny and injustice. Partly because it seemed to be all in vain and partly because his words were later distorted and taken out of context for propaganda purposes by people whose ideas he would have abhorred, therein lies his tragedy as well.

Notes

INTRODUCTION

1 For the continuing debate about Karamzin's place in nineteenth-century Russian letters, see Hans Rothe, 'Karamzin and His Heritage: History of a Legend,' in *Essays on Karamzin: Russian Man of Letters, Political Commentator, Historian, 1766-1826* ed. J.L. Black (The Hague 1974) 148-90.

CHAPTER 1   CREATIVE WRITER TO HISTORIAN 1766-1800

1 A number of monographs have been written on Karamzin over the last few years, all of which are listed in the bibliography for this book. None of them has followed the development of his political and social ideas throughout his career, but several have covered his early life in some detail. Thus, this chapter will deal almost exclusively with the evolution of his socio-political viewpoint in the eighteenth century. See Select Bibliography, section B for biographical information. Recent studies by Cross, Nebel, and Rothe cover his literary career well; those by Pipes, Mitter, and Rudolph Bächtold are the best to date on his early socio-political development. Roger B. Anderson of the University of Kentucky is completing a manuscript on Karamzin's prose writing. For Russian and Soviet publications on Karamzin, see subsequent notes.
2 For general biographical information, see above all M.P. Pogodin's two-volume study (1866) and those by Grot and Bulich. Longinov, Sipovsky, Starchevsky, and Tikhonravov deal with specific aspects of his early life.

3 N.M. Karamzin, *Izbrannye sochineniia* II (Moscow-Leningrad 1964) 769. Richard Pipes used the term 'middle' for this class. See his *Karamzin's Memoir on Ancient and Modern Russia* (Cambridge, MA 1959) 17-18.

4 See I.I. Dmitriev, *Vzgliad na moiu zhizn'* (Moscow 1866) 39, N.S. Tikhonravov, 'Professor I.M. Shaden,' *Sochineniia* III (Moscow 1898) 44-59, and Bulich. See also M.I. Demkov, *Istoriia russkoi pedagogii* II (St Petersburg 1897) 468-70, who said that Shaden had considerable influence over Karamzin; but he did not delineate in what way. A Soviet writer, N.A. Penchko, has described Shaden as 'one of the most reactionary conservatives' among the professors at Moscow University and calls him a leader of the 'materialistic orientation' school which, he claims, was so enthusiastically followed by Karamzin, Pogodin, and Shevryev. See *Dokumenty i materialy po istorii Moskovskogo Universiteta vtoroi poloviny XVIII veka* (Moscow 1960) 383. Schaden was selected by Catherine II to be part of a five-man committee to examine the performance of the private schools (*pensions*) in Moscow. The committee report painted a very bleak picture of the quality of almost all such schools, which were in the main run by foreigners. See K.V. Sivkov, 'Chastnye Pansiony i shkoly Moskvy v 80-x godakh XVIII v.,' *Istoricheskii arkhiv* VI (Leningrad 1951) 315-23.

5 On Freemasonry in Russia, see V.G. Vernadsky, *Russkoe masonstvo v tsarstvovanie Ekateriny* (Petrograd 1917); M.V. Longinov, *Novikov i moskovskie martinisty* (Moscow 1867). On Karamzin's relationship with Masonry, see Pogodin, *N.M. Karamzin, po ego sochineniiam, pis'mam i otsyvam sovremennikov. Materialu dlia biografii* (Moscow 1866); N.D. Kochetkova, 'Ideinoliteraturnye positsii masonov 80-90-x godov XVIII veka i N.M. Karamzin,' *XVIII vek: Sbornik* VI (Moscow-Leningrad 1964) 176-96; Ia. L. Barskov, *Perepiska moskovskikh masonov XVIII v., 1780-1792* (Petrograd 1915); G. Backvis, 'Nicolas Novikov et la Franc-maçonnerie russe au XVIIIe siècle,' *Revue de l'Université de Bruxelles* XII (May/July 1936) 365-90. See also G.H. McArthur, 'The Novikov Circle in Moscow, 1779-1792,' unpublished PHD dissertation, University of Rochester 1968.

6 Pogodin, *N.M. Karamzin, po ego...* I, 40

7 See Iu. V. Got'e, 'Pamiati Karamzina kak istorik,' *Istoricheskii izvestiia* Bk 1 (1917) 5-13; V.N. Karazin, 'Pokazanie o sebe,' in *Sochineniia, pis'ma i bumagi*, ed. D.I. Blagoi (Kharkov 1910) 613.

8 See N.I. Novikov, 'Blagorodnomu rossiiskomu iunoshestva,' in *Detskoe Chtenie dlia serdtsa i razuma* (2nd edition, 1819) Pt 1, 1-8

9 *Detskoe Chtenie* Pt 9, 116 (written in 1787)

10 See M.M. Shprygova, 'Voina Amerika za nezavisimost' v osveshchenii "Moskovskikh vedomosti" N.I. Novikova,' *Istoricheskie nauki: Nauchnye doklady vysshei shkoly* 3 (1961) 14-89. For Karamzin's own views on Novi-

kov, see his 'Note about N.I. Novikov' ('Zapiska o N.I. Novikov,' 1818), *Izbrannye sochineniia* II 231-2, and *Pis'ma N.M. Karamzina k I.I. Dmitrievy*, ed. Ia. Grot and P.P. Pekarsky (St Petersburg 1862) 79, 460, 465, 471. Karamzin's 'Note on Novikov' has been translated into English in H.B. Segel, ed., *The Literature of Eighteenth Century Russia* I (New York 1967) 47-472.

11 Pogodin, *N.M. Karamzin, po ego...* I 18

12 N.M. Karamzin, *Polnoe sobranie stikhotvorenii*, ed. Iu. Lotman (Moscow-Leningrad 1966) 81. Hereafter this title will be referred to as *PSS*. Karamzin renewed his acquaintance with Novikov when the great publisher was released from prison, but the relationship was not particularly close. See 'Posledniia snosheniia N.M. Karamzina s N.I. Novikovym' (1816), *Russkii arkhiv* (1890) 367-75.

13 Novikov, 'O vospitanii i nastavlenii detei...,' in *Izbrannye sochineniia* (Moscow 1951) 417-38; on the book *O dolzhnostiakh cheloveka i grazhdanina*, which was in its eleventh edition by 1817, see Demkov, 382-404, and P. Stolpiansky, 'Istoriia odnoi knigi,' *Vestnik vsemirnoi istorii* 6 (1901) 189-210.

14 L.N. Tolstoi, *Sobranie sochinenii* XIX (Moscow 1965) 125

15 On Dmitriev, see H. Swidzinska, 'I.I. Dmitriev: A Classicist and a Sentimentalist in the Context of the World and Russian Fable,' unpublished PHD dissertation, University of Pittsburgh 1972. See also Dmitriev, 'Vzgliad na moiu zhizn'' (1823), in *Sochineniia Ivana Ivanovicha Dmitrieva* (St Petersburg 1895), [reprint, London 1974] 23-6, 148-51, 167-9.

16 Karamzin spoke of Sterne as 'original, inimitable, sensitive, good, witty, dear Sterne' and, later, 'Sterne is incomparable!'; *Moskovskii zhurnal* Bk I, Pt 1 (Moscow 1791), 2nd edition, 1803, 56; Bk I, Pt 5, 231-2. For Karamzin and Shakespeare, see André Lirondelle, *Shakespeare en Russie, 1748-1840* (Paris 1912), and for the influence of Lenz on Karamzin, see Hans Rothe, *N.M. Karamzins europäishe Reise: Der Beginn des russichen Romans* (Berlin 1968) 56-62, and Pogodin, *N.M. Karamzin, po ego...* I 37. For the idea that Lenz was Karamzin's main teacher in Moscow, where they lived together, see Rothe, 'Karamzinstudien,' *Zeitschrift für slavische Philologie* XXIX 1 (1960) 106-7. For Ossian (Macpherson) and Karamzin, see V.I. Maslov, *Ossianism Karamzina* (Priluki 1928). A recent study on Lenz is M.N. Rosanov, *Jakob M.R. Lenz, der Dichter der Sturm-und Drang periode* (Leipzig 1972). On Petrov, see Dmitriev, 'Vzgliad na moiu zhizn',' 26-7.

17 *Russkii arkhiv* (1863) 888, (1866) 1762

18 *Sochineniia Karamzina*, ed. A. Smirdin, III (Petersburg 1848) 361. Hereafter this title will be referred to as Smirdin.

19 'Perepiska Karamzina s Lafaterom, 1786-1790,' *Zapiski imperatorskoi akademii nauk* 73 (St Petersburg 1893) 4

20 *Izbrannye sochineniia N.M. Karamzina*, ed. L. Polivanov, I (Moscow 1884) 13.

See also Cross, 'Karamzin's Versions of the Idyll,' *Essays on Karamzin...*
75-90.
21 PSS 61-2
22 See *Emilia Galotti: ein Trauerspiel in fünf Auszägen* (Berlin 1869) 35, 74;
Karamzin, *Izbrannye sochineniia* II (1964) 83, 106; I 129.
23 See P.P. Privalova, 'O sotrudnikh zhurnala *Detskoe Chtenie dlia serdtsa i
razuma,*' *XVIII vek: epokha klassitsizma* (Moscow-Leningrad 1964) 258-68,
and S. Skvartsova, 'N.M. Karamzin, i zhurnal *Detskoe Chtenie dlia serdtsa i
razuma,*' in *Materialy XVII-nauchnoi studencheskoi konferentsii, Poetika,
istoriia, literatura, lingvistika* (Tartu 1967) 43-7. Like so many aspects of
Karamzin's career, his role in the publication of *Readings for Children* has
been a matter of some dispute. For many years it was referred to as 'Karamzin's journal,' but the impression that he dominated it was largely a result of
the tendency on the part of his devotees to exaggerate his contribution to
everything. Vasily Sopikov, for example, in his otherwise valuable *Opyt
Rossiiskoi bibliografii, ili polnyi slovar' sochinenii i perevodov ... do 1813*,
5 pts (St Petersburg 1813-21), credited the journal solely to Karamzin (see
Pt II, 1814, no. 3604). Although Karamzin was certainly active in the publication and was its acting editor throughout 1787 and the early months of
1788, Petrov served as its main editor. See 'Perepiska Karamzina s Lafaterom...' 18-20; *Russkii arkhiv* (1866) 1785.
24 *Detskoe Chtenie* Pt 9 (1787) 99. On the journal, Genlis, and Karamzin, see
Cross, *N.M. Karamzin: A Study of His Literary Career, 1783-1803* 21-9. The
tradition has been to say that Karamzin translated fifteen of the Genlis tales,
but Cross demonstrates that only thirteen were actually hers.
25 *Detskoe Chtenie*, Pt 9 (1787) 98-100
26 *Ibid.* 186. For the extent of the reception of *Readings for Children* in Russian society, see Privalova, '*Detskoe Chtenie dlia serdtsa i razuma* v otsenka
chitatelei i kritiki,' *XVIII vek: sbornik* 7 (Moscow-Leningrad 1966) 254-60.
27 *Detskoe Chtenie* XV (1788) 40-1; see also IX 174. For the demonstration of
Karamzin's authorship of *Pustynnik,* see Cross, 'Karamzin's First Short Story?'
in *Russia: Essays in History and Literature*, ed. Lyman H. Letgers (Leiden
1972) 38-55.
28 Smirdin III 363
29 Pogodin, 'Moskovskii zhurnal Karamzina,' *Russkii vestnik* 7 (1866) 237.
Karamzin's relationship with individual Masons is best outlined in Barskov.
30 See G.P. Shtorm, 'Novoe o Pushkine i Karamzine,' *Izvestiia Akademii nauk
SSSR: otdelenie literatury i iazyka* XX 2 (1960) 144-51, for the view that has
Karamzin as an agent of the Masons in Europe; see also Pogodin, *N.M. Karamzin, po ego...* I 68, and M. Dmitriev, 'Melochi iz zapasa moei pamiati,' *Moskvitianin* 1/2 (1854) 175.

31 Karamzin insisted that the *Moscow Journal* would be neither theological nor mystical, but would have 'taste.' In 1816, he still claimed that he was no mystic himself.

32 See Barskov, *Perepiska moskovskikh masonov* 70, 86-7, 94, 99, 100-1, 106; Pogodin, *N.M. Karamzin, po ego...* I 168; *Russkii istoricheskii zhurnal* (1917) 136-7, Cross, *N.M. Karamzin...* 35-7, and Dmitriev 47-9.

33 He used such flowery phrases as 'my Fatherland! My love for you glows in my heart...,' etc.

34 *Arzamas i arzamasskie protokoly*, ed. M.S. Borovkova Maikova (Leningrad 1933) 240-1

35 *Moskovskii zhurnal* Pt 3 (1791), 2nd edition, 1801, 106-7. See also Cross, 'N.M. Karamzin and Barthelemy's *Voyage du jeune Anacharsis*,' *Modern Language Review* LXI 3 (1966) 467-72.

36 See Roger B. Anderson, 'Karamzin's Letters of a Russian Traveller: An Education in Western Sentimentalism,' *Essays on Karamzin...* 22-39.

37 *Izbrannye sochineniia* II 593

38 Pipes, in *Karamzin's Memoir...* 35-7, said that 'Karamzin was indifferent to the Revolution and to all that it entailed.'

39 *Izbrannye sochineniia* I 126-7. Machiavelli had written in *The Prince*: 'a Prince ... cannot observe all those things for which men are esteemed, being often forced, in order to maintain the state, to act contrary to faith, friendship, humanity and religion.' *The Prince*, trans. W.K. Marriott (Chicago 1952) 25

40 *Ibid.* 189. For Karamzin's feeling about Schiller, see F.W. Neuman, 'Karamzins Verhältnis zu Schiller,' *Zeitschrift für slavische Philologie* IX (1932) 359-66. For the evolution of Karamzin's political viewpoint during the French Revolution, see items listed under Pipes, Mitter, and Kisliagina in bibliography, section E. Kisliagina also wrote: 'K voprosu o razvitii sotsial'no politicheskikh vzgliadov N.M. Karamzina v 90-x godakh XVIII burzhuaznaia revoliutsiia,' *Vestnik Moskovskogo universiteta* 3 (1968) 35-44. Iu. Lotman's 'Evoliutsiia mirovozzreniia Karamzina (1789-1803),' *Uchenie zapiski Tartuskogo gosudarstvennogo universiteta* 51 (1957) 197-223, was the first serious Soviet attempt to re-evaluate Karamzin's political stand and is still the most successful. A more recent but less rewarding effort is that by M.V. Ivanov, 'Problemy istorii i frantsuzskaia revoliutsiia v tvorchestve Karamzina 1790-x godov,' *Russkaia literatura* 2 (1974) 134-43. See also V.I. Fedorov, 'K kharakteristike sotsial'no-politicheskikh vzgliadov N.M. Karamzina,' *Uchenye zapiski Moskovskogo gosudarstvennogo pedagogicheskogo instituta* (Moscow 1963) 35-51. For one pre-Soviet writer who dealt with this theme, see A.K. Borozhdin, 'Literaturnye i obshchestvennye vzgliady Karamzina,' in *Literaturnye kharakteristiki: Deviatnadtsatyi vek* I (St Petersburg 1903) 20-78.

41 *Izbrannye sochineniia* II 97-100. See also G.P. Gooch, *Catherine the Great and Other Studies* 101-2.

42 On Prussia: 'My God! What cautiousness.' *Izbrannye sochineniia* I 121. On Switzerland: 'And I am already in Switzerland, country of picturesque nature, land of freedom and well-being! The very air seems to contain something invigorating.' *Ibid.* 207

43 *Ibid.* 211-14, 243, 271-2

44 *Ibid.* 228

45 *Ibid.* 245-7

46 *Ibid.* 291

47 *Ibid.* II 93-6. See also I 382, where he speaks (in 1801) of republics once again.

48 *Ibid.* II 117. The original appeared in *Moskovskii zhurnal* Pt 4 (December 1791) 356. On Karamzin and Radishchev, whom he failed to mention even once in his works and correspondence, see Erwin Wedel, 'Radishchev und Karamzin,' *Die Welt der Slaven* IV 1 (1959) 38-65.

49 'Karamzin's Versions of the Idyll,' *Essays on Karamzin...* 75-90

50 *Izbrannye sochineniia* I 282, 506-7

51 *Moskovskii zhurnal* Pt 2 (1792) 2nd edition, 1802, 76. For a survey of Russian press opinions on the French Revolution, see A. Kaganova, 'Frantsuzskaia burzhuaznaia revoliutsiia kontsa XVIII v. i sovremennaia ei russkaia pressa,' *Voprosy istorii* 7 (1947) 87-94, and M.M. Shtrange, *Russkoe obshchestvo i frantsuzskaia revoliutsiia, 1789-1794 gg.* (Moscow 1956) 151-81.

52 *Moskovskii zhurnal* Pt 8 (1791) 2nd edition, 1801, 327

53 *Izbrannye sochineniia* I 353

54 *Moskovskii zhurnal* Pt 5 (1791) 2nd edition, 1801, 145

55 'To Mercy' (1792) is perhaps the best known of these poems. Written when Novikov was arrested in April 1792, the first published version was somewhat abridged from Karamzin's initial draft. See *PSS*, 20-1, 110-11, 369. For this and other such poems, see V.V. Vinogradov, 'Ischeznuvshii tekst: "Raznye otryvki (iz zapisok odnogo molodnogo rossianina)" N.M. Karamzina,' *Problema avtorstva i teoriia stilei* (Moscow 1961) 265-7.

56 *Moskovskii zhurnal* Pt 6 (1792) 2nd edition, 1802, 206-8. See also Vinogradov, 264ff.

57 *Izbrannye sochineniia* I 90-1, 120, 164, 343, 415-18. See also J.L. Black, 'Karamzin's Views on Peter the Great,' *The New Review: A Journal of East European History* VI 4 (1966) 20-37.

58 *Moskovskii zhurnal* Pt 3 (1791) 2nd edition, 1801, 206-8. For a study of this and other such tales, see L.V. Krestova, 'Drevnerusskaia povest' kak odin iz istochnikov povestei N.M. Karamzina "Raiskaia ptichka," "Ostrov Borngol'm," "Marfa Posadnitsa",' *Issledovanniia i materialy po drevnerusskoi literature* (Moscow 1961) 193-226, and Cross, *N.M. Karamzin...* 96-142.

59 *Moskovskii zhurnal* Pt 5 (1792) 2nd edition, 1802, 292-323

60 *Ibid.* 303

61 *Izbrannye sochineniia* I 622. On *Natal'ia* and other tales, see P.Z. Kanunova, '"Natal'ia boiarskaia doch"' kak pervyi opyt istoricheskoi povesti N.M. Karamzina,' *Uchenye zapiski Tomskogo gosudarstvennogo universiteta* 48 (1964) 174-94, and *Iz istorii russkoi povesti (Istoriko-literaturnoe znachenie povestei N.M. Karamzina)* (Tomsk 1967).

62 *Izbrannye sochineniia* I 644

63 This point has been made by Witold Kośny in his 'Zum Problem der historischen Erzahlüng bei N.M. Karamzin,' *Die Welt der Slaven* XIII 3 (1968), and by Kanunova, *Iz istorii...* 71-99.

64 See K.S. Serbinovich, 'Nikolai Mikhailovich Karamzin, Vospominaniia,' *Russkaia starina* II (St Petersburg 1874) 46. Serbinovich was a close associate of Karamzin during the writer's last years. He translated for him and helped Bludov prepare the final volume of the *History of the Russian State* for publication after Karamzin's death.

65 *Moskovskii zhurnal* Pt 5 (1792), 2nd edition, 1802, 372

66 Karamzin, *Izbrannye sochineniia* I 415-16, 418-19; see also II 173, 197. Levesque's *Histoire de la Russie, tirée des chroniques originales et des meilleures histoires de la nation, avec l'histoire des différents peuples soumis à la domination des Russes* I-V (Paris 1782-3) had been translated into Russian in 1787. In 1784, it was translated into Italian; so was the first part of LeClerc's *Histoire physique, morale, civile et politique de la Russie ancienne et moderne* (Paris 1783-93). Boltin and Karamzin were following a tradition set by Lomonosov, who had attacked the historical writings on Russia by A.L. Schlözer, G.F. Müller, and Voltaire for much the same reasons. On Levesque, see André Mazon, 'Pierre-Charles Levesque, humaniste, historien et moraliste,' *Revue des études slaves* 42 (Paris 1963) 7-66. On the Boltin-Shcherbatov dispute, see the works on Russian historiography by S.L. Peshtich, L.V. Cherepnin, V.E. Illeritsky, V.I. Astakhov, and the nineteenth-century writer, V.S. Ikonnikov. Above all, see Peshtich, *Russkaia istoriografiia XVIII veka* III (Leningrad 1971) 5-77. See also Hans Rogger, *National Consciousness in Eighteenth-Century Russia* (Cambridge, MA 1960) 222-38.

67 On the general issue of Karamzin's inner crisis during these years, see R. Neuhäuser, 'Karamzin's Spiritual Crisis of 1793 and 1794,' *Essays on Karamzin...* 56-74.

68 *PSS* 118, 131

69 *Izbrannye sochineniia* I 272-3, 285-91, 316-18, 349-50

70 *Ibid.* 381

71 As Pogodin was to point out later, an astonishing aspect of the life of the *Moscow Journal* was that it never seemed to have attracted the attention of

Catherine II. Karamzin once referred to the 'gloominess' of the year 1791 (*Izb. soch.* II 114), and his friendship with Novikov may well have put him in a delicate political position, but the apparent disinterest in the journal on Catherine's part must have been a blow to his pride. It is also indicative of the tenseness of the times and a sign that the mutual regard between Catherine and Russia's world of letters had come to an end.

72 *PSS* 110-11
73 *Izbrannye sochineniia* II 121-2
74 'Rousseau, I do not believe your system!' *Ibid.* 129, 140. See also Fernard Girardin, *Karamzine et J.J. Rousseau* (Paris 1912).
75 *Izbrannye sochineniia* 127-8
76 *Ibid.* 140-1, 132-5
77 *Ibid.* 120
78 *PSS* 135
79 *Pis'ma Karamzina k Dmitrievu* 98
80 Smirdin III 361
81 Written in 1793 but not published until 1795; Cross has suggested that this essay was inspired by Barthelemy. See *Modern Language Review* (1966) 470.
82 Smirdin III 435
83 See Rothe, *Karamzins...* 298.
84 *Izbrannye sochineniia* II 245-59, and Neuhäuser 68-70
85 Smirdin III 435
86 See Vinogradov, *Problema...*; N.K. Piksanov, '"Bednaia Aniuta" Radishcheva i "Bednaia liza" Karamzina,' *XVIII vek: sbornik 3* (Moscow-Leningrad 1958) 309-25; Jean-Louis van Regemorter, 'Deux Images idéales de la paysannerie russe à la fin du XVIIIᵉ siècle,' *Cahiers du monde russe et soviétique* IX 1 (1968) 5-19 (on Karamzin and Radishchev); V.P. Stepanov, 'Povest' Karamzina "Frol Silin",' *XVIII vek: sbornik 8* (Moscow 1969) 229-44.
87 Smirdin I 339, 406; III 350-1, 570, 573-4, 591
88 Demkov 370-1; L.L. Dodon, 'Uchebnaia literatura russkoi narodnoi shkoly vtoroi poloviny XVIII veka i rol' F.I. Iankovicha v ee sozdanii,' *Uchenye zapiski kafedra pedagogika* 118 (Leningrad Pedagogical Institute 1955) 185-207
89 *PSS* 185-90
90 *Pis'ma Karamzina k Dmitrievu* 70; Smirdin III 710-12
91 *Pis'ma Karamzina k Dmitrievu* 478. The fact that the *Letters* were not, as Karamzin claimed, notes that he had written to friends in Russia from Europe during his tour, but were written after his return and changed often, was first demonstrated by V.V. Sipovsky, *N.M. Karamzin, avtor 'Pis'ma russkago puteshestvennika'* (St Petersburg 1899). *Le Spectateur du Nord: Journal politique, littéraire et moral* was published in Hamburg in twelve

volumes, 1797-9. Karamzin's 'Lettre au *Spectateur* sur la littérature russe,' signed 'N.N.,' was printed in volume IV (October 1797) 53-71.

92 *Izbrannye sochineniia* II 281-3
93 *Spectateur du Nord* 3 (1797) 69-70. Karamzin's essay was also reprinted in *Pis'ma Karamzina k Dmitrievu*, appendix 8, and has been translated into English for Segel I 430-41.
94 *Pis'ma Karamzina k Dmitrievu* 91
95 *Russkii arkhiv* (1872) 1325-6
96 The *Aonides* was published by Karamzin in three books, 1796-9. See Cross, *N.M. Karamzin...* 172-92.
97 *Pis'ma Karamzina k Dmitrievu* 036
98 *Ibid.* 99
99 N.M. Karamzin, *Panteon inostrannoi slovestnosti* II (Moscow 1798) 2nd edition, 1818, 306-7, 258; I 125-6. See also Cross, *N.M. Karamzin...* 160-6.
100 *Russkii arkhiv* (1866) 1763-4
101 See Cross, 'Karamzin in English: A Review Article,' *Canadian Slavic Studies* III 4 (1969) 716-27; T.A. Bykova, 'Perevody proizvedenii Karamzina na inostrannye iazyki otkliki na nikh v inostrannoi literature,' *XVIII vek: sbornik 8* (Leningrad 1969) 324-42; P. Berkov, 'Izuchenie russkoi literatury vo Frantsii,' *Literaturnoe nasledstvo* 33/34 (1939) 721-68. For Karamzin's *Julia* in Europe, see *Le Spectateur du Nord* (February 1797) 184-203.
102 *Pis'ma Karamzina k Dmitrievu* 42-9 and Neuhäuser 67-8
103 'Protei, ili nesoglasiia stikhotvortsa' (*Aonides*) *PSS* 242-51
104 *PSS* 215
105 *Ibid.* 255. In 1797, the poem 'Tacitus' ('Tatsit') implied that a tyrannical government did not have the right to exist. *Ibid.* 239

CHAPTER TWO   THE SAGE AND POLITICAL PUNDIT 1800-3

1 Although Paul Miliukov claimed that Karamzin was in no way interested in writing a Russian history at this time, the idea certainly had occurred to Karamzin. Most of Miliukov's contentions were based on his feeling that Karamzin was a poor historian who intended only to produce a great work of literature. Miliukov, *Glavnyia techeniia russkoi istoricheskoi mysli* I (Moscow 1897) 120. For Karamzin's reference to 'gloire,' see *Neizdannyia sochineniia i perepiska Nikolaia Mikhailovicha Karamzina* Pt I (St Petersburg 1862) 203.
2 *Ibid.* 202-3
3 *Russkii arkhiv* (1872) 1323-7
4 See Demkov, *passim*, and M.F. Vladimirsky-Budanov, *Gosudarstvo i narodnoe obrazovanie v Rossii XVIII-go veka* (Yaroslavl' 1874) 155.

5 Peshtich I 96; P. Pekarsky, *Nauka i literatura v Rossii pri Petre Velikom* (St Petersburg 1862) 315-17; Demkov 69-74; Tatishchev, *Istoriia rossiiskaia* I (Moscow-Leningrad 1962) 81, and *Izbrannye trudy po geografii Rossii* (Moscow 1950) 77. See also Tatishchev's essay, *Razgovor dvukh priiatelei o pol'ze nauk i uchilishch* (Moscow 1887). Written in 1733, this essay contains his best reflections on education, history, and politics. Rogger, 194-202

6 The *Kratkaia rossiiskaia istorii* (St Petersburg 1799) was printed specifically for use in the public schools. Stritter had been commissioned to do such a text in 1783 but it was fifteen years before a German version appeared, and a Russian translation was not ready until 1800. See Stritter, *Istoriia Rossiiskago Gosudarstva* I-III (St Petersburg 1800-3). See Dodon 187-9. This writer has seen only the 1805 (3rd) edition of the *Kratkaia rossiiskaia istorii*; apparently it was in a ninth edition by 1827. Peshtich (II 63-4) says that it was written by one Shelekhov, and the bibliographers Sopikov and Smirdin attribute it to T. Kiriak, but the strongest evidence points to De Mirievo.

7 Lomonosov, *Kratkii Rossiiskii letopisets s rodosloviem* (St Petersburg 1760) and *Drevniaia Rossiiskaia istoriia* (St Petersburg 1766) are both printed in his *Polnoe sobranie sochinenii* VI (Moscow-Leningrad 1952) 287-358, 163-286. See also Peshtich II 164-210. For Catherine II's *Nakaz*, see *Documents of Catherine II*, ed. W.F. Reddaway (Cambridge 1931), here, no. 348, 271. The 'Notes on Russian History' ('Zapiski kazatel'no Rossiiskoi istorii') had comprised almost 1400 pages in the journal *Sobesednik liubitelei rossiiskogo slovo* (1783-4), which Catherine edited with Princess Dashkova.

8 *Pis'ma Karamzina k Dmitrievu* 102. Golikov had written a thirty-volume panegyric to Peter I, 1788-97.

9 *Pis'ma Karamzina k Dmitrievu* 102 (20 September 1798)

10 *Vestnik evropy* 1 (1802) 3-5

11 In a letter to his brother. Smirdin III 712-13. See also a letter to Murav'ev, *ibid.* 680.

12 *Izbrannye sochineniia* I 441

13 *Ibid.* 480, 397, 343, 415-16

14 *Pis'ma Karamzina k Dmitrievu* 115-16

15 *Izbrannye sochineniia* II 159, 171. In the 1790s Emin had been one of Karamzin's detractors.

16 *Ibid.* II 157

17 See A.L. Schlözer, *Probe russischer Annalen* (Bremen and Göttingen 1768) 51-2. He repeated this in *Nestor: Russkiia letopisi na drevle-slavenskom iazyke...*, translated from the German by D. Iazykov (St Petersburg 1809) rzt. Capital letters are Schlözer's.

18 *Izbrannye sochineniia* II 156-7

19 In a letter to Alexander, Karamzin wrote of the 'common joy' which Russians experienced when the new sovereign came to the throne. The letter was reprinted as the frontispiece of the 1892 edition of the *History of the Russian State* (see below, appendix).

20 He admitted this in one of the odes to Alexander, *PSS*, 270. In the same letter to Alexander cited above, Karamzin thanked the emperor for gifts sent to him in appreciation of the odes. Karamzin replied: 'the history of Russia will be the object of my diligent labours.'

21 Pypin, *Obshchestvennoe dvizhenie v Rossii pri Alexandre I* 4th edition (St Petersburg 1908) 208-9; N.P. Barsukov, *Zhizn' i trudy M.P. Pogodina* I (St Petersburg 1888) 82

22 Smirdin I 276-7

23 *Ibid.* 199, 205, 210. For citations from Montesquieu, see *Esprit des lois* Bk XI, chapters 3 & 6.

24 Smirdin I 282-300, 302-3, 308, 311

25 Boltin, *Kriticheskiia primechaniia general-maiora Boltina na pervy-vtoroi tom istorii kniazia Shcherbatova* I (St Petersburg 1793) 319, II (1794) 460. See also Hans Rogger, 'The "Nationalism" of Ivan Nikitich Boltin,' in *For Roman Jacobson*, ed. Morris Hale (The Hague 1956) 423-9, and A. Lipski, 'Boltin's Defense of Truth and the Fatherland,' *California Slavic Studies* II (1963) 39-52.

26 Boltin, *Primechaniia na istoriiu drevniia i nuneshniia Rossii g. Leklerka* II (St Petersburg 1788) 542

27 *PSS* 299, 410

28 Smirdin I 500-1

29 *Vestnik evropy* Pt 1 (1802) 5

30 On Popugaev, see *Russkie Prosvetiteli (ot Radishcheva do Dekabristov)* I (Moscow 1966) 323-5, 418-23. Pisarev's book was entitled *Predmety dlia khudizhnikov, izbrannyia iz Rossiiskoi istorii, basnosloviia i iz vsekh Ruskikh sochinenii v stikhakh proze* 2 pts (St Petersburg 1807).

31 *Pis'ma Karamzina k Dmitrievu* 92

32 'Pis'ma N.M. Karamzina k kniazia P.A. Viazemskomu, 1810-1826,' *Starina i novizna* Bk I, section 2 (1897) 114, 116. On the extent of the interest in folklore during the first three decades of the nineteenth century, see Peter K. Christoff, *The Third Heart: Some Intellectual-Ideological Currents and Cross-Currents in Russia, 1800-1830* (The Hague 1970).

33 Smirdin I 424. In the *Messenger of Europe*, Karamzin praised Ivan Bogdanovich for 'preserving the precious remnants of our ancestors' thoughts,' and regretted that older people had not been interviewed for their accounts of the times in which they had lived. Finally, he said, 'how good it would be to

collect all the Russian fables which are related either to history or to old customs!' Smirdin I 641, 424-5; *Vestnik evropy* no. 12 (1802) 60; for an outline of this and other themes in the journal, see Cross, 'N.M. Karamzin's *Messenger of Europe (Vestnik yevropy)*, 1802-03,' *Forum for Modern Language Studies* V 1 (1969) 1-25.

34 *Izbrannye sochineniia* II 283
35 *PSS* 299, 410
36 *Izbrannye sochineniia* II 283-4
37 *Vestnik evropy* 1 (1802) 486, 496. See also A.D. Galakhov, 'Karamzin kak optimist,' *Otechestvennye zapiski* 116, no. 1 (1858) 107-46.
38 *Izbrannye sochineniia* I 680. On 'Martha' see V.I. Fedorov, 'Istoricheskaia povest' N.M. Karamzina "Marfa Posadnitsa",' *Uchenye zapiski Moskovskogo gorodskogo pedagogicheskogo instituta* 62, no. 6 (1957) 109-29.
39 *Izbrannye sochineniia* I 727
40 *Ibid.* 683
41 Smirdin III 52-3; *Izbrannye sochineniia* II 178-9
42 Smirdin I 416
43 *Izbrannye sochineniia* I 727, 273. There were over thirty entries on Napoleon during Karamzin's time as editor of the journal. He also wrote an essay which dealt with Oliver Cromwell in the same manner, that is, praise for his stress on law and order in a time of chaos. See *Vestnik evropy* Pt 2 (1802) 260-1.
44 Smirdin III 585-8
45 Pipes, *Karamzin's Memoir on Ancient and Modern Russia* 39-44
46 'Al'bom N.M. Karamzina,' ed. N. Lyshin, *Letopisi russkoi literatury* I section 2 (Moscow 1858). See especially 180-1.
47 Smirdin I 434
48 Karamzin, *Neizdannyia sochineniia* 3-4
49 Smirdin III 352-4. Karamzin italicized this sentence.
50 *Ibid.* 348-51
51 *Vestnik evropy* II (1802) 52-5; VI 147-63; Smirdin III 607-8, 505-9. Karamzin's main objections to Schlözer senior appeared in the essay 'O tainoi kantseliarii,' *Vestnik evropy* (1803), which is reprinted in Smirdin (I 419-26). Christian von Schlözer, the eldest son of August, was appointed to the Academy as an historian of Europe and Russia in 1801. Karamzin attended and commented upon a public lecture delivered by Christian in Moscow in 1803. Praising the young German's scholarly ability, Karamzin regretted that the lecture was given in German, Smirdin III 614-15. See also Cross, *N.M. Karamzin...* 129.
52 'O novom obrazovanii narodnago prosveshcheniia v Rossii,' Smirdin III 352
53 *Memoir on Ancient and Modern Russia* 158-9

54 Karamzin, 'O vernom sposobe imet v Rossii dovol'no uchitelei' (1803), Smirdin III 341. On the educational theme in the journal *Patriot* see M.F. Shabaeva, *Ocherki istorii shkoly i pedagogicheskoi mysli narodov SSSR* (Moscow 1973) 290-4.

55 On Tatishchev's ideas, see Rudolph Daniels, *V.N. Tatishchev: Guardian of the Petrine Revolution* (Philadelphia 1973) 47. Karamzin wrote favourably of Peter III in the eulogy to Catherine II and in an essay of 1803, 'Travels around Moscow' ('Puteshestvie vokrug Moskvy'), in which he said, 'I, as a Russian and *dvoriane*, wished to see the place which pleased Peter III, where he signed two glorious and immortal laws....' Smirdin I 336, 451. Karamzin drew a much harsher picture of Peter III in the *Memoir* (see 130, 132, 137).

56 Smirdin III 581

57 *Ibid.* 343, 348, 351, 401, 575

58 *Ibid.* I 398

59 *Ibid.* I 502; III 602-4

60 *Ibid.* I 410, 418 (from *Vestnik evropy* no. 18, 1803)

61 Schlözer, *Probe russischer Annalen* 44

62 Smirdin III 603, 526-7. See also *Izbrannye sochineniia* II 280.

63 Smirdin III 209. For this general theme, see V.A. Teplova, '*Vestnik evropy* Karamzina o Velikoi frantsuzskoi revoliutsii i formakh pravleniia,' *XVIII vek: sbornik 8* 268, 280, and P.A. Orlov, 'Respublikanskaia tema v zhurnala Karamzina *Vestnik evropy* (K voprosu ob evoliutsii mirovozzreniia pisatelia),' *Nauchnye doklady vysshei shkoly: Filologicheskie nauki* 3 (1969) 15-24.

64 *Vestnik evropy* 1 (1802) 44. He added in a footnote, 'and Peter the Great?'

65 Smirdin III 886, 598

66 *Ibid.* 502, 332-9

67 *Vestnik evropy* 1 (1802) 3

68 Smirdin I 549, 552

69 See Iu. Lotman, 'Evoliutsia mirovozzreniia Karamzina (1789-1803)' 150-5; Cross mentions this also in his article on the *Messenger of Europe* 21. Karamzin's version of Portalis's speech appeared in no. 3 (1802) of the journal 65-77. On England, see *Vestnik evropy* 4 (1802) 73.

70 *PSS* 286-9; *Vestnik evropy* 5 (1809) 59-60

71 *Ibid.* 4 (1802) 60-1. See also no. 9 (1803) 124.

72 On the matter of Karamzin's feelings towards Herder, see Bittner, 'Herdersche Gedanken in Karamzins Geschichtsschau,' *Jahrbücher für Geschichte Osteuropas* VII (1959) 237-69. For a discussion of Bittner's treatise, see J.L. Black, 'N.M. Karamzin's Views on Peter the Great,' *New Review* VI (December 1966) 20-37.

73 *Izbrannye sochineniia* II 280. For Tatishchev, see Daniels, 36-42, 94-5.

74 'Pis'ma Karamzina k Viazemskomu' (21 August 1818) 60
75 *Vestnik evropy* 1 (1802) 72, 86; 3 (1802) 101; 21 (1802) 52. In the *History of the Russian State*, he wrote that 'republics sustain themselves by virtue, but without it they fall.' VI (1818) 127
76 *Vestnik evropy* 20 (1802) 319-20
77 'Obshchestva v amerike,' *ibid.* 6 (1802) 315-18. This essay was reprinted again by Karamzin in 1818, in the second edition of the *Pantheon of Foreign Literature.* He had not included it in the first edition because of the strict censorship demanded by Paul. It has been translated for the *Laurentian University Review* IV 3 (1972) 43-4.
78 *Vestnik evropy* 7 (1802) 256. His analogy vis-à-vis the United States was made clear in two articles about Canada, which he praised in contrast to its American neighbours. See 'An Englishman's Letter from Quebec,' where he extolled the benefits of hard work, cleanliness, and paternal (monarchical) government. *Vestnik evropy* 16 (1803) 272-6
79 *Ibid.* 1 (1802) 12
80 *Ibid.* 10 (1803) 130
81 *Izbrannye sochineniia* I 415; *Neizdannye sochineniia* 109
82 Smirdin III 712
83 Pogodin, *N.M. Karamzin, po ego...* II 18-19; Smirdin III 680; *Russkii arkhiv* (1869) 2019. M.N. Murav'ev remained Karamzin's patron at court until his death in 1807. Karamzin helped edit and wrote an introduction to a collection of some of Murav'ev's works which were published in Moscow in 1820. See V.D. Levin, 'Karamzin, Batiushkov, Zhukovskii – redaktory sochinenii M.N. Murav'eva,' *Problemy sovremennoi filologii* (Moscow 1965) 182-90. On the position at Vilna, see 'Pis'ma N. Karamzina k popechiteliu Vilenskogo universiteta kniaziu A. Chartoryiskomu,' *Russkaia literatura* 2 (1967) 116. Prince Adam Czartoryski, Alexander's long-time friend, had replaced Novosiltsov as curator in 1804.
84 Cited in I.A. Shliapkin, *Pervyi ruskii istorik N.M. Karamzin* (Petrograd 1917) 23-4
85 Smirdin III 419-23, 694-5
86 *Literaturnoe nasledstvo* 60 (1956) 328-33. On the extent of Karamzin's popularity at home during these years, see Cross, *N.M. Karamzin...* 218-19. See also A. Fomin, 'A.I. Turgenev i A.S. Kaiserov,' *Russkii bibliofil* 1 (1902) 26-30.
87 *Literaturnoe nasledstvo* 60 (1956) 329. Kaiserov wrote a strongly anti-Karamzin pamphlet in 1799. In his memoir, F.F. Vigel' reported that in 1800 'envy and slander were already gathering to ruin him [Karamzin].' *Zapiski* I (Moscow 1928) 130
88 Smirdin III 585

CHAPTER THREE   HISTORIAN AND MAN AT COURT:
KARAMZIN AND RUSSIAN SOCIETY 1803-26

1 *Russkii arkhiv* (1869) 1090. Izmailov's *Patriot* carried an article on Karamzin
   (no. 3, 1804). The *Moskovskii merkuri* was a monthly and failed to appear
   only because of the death of its editor. P.I. Shalikov tried to revive a version
   of Karamzin's *Aglaia* in 1808-10, with little success. See A.V. Zapadov, *Istoriia russkoi zhurnalistiki XVIII-XIX vekov* (Moscow 1966) 113-22. See also
   'Dva pis'ma N.M. Karamzina k V.V. Izmailovu,' *Russkii arkhiv* (1870) 599-
   600.

2 On this general subject, see Christoff, *The Third Heart* 31-3, Zapadov, 115-22,
   N.I. Mordovchenko, *Russkaia kritika pervoi chetverti XIX veka* (Moscow
   1959) 114-19, 262-5, and Marc Raeff, 'Filling the Gap between Radishchev
   and the Decembrists,' *Slavic Review* XXVI 3 (September 1967) 395-413. On
   the literary salons of this era, see N.L. Brodsky, *Literaturnye salony i kruzhki:
   pervaia polovina XIX veka* (Moscow-Leningrad 1930).

3 P. Viazemsky, *Polnoe sobranie sochinenii* X (St Petersburg 1886) 288, 291-3.
   A recent Soviet publication by M.I. Gillel'son, *P.A. Viazemskii: zhizn' i tvor-
   chestvo* (Leningrad 1969), suggests that Viazemsky was not so 'Karamzinist'
   as it has usually been assumed. The book is an important one and its interpretation has merit as far as the two writers' literary positions are concerned.
   However, in their socio-political viewpoints the younger man was very much a
   disciple of Karamzin. For Karamzin's feelings about literature and letters
   spreading beyond the confines of the noble class, see *Vestnik evropy* Pt 1
   (no. 1, 1802) 4.

4 Shishkov, 'Razsuzhdenii o starom i novom sloge rossiiskago iazyka,' *Sobranie
   sochinenii i perevodov* II (St Petersburg 1824) 1-356. There are a number of
   studies which touch upon the Shishkov-Karamzin dispute. In fact, Raeff com-
   plains that literary histories of the period between 1790 and 1815 tend all too
   often to be limited to the 'philological debate between Karamzin and Shishkov'
   (*Slavic Review* [1967] 395). Given the rather picayune point that Karamzin
   did not really involve himself in the discussion, the complaint is a valid one.
   Besides the writing of the combatants and their supporters, see P. Shchebal'sky,
   'A.S. Shishkov, ego soiuzniki i protivniki,' *Russkii vestnik* 90 (1870) 192-254,
   'Anekdot o Shishkove,' *Russkii arkhiv* (1863) 217, and Iu. N. Tynianov, *Push-
   kin i ego sovremenniki* (Moscow 1968) 24-33.

5 On the growth of Russian criticism, see Mordovchenko, *Russkaia kritika*, and
   Istoriia russkoi kritiki I (Moscow-Leningrad 1958) 94. Even Novikov was criti-
   cized in 1805 for being too 'soft,' *Severny vestnik* V 3 (1805) 277-8. For
   Karamzin's own views on criticism, see Smirdin III 645-6. Dmitriev's concern

was expressed in a letter to Iazykov, 20 December 1803; see *Russkii arkhiv* (1869) 1084.

6 *Moskovskii merkuri* Pt IV (1803) 163, 189-91. See also *Sochineniia i perevody Petre Makarova* I Pt 2 (Moscow 1817) 38-40. In 1816, Makarov still defended Karamzin's use of foreign words, but recommended that they be screened carefully so that they suited Russia's needs. On this matter, see Roger B. Anderson, 'Karamzin's Concept of Linguistic "Cosmopolitanism" in Russian Literature,' *Studies by Members of SCMLA* XXXI 4 (1971) 169. On the question of whether or not there was such a thing as a 'Karamzinist' era in the history of Russian literature, see the two articles by G.P. Makogonenko. In the first, he insisted that there had been no such era, but after being criticized by colleagues among Soviet literary historians, he retracted: 'Byl li karamzinskii period v istorii russkoi literatury?' *Russkaia literatura* 4 (1960) 3-32 and 'Literaturnaia pozitsiia karamzina v XIX veke,' *ibid.* 1 (1962) 68-107

7 In the Soviet publication, *Arzamas i arzamasskie protokoly* (Leningrad 1933), the debate was treated as a matter of 'enlightenment' versus 'feudal church ideology.'

8 In his article, 'Arzamas: Portrait of a Literary Society,' B. Hollingsworth points out that Griboedov, Krylov, Katenin, and others did back Shishkov in the matter of language, *Slavonic and East European Review* XLIV 103 (1966) 306-26. See also N. Gerzhenson, *Griboedovskaia Moskve* (Moscow 1916), M. Dmitriev, *Melochi iz zapasa moei pamiati* 2nd edition (Moscow 1869) 73, and *Graf' Bludov i ego vremia*, ed. E. Kovalevsky (St Petersburg 1866).

Shishkov's work was reprinted in 1813. Another of his works, *Razgovory o slovestnosti* (St Petersburg 1811), received far less attention and did not centre on Karamzin. It was reviewed quite favourably by Kachenovsky in *Vestnik evropy* 12 (1811) 285-305; 13 (1811) 34-57.

9 See Christoff, *The Third Heart*. Shishkov, whose wife was Lutheran, even hired a French tutor for his two nephews and spoke only in French to them. F.F. Vigel' also called Shishkov a Slavophile. *Zapiski* 55

10 See *Moskvitianin* Pt 2 (1847) 130, for Karamzin's acceptance speech (14 July 1810).

11 See Pogodin, *N.M. Karamzin, po ego...* II 62ff., for the Golenishchev-Kutuzov-Karamzin dispute. See also *Pis'ma Karamzina k Dmitrievu*, 056; 'Pis'ma I.I. Dmitrieva k P.A. Viazemskomu' 237. Always Karamzin's first defender, Viazemsky made a speech to an Arzamas meeting which was, in effect, a bitter diatribe against Kutuzov. For Karamzin's early denigration of Kutuzov, see *Vestnik evropy* 4 (1803) 275. On Khvostov, see *Pis'ma Karamzina k Dmitrievu* 379-80, and Khvostov, *Stikhi N.M. Karamzinu* (Moscow 1810).

12 A.G. Tartakovsky, *Voennaia publitsistika 1812 goda* (Moscow 1967) 47; Shishkov, *Razsuzhdenie o liubvi k otechestvu* (St Petersburg 1812)

13 *Pis'ma Karamzina k Dmitrievu* 098, 250. He said exactly the same thing in a letter to his wife. See *Neizdannyia sochineniia* 148.

14 The editor was N.N. Makarov who, at age seventeen and with I.V. Smirnov, founded the *Journal for Sweethearts* (*Zhurnal dlia Milykh*) to attack Shishkov.

15 *Arzamas i arzamasskie protokoly* 24-5

16 'Pis'ma I.I. Dmitrieva k P.A. Viazemskomu' 20. On Uvarov, besides his own works, see C.J.H. Whittaker, 'Count S.S. Uvarov: Conservatism and National Enlightenment in Pre-Reform Russia,' unpublished PHD dissertation (Indiana University 1971).

17 *Neizdannyia sochineniia* 160, 165. For the opinion that the main purpose of the organization was to defend Karamzin, see Vigel', *Vospominaniiakh* II (Moscow 1866) 163-73; III 38-54.

18 'Pis'ma N.M. Karamzina k A.I. Turgenevu (1806-1826),' ed. V. Saitov, *Russkaia starina* 97 (1899) no. 28, 472 (letter of 30 March 1816)

19 S.S. Uvarov, 'Literaturnyia vospominaniia,' *Sovremennik* 27, section 2 (1851) 37; Viazemsky, *Polnoe sobranie sochinenii* X (1886) 245-7. Shakhovskoi wrote a satirical play in 1807, 'The New Sterne: A Comedy in One Act' ('Novyi Stern, komediia v l deistvii'), to which the historiographer's friends took umbrage. See Hollingsworth 313.

20 For a reproduction of the diploma, see 'Diplom, podnesennym obshchestvom "Arzamas" N.M. Karamzina,' *Starina i novizna* 12 (1907) 334-5, and this volume, appendix p 256.

21 *Arzamas i arzamasskie protokoly* 279

22 *Russkii arkhiv* (1869) 831

23 Viazemsky's comment is cited in Gillel'son, *P.A. Viazemskii* 30.

24 *Arzamas i arzamasskie protokoly* 240

25 Gillel'son, *P.A. Viazemskii*, 37-8

26 *Russkii arkhiv* (1871) 158

27 *Poliarnaia zvezda*, ed. A. Bestuzhev, K. Ryeev, 1823-25 (reprint, Moscow-Leningrad 1960) 278; *Trudy Ia. K. Grota* III (St Petersburg 1899) 147. For Pushkin's relationship with Arzamas and for his opinion about Karamzin's presence in Russia's literary scene, see Tynianov *Pushkin*, 58-63, 212-17; *Russkii arkhiv* (1869) 440. Karamzin carried on a constant correspondence with Zhukovsky, which reflects most of his attitudes towards contemporary Russian and European literature. See 'Pis'ma N.M. Karamzina k V.A. Zhukovskomu,' *Russkii arkhiv* (1869) no. 6, 1827-36; (1869) no. 7, 1383-6; (1870) no. 8, 1682-90; (1875) no. 3, 493-7; (1900) no. 3, 5-54.

28 See Hans Rothe, 'Karamzin and his Heritage: History of a Legend,' in *Essays on Karamzin...* 148-90, and 'Philologische Ausgrabungen oder Katenin und

die Nachwelt,' *Zeitschrift für slavische Philologie* XXXVI 2 (1972) 237-65.
'Pis'ma I.I. Dmitrieva k P.A. Viazemskomu,' 195-6. In this case Dmitriev was
complaining about Nicholas Polevoi's *Telegraf* and making fun of Belinsky
who, it seems, had reviewed an old translation of Shakespeare's *Julius Caesar*
in glowing terms without realizing that it was Karamzin's.

29 On his rejection of Derzhavin's request, see *Neizdannyia sochineniia* 160
(letter to his wife, 18 February 1816).

30 For Dmitriev's viewpoint, see *Russkii arkhiv* (1869) 1086, and 'Pis'ma I.I.
Dmitrieva k P.A. Viazemskomu' 129; for that of Dashkov, see *Russkii arkhiv*
(1869) 589-93. Murav'ev was dead by this time, but Dashkov said that he had
contributed more to Russian letters than had Karamzin.

31 *Vestnik evropy* 1 (1808) 8

32 Pogodin, *N.M. Karamzin, po ego...* II 46-7, 53

33 Smirdin III 720 (in a letter to his brother, 12 April 1811); 'Pis'ma Karamzina
k Viazemskomu' (17 March 1811) 6. Richard Pipes discussed the circumstances
of Karamzin's presence at these meetings and outlines a history of the text of
the *Memoir* in his study of that work. He lists the various places and forms in
which parts of the text appeared before the first full printing of 1870 (see
Memoir 93-100). Pipes omitted the long extract which appeared in N.G.
Ustrialov's, *Istoriia tsarstvovaniia Petre Velikago* I (St Petersburg 1858). Hans
Rothe suggests that Karamzin's appearance at Tver, and the *Memoir* itself, indicate that he was willing to partake in 'intrigue' against the emperor's policy
makers (*N.M. Karamzins...* 433), but this strikes me as too strong a statement.
In recalling these meetings at Tver, F.P. Lunianovsky said: 'Often Nicholas
Karamzin read the *History of the Russian State* to us, still in manuscript form
... we listened with close attention, all the more since the Historiographer
seemed to love to listen to himself.' *Russkii arkhiv* (1872) 502. De Maistre,
too, wrote of the meetings in Tver and said that in 1810 'Mr Karamzin, a
famous writer, gave history lectures there....' *Russkii arkhiv* (1871) 0192. See
also Pogodin, *N.M. Karamzin, po ego...* II 58, 68, and Dmitriev 112.

34 *Memoir* 105 (all references refer to Pipes's edition)

35 *Ibid.*

36 Smirdin I 283-4; *Memoir* 129, 145

37 *Ibid.* 132

38 *Ibid.* 141, 145, 205. Interestingly, Admiral Mordvinov, president of the
commerce department, also forwarded a memorandum to Alexander in
1810 in which he suggested that territorial aggrandizement (Finland) was a
major error in judgement and argued for a basically defensive position.

39 'Pis'ma Karamzina k Turgenevu' 233. See also *Pis'ma Karamzina k Dmitrievu*
129, 305-7, 310. When the *History* was first published, Speransky was very
enthusiastic about it and compared Karamzin favourably with Hume (in a

letter to A.A. Stolypin, 5 March 1818). See *Russkii arkhiv* (1869/1870) 919. Karamzin and Speransky were contrasted in an article by V.Z. Zavitnevich, 'Speranskii i Karamzin kak predstaviteli dvukh politicheskikh techenii v tsarstvovanie imperatora Aleksandra I,' *Trudov Kievskoi dykhovnoi akademii* XIVIII 11 (1907) 347-95.

40 Smirdin I 524
41 Pogodin, *N.M. Karamzin, po ego...* II 80-2. He cited somewhat circumstantial evidence from Serbinovich, Ivan Dmitriev, and Bludov.
42 'Al'bom N.M. Karamzina' 164. The album was presented to Catherine as a birthday gift. On this and her salon at Tver, see Irène de Vries-Bsse. de Gunzburg, *Catherine Pavlovna: Grande-Duchesse Russe* (Amsterdam 1941), and Pogodin, *N.M. Karamzin, po ego...* II 88-92.
43 'Pis'ma N.M. Karamzina k S.S. Uvarovu,' *XVIII vek: sbornik 8* 353. Uvarov had recently sent to Karamzin a copy of his small booklet, *O prepodovannii istorii, otnositel'no k narodnom vospitaniia* (*About the Teaching of History, in Relation to Popular Education*), (St Petersburg 1813).
44 *Russkii arkhiv* (1869/1870) 919; (1871) 434; Pogodin, *N.M. Karamzin, po ego...* I 475-6; II 95
45 Karamzin once again lauded the appointment of Speransky, in 1826, to the task of codifying Russia's laws. In this, Nicholas was adopting a policy suggested in the *Memoir*, that is, that one man be assigned the job and not a committee.
46 *Pis'ma Karamzina k Dmitrievu* 225 (letter written in 1817)
47 *Russkii arkhiv* (1869) 1437; (1880) 239; Pogodin, *N.M. Karamzin, po ego...* II 95, 98-101
48 *Pis'ma Karamzina k Dmitrievu* 174 (letter of 15 June 1813)
49 *Ibid.* 186 (letter of 9 September 1813). Dmitriev (1760-1837) had been made a state councillor (1797) and an attorney general in 1798, but had retired in the next year. In 1806, he was named to the senate in Moscow, where he lived from 1802 until 1809. Then he moved to St Petersburg as a member of the State Council. He made several enemies in the ministry, for he attempted to clean out 'idle persons' and demanded efficiency. Given permission to retire by 1814, he moved back to Moscow. See *Zhurnal Ministerstva narodnogo Prosveshcheniia* (April 1902) 369-70, and Swidzinska, 'I.I. Dmitriev...' 173-243.
50 'Pis'ma Karamzina k Viazemskomu' 33 (letter of 28 August 1817)
51 Pogodin, *N.M. Karamzin, po ego...* II 116-18
52 See especially 'Pis'ma Karamzina k Viazemskomu' 15, 44, 50, for Karamzin's comments about life in St Petersburg. For his sentiments about Moscow, see *Zapiska o Moskovskikh dostopamiatnostiakh* (*Note about Moscow's Memorials*), which he wrote in 1817. Smirdin I 427-47. Karamzin had not intended

this essay for publication, but V.N. Karazin printed it without asking permission in the *Ukrainskii vestnik* 5/6 (1818), with 'many mistakes' according to Karamzin, so the historian included it in his own *Sochineniia* IX (1820). See Pogodin, *N.M. Karamzin, po ego...* I 18. For Karamzin's comments about Peter I and St Petersburg, see *Memoir* 124, 126-7. Pogodin printed the correspondence between Karamzin and the emperor, *N.M. Karamzin, po ego...* II 112-15.

53 On his conflict with Arakcheev, see Michael Jenkins, *Arakcheev: Grand Vizier of the Russian Empire* (New York 1969) 178-9. On A.A. Besborodko, one of Catherine II's most capable diplomatic advisers, see *Pis'ma Karamzina k Dmitrievu* 397 (letter of 2 June 1825).

54 'Pis'ma Karamzina k Turgenevu' 237; *PSS* 300-10

55 *Pis'ma Karamzina k Dmitrievu* 44, 47-8, 212. Labzin made many enemies at court because of his domineering and arrogant manner. He made the mistake of opposing Golitsyn and so found himself banished from Moscow by the 1820s. In December 1818, Karamzin complained to his brother that he was too old for the court and that he had only Capodistrias as a friend (Smirdin III 730-1). Novosiltsev replaced M.N. Murav'ev, who died in 1808, as Karamzin's sponsor at court. See 'Pis'ma N.M. Karamzina k stats' sekretari N.N. Novosil'tsevu, May 3, 1808,' *Moskvitianin* I (1847) 139-40. On Karamzin and Golitsyn, see *Pis'ma Karamzina k Dmitrievu* 198, 202, 218, 336-7. Karamzin did not have to subject his work to the censors. *Ibid.* 198

56 Gogol' wrote this in 1846. See his *Sobranie sochinenii* (Moscow 1967) 256.

57 *Pis'ma Karamzina k Dmitrievu* 236, 249

58 'Pis'ma Karamzina k Viazemskomu' (11 September 1818) 61

59 The 'Opinion of a Russian Citizen' ('Mnenie Russkago grazhdanina') was printed first in *Neizdannyia sochineniia* 3-9 and then again in *Starina i novizna* Bk 2, section 2 (1897) 13-17. It has been translated for *Essays on Karamzin...* 193-6. Karamzin admitted in a diary note left for his sons that Alexander did not ask for or follow his advice: 'It is true that Russia kept its Polish province, but more due to circumstances than to my advice.' *Neizdannyia sochineniia* 18-19. See also A. Fateev, 'Sud'ba Zapisok Karamzina o Rossii i Pol'she pri Imperatore Nikolae I,' *Zapiski Russkogo Istoricheskogo Obshchestva v Prage* (Prague 1927) 114-19, and J.L. Black, 'Interpretations of Poland in Nineteenth Century Russian Nationalist-Conservative Historiography,' *The Polish Review* XVII 4 (1972) 20-41.

60 N.I. Turgenev, *La Russie et les Russes* (Paris 1847) 88, and Herzen, *Sobranie sochinenii* VII (Moscow-Leningrad 1959) 294

61 'Pis'ma Karamzina k Viazemskomu' (letter of 16 February 1821) 110. J.G. Garrard has recently published a very interesting article in which he poses the possibility that Karamzin and Mme de Staël might have met in Moscow.

See 'Karamzin, Mme de Staël, and the Russian Romantics,' *American Contributions to the 7th International Congress of Slavists* (Warsaw 1973) II, Literature and Folklore, ed. Victor Terras (The Hague 1973) 233.

62 For his pessimistic view on The congresses in Europe, see 'Pis'ma Karamzina k Viazemskomu' (16 February 1821) 110.

63 *Pis'ma Karamzina k Dmitrievu* 332ff., 378. Karamzin's petition to Golitsyn about the censors' attempt to 'correct!' V.L. Pushkin can be found in a letter of 7 September 1822. *Ibid.* 336-7. See also 'Karamzin i V.L. Pushkin' (1801), *Russkii arkhiv* (1863) 295-8.

64 *Ibid.* 323 (letter of 9 February 1822). Karamzin had already shown his low regard for Runich in a letter to his wife in 1816. See *Neizdannyia sochineniia* 146. In a letter to Viazemsky, 15 October 1825, Karamzin expressed 'horror' at what he had heard of Magnitsky's action. See *Starina i novizna* VII (1903) 12. See, too, James T. Flynn, 'Magnitsky's Purge of Kazan University: A Case Study in the Uses of Reaction in Nineteenth Century Russia,' *Journal of Modern History* XLIII 4 (1971) 598-614.

65 See Gillel'son *P.A. Viazemskii* 39, 352 and 'Pis'ma Karamzina k Viazemskomu' (8 July 1812) 80.

66 Smirdin I 339, 406; III 350-1, 570, 573-4, 591. The letters to Balashev are included in Smirdin (III 706-8). See also 'Pis'ma Karamzina k Viazemskomu' (30 October 1818) 65, 188.

67 *Pis'ma Karamzina k Dmitrievu* 279, 400-1, 0171; *Pis'ma N.M. Karamzina k A.F. Malinovskomu i pis'ma A.S. Griboedova k S.N. Begichevu* (Moscow 1860) 12; 'Pis'ma Karamzina k Viazemskomu' 65; Smirdin III 706; Serbinovich 'Vospominaniia' 259

68 'Pis'ma Karamzina k Viazemskomu' 49

69 This Hegelian idea reappeared all through Karamzin's correspondence. He once remarked to Viazemsky that 'I love freedom, although I am not a liberal,' and to Dmitriev that what people need is 'freedom of the soul, although I am not a liberal.'

70 'Pis'ma Karamzina k Viazemskomu' (letter of 25 February 1820) 96

71 *Neizdannyia sochineniia* 28, 185-7

72 'Pis'ma Karamzina k Viazemskomu' 107, 151-8; 'Pis'ma Karamzina k Turgenevu' 230

73 *Vestnik evropy* 2 (1802) 75; *Pis'ma Karamzina k Dmitrievu* 285; 'Pis'ma Karamzina k Turgenevu' 480

74 'Pis'ma Karamzina k Viazemskomu' 107; *Pis'ma Karamzina k Dmitrievu* 306

75 'Russian policy is very wise; we keep out of war until the last possible moment.' *Atenei* 27 (1858) 61 (letter to Turgenev, 1821). Karamzin praised men like Lord Byron for their romantic and real contribution to the popular Greek cause, and often condemned 'Turkish barbarism.' See *Pis'ma Karamzina k*

Dmitrievu 309, 312. For Karamzin's overall view on war and Russian partici-
pation in European affairs, see J.L. Black, 'Karamzin, Napoleon, and the
Notion of "Defensive War" in Russian History,' *Canadian Slavonic Papers*
XII 1 (1970) 30-46.

76 'Pis'ma Karamzina k Viazemskomu' 120

77 *Pis'ma Karamzina k Dmitrievu* 286-7, 337; *Russkii arkhiv* (1866) 1090,
1098, 1099; (1879) 325. In 1816, Karamzin wrote often of the Arzamas,
among them Pushkin, whom he called 'witty.' Six years later he remarked
that a new poem of Pushkin's was 'bad' but still had 'lively lines.' Simon
Vorontsov (1744-1834) was for a long time Russian ambassador to England.
See also 'Pis'ma Karamzina k Viazemskomu' (17 May 1820) 101.

Pushkin's relationship to Karamzin has often been remarked upon and has
been the subject of several articles. See, for example, V.E. Vatsuro, 'Podvig
chestnogo cheloveka,' *Prometei* 5 (1968) 9-51, who discusses the influence
of Karamzin's *History of the Russian State* on the writing of Pushkin. Others
include L.N. Luzianina, 'Istoriia gosudarstva Rossiiskogo N.M. Karamzina i
tragediia Pushkina *Boris Godunov* (k probleme kharaktera letopistsa),' *Russkaia literatura* 1 (1971) 45-57; B.V. Tomashevsky, 'Epigrammy Pushkina na
Karamzina,' *Pushkin, issledovanniia i materialy* I (Moscow-Leningrad 1956);
M.B. Rabinovich, '*Boris Godunov* Pushkina, *Istoriia* Karamzina i letopisi,'
Pushkin v shkole, Sbornik statei (Moscow 1951) 307-17; I. Toibin, '*Istoriia
gosudarstva Rossiiskogo* N.M. Karamzina v tvorcheskoi zhizni Pushkina,'
Russkaia literatura 4 (1966) 37-49; V.I. Butakova, 'Karamzin i Pushkin
(Neskol'ko sopostavlenii),' *Pushkin i ego sovremenniki* XXXVII (Leningrad
1928) 127-35; N.M. Danilov, *Pushkin i Karamzin: k 150-letnemu iubileiu so
dnia roshdeniia N.M. Karamzina* (Kazan 1917). See also n85, below.

78 *Pis'ma Karamzina k Dmitrievu* 253, 270; *Literaturnoe nasledstvo* 60 (1956)
181; *Neizdannyia sochineniia* 12

79 'Pis'ma Karamzina k Viazemskomu' (21 August 1818) 60. See also 108.

80 L.N. Tolstoi, *Sobranie sochinenii* XVII (Moscow 1958) 493

81 'Pis'ma Karamzina k Turgenevu,' no. 68, 233 (18 December 1825). In a
letter to Nicholas dated 22 March 1826, Karamzin praised the ruler for doing
what Alexander would have done under similar circumstances. *Russkii arkhiv*
(1904) 122. For Karamzin and Nicholas I, see 'Imperator Nikolai Pavlovich i
Karamzin v poslednie ego dni, ikh perepiska,' *Russkii arkhiv* (1906) 122-7,
and n59, above.

82 'Pis'ma Karamzina k Turgenevu' 229 (6 September 1825)

83 See *Perepiska Ia. K. Grota s P.A. Pletnevym* III (St Petersburg 1886) 400;
Ia. K. Grot, 'Ocherk deiatel'nosti i lichnosti Karamzina, 1866' 12-166; Viazemsky, *Polnoe sobranie sochinenii* VII (1882) 133.

84 *Russkii arkhiv* (1869) 619

85 For Shevyrev's opinion of Karamzin, see 'Pis'ma M.P. Pogodin, S.P. Shevyrev
    ... k Viazemskomu,' ed. N.P. Barsukov, *Starina i novizna* Bk 4 (1901) 147;
    see also F. Tiutchev, *Polnoe sobranie sochinenii* (St Petersburg 1913) 203.
    On the Karamzin salon, see *Pushkin v pis'makh Karamzinykh, 1836-1837*
    (Moscow 1960).

86 V.G. Belinsky, *Polnoe sobranie sochineniia* IX (Petrograd 1917) 219; XIII
    107. In a letter to Zhukovsky (6 August 1826), Viazemsky said: 'He was a
    kind of life-giving, radiant focus of our circle, of all the fatherland. The death
    of Napoleon in contemporary history, the death of Byron in the world of
    poetry, the death of Karamzin in Russia, leaves a huge vacuum which we will
    not be able to fill.' *Polnoe sobranie sochinenii* IX (1884) 89. Strangely, Via-
    zemsky never wrote a major work on Karamzin, though he began to do so in
    1826 but changed his mind and prepared a study on Fonvizin instead. A. Star-
    chevsky, who did write a book on Karamzin (*Nikolai Mikhailovich Karamzin*,
    St Petersburg 1849), wondered about this in an article written for *Istoricheskii
    vestnik* in 1888 (no. 10, 125).

CHAPTER FOUR   THE *HISTORY*: TEXTBOOK FOR EMPERORS AND CITIZENS

1 'I do not write for the book-selling market. I write either for posterity or not
   at all,' *Pis'ma Karamzina k Dmitrievu* (letter of 20 April 1814), 180-1. Parts
   of the second half of this chapter were contained in my article, 'Nicholas
   Karamzin's Scheme for Russian History,' in *Eastern Europe: Historical
   Essays*, ed. H.C. Schlieper (Toronto 1969) 16-33.

2 Smirdin I 424, 416

3 N.M. Karamzin, *Istoriia gosudarstvs Rossiiskago* IX (St Petersburg 1892) 5
   (hereafter, *History*). This writer had access to several editions of the *History*.
   Those of 1892 and 1897 were used most often in the early stages of research,
   the first edition being only a recent acquisition. For that reason, the references
   herein will be to more than one printing of the work.

4 *PSS* 367; *Moskovskii zhurnal* 3 (1791) 1802 edition, 112

5 On this point, see E. Heier, *L.H. Nicolay (1737-1820) and His Contemporaries*
   (The Hague 1965) and 'William Robertson and Ludwig Heinrich von Nicolay,
   His German Translator at the Court of Catherine II,' *Scottish Historical Review*
   XLI (October 1962) 135-40.

6 *Izbrannye sochineniia* I 415-16

7 *Vestnik evropy* 5 (1803) 47. In the *Letters*, Karamzin had said: 'It is important to note that one country produced both the best novelists and the best
   historians. Richardson and Fielding taught the French and the Germans to
   write novels as descriptions of life, and Robertson, Hume and Gibbon spread
   the attractiveness of the most interesting novels into history by means of wise

organization of events, descriptions of characters and adventures ... after Thucydides, no one can compare with the historical triumvirate of Britain' (*Izb. soch.* I 574). Even Karamzin's reference to Richardson and Fielding in this instance had a decidedly historical connotation, for those writers had written 'histories' of their fictional heroes. Witold Kośny mentioned this in his article, 'Zum problem der historischen Erzählung bei N.M. Karamzin.'

8 *History* I (1818) xvii. In another place in the *History*, Karamzin boasted that the Englishman was 'astonished' to see that a 'barbarian' Russian monarch, Feodor, held views on free trade that were far in advance of those held by the 'renowned' English Queen Elizabeth, *History* IX (1821) 29-30 n50.

9 Smirdin I 727

10 *Ibid.* 713. The foreword to the *History* has been translated into English. See Marc Raeff, ed., *Russian Intellectual History: An Anthology* (New York 1966) 117-24.

11 *History* I (1818) xvii

12 *Vestnik evropy* 1 (1802) 22

13 *History* I (1818) xvi

14 *Neizdannyia sochineniia* 205

15 Serbinovich 'N.M. Karamzin: Vospominaniia,' *Russkaia starina* (1874) 244

16 'Pis'ma Karamzina k Turgenevu,' appendix I 234

17 For the empress's letter, see Pogodin, *N.M. Karamzin, po ego...* II 121; for Rumiantsev's note, see *Russkii arkhiv* (1869) 598.

18 *History* IX (1821) 439 n762

19 M.V. Lomonosov, *Polnoe sobranie sochinenii* VI (Moscow-Leningrad 1952) 170

20 Smirdin III 455

21 *History* I (1818) 122, 113, 148, 156

22 *Ibid.* II (1892) 45

23 *Ibid.* (1818) 299

24 *Ibid.* VI (1892) 220

25 After Karamzin's imitation of Shcherbatov's treatment of this era, such a division of Ivan's reign became the norm for Russian history books in the nineteenth century.

26 *History* I (1897) 30; (1818) 112

27 *Ibid.* II (1818) 63

28 *Ibid.* I (1897) xxii

29 *Ibid.* (1818) 29-30 n64

30 *Ibid.* 73-8

31 *Ibid.* VI (1892) 79; (1818) 127-9

32 *Ibid.* IV (1892) 143; VI 16, 13

33 *Ibid.* VI (1892) 85; (1818) 127

34 *Ibid.* (1818) 95
35 *Ibid.* I (1897) 50; W.F. Reddaway, ed. *Documents of Catherine the Great* (Cambridge 1931), 'Instructions' (no. 250) 256
36 *History* V (1892) 77. Montesquieu, *The Spirit of Laws*, trans. T. Nugent (Chicago 1952) 10-11
37 *History* V (1818) 367; VIII (1818) 6
38 *Ibid.* V (1892) 232; VIII 6
39 *Ibid.* I 158
40 *Ibid.* (1897) 159-60, 120-1
41 *Ibid.* II (1892) 88-9
42 *Ibid.* III 143; V (1818) 363-4
43 *Ibid.* III (1892) 19
44 *Ibid.* IV 192
45 *Ibid.* V (1818) 73-4
46 *Ibid.* 79
47 *Ibid.* (1892) 152, 158
48 According to Karamzin, Moscow was so deserted that Vasily's stronghold, Kolomna, became the capital for the Great Prince: 'This was a unique case in our history and resulted not so much from a special love for Vasily as from zeal for the principle that the son must succeed the father to the rank of Great Prince.' *Ibid.* 161
49 *Ibid.* 219-20 n363; (1818) 345
50 *Ibid.* V 362-9; the *Kratkaia Rossiiskaia istoriia*, which was written for national schools in 1799, was the only history school textbook to carry this theme in the nineteenth century.
51 *History* VI (1892) 1
52 *Ibid.* 216
53 *Ibid.* IV 153
54 He claimed that in the *veche* 'passion ruled over wisdom.' *Ibid.* VI 22
55 *Ibid.* (1818) 45, 128-9
56 *Ibid.* (1892) 90, 97-100
57 *Ibid.* (1818) 321-6; (1892) 217-19, 230
58 *Ibid.* VII (1892) 4. See also pages 75 and 114, where he spoke of Vasily as a 'follower of Ivan in everything.'
59 'Vasily sought a midpoint between cruel terror and harmful weakness' and later, 'Ivan III created, Ivan IV glorified and almost ruined, Vasily preserved and maintained the state....' *Ibid.* 107-8
60 *Ibid.* 19, 74, 77
61 *Ibid.* 124
62 *Ibid.* 126, 130-2. The traveller was Baron Sigismund von Herberstein.
63 *Ibid.* VIII 10, 32-3

64 *Ibid.* 63
65 *Ibid.* 195
66 See Machiavelli, *The Prince* (Chicago 1952) 25, 94; Montesquieu xxii.
67 *History* IX (1821) 437. Interestingly, the 1892 edition omitted the phrase about breaking the 'iron sceptre' (IX [1892] 273), which may have been somewhat too revolutionary in implication. Karamzin's first edition was not submitted to the censors.
68 *Ibid.* (1821) 439-41
69 *Ibid.* (1892) 170
70 'But we will be fair to tyrants as well.' *Ibid.* (1821) 219; (1892) 275
71 In the 'Opinion of a Russian Citizen,' *Neizdannyia sochineniia* 4; *Starina i novizna* Bk 2 (1897) 14
72 *History* X (1892) 6-8
73 *Ibid.* XI 11
74 *Ibid.* X (1892) 141
75 In one place, Karamzin actually noted the similarity between Godunov and Ivan IV. According to Karamzin, the psychological problem in Ivan's life was the death of his wife; that in Godunov's career was a growing sense of guilt over the Tsarevich Dmitry's death – a highly unlikely sentiment indeed.
76 *History* XI (1892) 72
77 *Ibid.* 96
78 *Ibid.* XII 5
79 *Ibid.* (1829) 127
80 *Ibid.* (1829) 191; XII (1829) 124, 137, 313
81 He was speaking of the attempt on the part of some of the Russian nobility to have a Polish prince named tsar of Russia. *Ibid.* XII (1829) 241
82 See, for example, V (1892) 149; VIII 39-40
83 *Ibid.* VIII 10
84 *Ibid.* II 88-9, 97-8
85 *Ibid.* VIII 43. A recent Soviet article shows very clearly that Karamzin assigned a dynamic role to the mass of Russian people in his nation's history. Its author, L.N. Luzianina, is careful to point out, justifiably, that Karamzin was simply trying to prove that Russians chose autocracy of their own accord. See 'Ob osobennostiakh izobrazheniia naroda v *Istorii gosudarstva Rossiiskago* N.M. Karamzina,' *Uchenye zapiski Leningradskogo universiteta* 355 (1971), philosophy series, issue 76, 3-17.
86 *History* XI (1892) 57-8; (1824) 108-9
87 *Ibid.* VI 22
88 Smirdin I 276
89 *History* VI (1818) 326. For further details on Karamzin's views about the role of the prince in Russian history, see Pipes, 'Karamzin's Conception of

the Monarchy,' and R. McGrew, 'Notes on the Princely Role in Karamzin's *Istorija Gosudarstva Rossiiskogo*,' *American Slavic and East European Review* XVIII (1959) 12-25.

90 *History* I (1897) 49, 156; IV (1892) 192; *Memoir* 22
91 *History* IX (1892) 285
92 *Ibid.* IV 137-8; V 134; IX 192, 197. See also Black, 'Karamzin, Napoleon and the Notion of "Defensive War" in Russian History.'
93 *History* V (1818) 3; VI 325
94 *Ibid.* VI 326
95 See, for example, *ibid.* III (1892) nn77, 110, 198; IV n103; XIII 191; *Neizdannyia sochineniia* 6. Karamzin was very worried at this time, for his emperor was in Warsaw.
96 'Pis'ma Karamzina k Viazemskomu' 16. Alexander was not swayed by Karamzin but he was interested enough to show the 'Opinion' to a German ambassador, E.A. Engelhardt, who agreed with its basic premises. *Russkii arkhiv* (1869) 303-4
97 *Neizdannyia sochineniia* 29; *History* XI (1929) 522. Certainly it would not be unreasonable to charge Karamzin with hypocrisy on reading his pious intonation to Viazemsky in 1818, to the effect that 'we must love them [Poles] as Christians and men,' but he added that it would also not be advisable to trust them. 'Pis'ma Karamzina k Viazemskomu' 55
98 *History* III (1892) 18-19
99 *Ibid.* IV 153
100 *Ibid.* VIII 194; XII 133, 166; *Memoir* 117
101 *History* VIII (1892) 54, 87; III 54; II (1818) 71
102 *Neizdannyia sochineniia* 206
103 *History* IX (1892) 273-4
104 *Ibid.* II (1818) 65-6
105 'Pis'ma Karamzina k Turgenevu' 98
106 See, for example, *Pis'ma Karamzin k Dmitrievu* 339, 345, 350, 356.
107 *Izbrannye sochineniia* II 105-6
108 *History* I (1818) n316; *Neizdannyia sochineniia* 206
109 *History* I (1897) xx-xxvi. On this general question, see N. Bestuzhev-Riumin, 'Nravstvennoe chuvstvo v *Istorii* Karamzina,' *Nikolai Mikhailovich Karamzin: Ego zhizn' i sochineniia* (Moscow 1908) 107-10; I.I. Davydov, *Vzgliad na 'Istoriia gosudarstva Rossiiskago' Karamzina so storiny khudozhestvennoi* (St Petersburg 1855); N. Apostolov, 'Karamzin kak romanist-istorik' in *Ocherk po istorii russkogo istoricheskogo romana* (Petrograd 1916)
110 *Izbrannye sochineniia* II 229 (italics are Karamzin's)
111 *Ibid.* 144

112 Smirdin III 486, 690; *History* I (1818) 32
113 Smirdin III 746; *Moskvitianin* Pt 1 (1847) 139-40
114 Smirdin I 486
115 *History* I (1892) 222 n283; V (1818) 368. On other such inconsistencies see Horace W. Dewey, 'Sentimentalism in the Historical Writings of N.M. Karamzin,' *American Contributions to the 4th International Congress of Slavicists* (Moscow 1958).
116 *History* I (1818) n105. On Karamzin the scholar, see Black, 'The *Primechaniia*: Nicholas Karamzin as a "Scientific" Historian of Russia,' *Essays on Karamzin*... 127-47.
117 *Neizdannyia sochineniia* 118; for the outline, see 192-3. Smirdin III 723; *Pis'ma Karamzina k Dmitrievu* 180
118 Serbinovich 'Vospominaniia' 238
119 *Ibid.* 69-70, 245; Smirdin III 688-9. He made this remark in 1804.
120 Catherine Pavlovna had asked him to write the history of recent times. *Neizdannyia sochineniia* 119
121 *History* I (1818) xxvi. An important consequence of his emphasis on unity was that the *History* was not merely an account of the evolution of the Russian state system, but, more specifically, it was a history of the Great Russians. Thus the state and people were synonymous and even the history of the Siberian areas was treated only as a by-product of the expansion of the Russians. On this point, see N.A. Firsov, 'Karamzin ob istorii severovostochnoi Rossii,' *Uchenie zapiski Kazanskogo universiteta* 1 (1867) 28-51 (here 30-1).
122 *Izbrannye sochineniia* I 171-5, 177-8, 181
123 *History* IX (1892) 198; I (1818) xiv
124 '...national spirit ... had served Russia in the days of the pretenders.' *Memoir* 22
125 *Ibid.* 21, 95, 118
126 *Izbrannye sochineniia* II 238-9
127 'Pis'ma Karamzina k V.A. Zhukovskomu,' *Russkii arkhiv* (1869) 1285. In 1802, he translated Herder's *Gespräch über eine unsichtbar-sichtbare Gesellschaft.*

CHAPTER FIVE   THE *HISTORY* AND RUSSIAN SOCIETY
IN THE NINETEENTH CENTURY

1 See Rogger, 'The Uses of Russian History,' in *National Consciousness in Eighteenth Century Russia* 186-252; S.L. Peshtich, *Russkaia istoriografiia XVIII vek* I-III (Leningrad 1961-71); P.D. Erik, 'Prepodavanie istorii v russkoi shkole v XVIII v.,' *Prepodavanie istorii v shkole* 4 (1960) 67-74;

L.L. Dodon, 'Uchebnaia literatura ... i rol' F.I. Iankovicha,' *Ychenye zapiski kafedra pedagogiki* (1955); K.F. Kalaidovich, *Kratkoe nachertanie Rossiiskoi istorii* (Moscow 1814); P. Stroev, *Kratkaia Rossiiskago istoriia, v pol'zu rossiiskago iunoshestva* (Moscow 1814); Schlözer's *Nestor* was first published in German, 1802-5, and then translated into Russian, 1809-16; the official text for Russian schools after 1799 was the *Kratkaia Rossiiskaia istoriia*, written by de Mirievo and in its sixth edition by the time that Karamzin's study appeared. On the *Sinopsis*, see J.L. Black, 'History in the Service of the Russian State: The Seventeenth Century *Sinopsis*,' to appear in a *Festschrift* for J.P. Rudnyckyi, Winnipeg 1975. Two other important textbooks of Russian history were those prepared by Ivan Stritter, *Istoriia Rossiiskago Gosudarstva* Pts I-III (St Petersburg 1800-3), and Catherine II, *Zapiski kasatel'no rossiiskoi istorii* Pts I-III (St Petersburg 1801).

The first eight volumes of the *History of the Russian State* appeared in 1818, even though the frontispieces of the first three volumes cite 1816 and the rest 1817. The ninth appeared in 1821, tenth and eleventh in 1824, and the final volume posthumously in 1829.

2 On this point, see the collected works of the individual authors and S. Petrov, *Russkii istoricheskii roman XIX veka* (Moscow 1964); M.V. Cherepnin, *Istoricheskie vzgliady klassikov russkoi literatury* (Moscow 1968).

3 F.M. Dostoevsky, *Dnevnik pisatelia (1873 g.)* (Moscow-Leningrad 1929) 139; Forrest A. Miller, *Dmitrii Miliutin and the Reform Era in Russia* (New York 1965) 10; N.N. Strakhov, 'Vzdokh na grobe Karamzina,' *Kriticheskie stati (1861-1894)* (Kiev 1902) 205; Solov'ev, *Moi zapiski dlia detei moikh, s esli mozhno i dlia drugikh* (Petrograd 1915) 8-9. The subject of Karamzin's overall influence in nineteenth-century Russian letters is handled in detail by Hans Rothe, 'Karamzin and His Heritage: The History of a Legend,' in *Essays on Karamzin: Russian Man-of-Letters, Political Commentator, Historian, 1766-1826* (The Hague 1974) 148-90. On Kliuchevsky and Karamzin, see the very good recent book by M.V. Nechkina, *Vasilii Osipovich kliuchevskii: Istoriia zhizni i tvorchestva* (Moscow 1974) 63, 64, 67, 117-18, 481-4, 612.

4 L.N. Tolstoi, *Sobranie sochinenii* XIX (Moscow 1965) 120. Similar sentiments were expressed by the peasant folk poet, A.V. Kol'tsov, in a letter to Belinsky in 1839. See *Polnoe sobranie sochinenii A.V. Kol'tsova* (St Petersburg 1909) 194-5.

5 *Sovremennik* II (1836); in the eighties this was still a common practice. See, for example, *Riazanskii voevoda ili smert' Prokopova Liapunov: Istoricheskii povest'* (Moscow 1880), a novel based on volume nine of the *History*.

6 Odoevsky, *Sochineniia* (Moscow 1844) 361

7 Dobroliubov, *Sobranie sochinenii v deviati tomakh* I (Moscow-Leningrad 1961) 144-5; II (1962) 53, 97, 180

8 *Russkii arkhiv* (1872) 1222. For the impression their students had of Karamzin, Kachenovsky, and Solov'ev and others, see the book *Vospominaniia o studencheskoi zhizni* (Moscow 1899); for comments by St Petersburg students, see *Leningradskii universitet v vospominaniakh sovremennikov* I (Leningrad 1963); 'Lektsii F.I. Buslaeva E.H.V. Nasledniku Tsesarevichu Nikolaiu Aleksandrovichu (1859-1860),' *Starina i novizna* X (1905) 1-267, XII (1907) 10-306.

9 *Atlantic Monthly* X (1862) 552

10 N.A. Miller-Krasovsky, *Osnovnye zakony vospitaniia* (St Petersburg 1859) 38. See also 'Pis'ma Dmitrieva k Viazemskomu' 85-6. Ivanchin-Pisarev's book, *Dukh Karamzina ili izbrannye mysli, chuvstvovaniia sego pisatelia* (Moscow 1827), was unfavourably reviewed in *Moskovskii vestnik* 18 (1827) 176-85, and in *Moskovskii telegraf* 13 (1827) 76-81. Ivanchin-Pisarev also printed an epitaph to Karamzin in Polevoi's *Moskovskii telegraf* 12 (1826) 160. See also below, n37.

11 N. Ponomarev, *Materialu dlia bibliografii literatury o N.M. Karamzine: k stoletiiu ego literaturnoi deiatel'nosti (1783-1885)* (St Petersburg 1883) 46-51

12 *Zavoevanie Russi Mongolam* (St Petersburg 1889); *Nashestvie Tatar* (St Petersburg 1897). See also *Razskazy o russkoi starine: Iz Sochineniia Karamzina 'Istoriia gosudarstva Rossiiskago'* (Moscow 1903) and *Pervye russkie kniaz'ia Riurik, Sineus, Truvor', Oleg i Igor* (Moscow 1905).

13 See also Buslaev who recommended the *History* to literature teachers, *O prepodavanii otechestva iazyka* Pt I (Moscow 1844) 143-77. The abridgement of Karamzin's *History* was made by D.A.W. Tappe, as *Sokrashchenie Rossiiskoi istorii N.M. Karamzina* (St Petersburg 1819). The second edition, 1824, was unchanged.

14 Kaidanov, *Nachertanie istorii Gosudarstva Rossiiskago* (St Petersburg 1829) 469 pp. A reviewer for *Atenei* said that the text was based on Karamzin's 'immortal creation' (January 1830, 108-9). Kaidanov wrote a shorter version of the text in 1834. Also in 1829 a *Rodoslovnye vlodotel'nykh kniazei Rossiiskikh* was drawn up from the *History* and included in the general school program for history. *Atenei* reviewed another *Istoriia gosudarstva Rossiiskago* (St Petersburg, 2 pts, 1829), but mentioned no author. It was given unfavourable reviews (January 1830, 196-7). Konstantinov's text, *Uchebnaia kniga istorii gosudarstva Rossiiskago* I-II (St Petersburg 1830), carried Russian history up to the reign of Nicholas I, but its early parts might well have been written by Karamzin. For Uvarov's early regard for history, see his *Prepodavanii istorii otnositel'no k narodnomu vospitaniiu* (St Petersburg 1814).

15 See I. Baikov, *Kratkoe izulechenie iz Istorii gosudarstva Rossiiskogo dlia iunoshestva* (St Petersburg 1830). The notebooks were called *Detskii Karam-*

zina, ili Russkaia Istoriia v kartinakh, edited by A. Prevo (St Petersburg 1835). A second edition came out the next year and another in the same year under a different title, *Zhivopisnyi Karamzin*. They were reviewed in *Biblioteka dlia Chteniia* XIV Pt 6 (1836) 14-15. In 1844, B. Fedorov printed *Russkaia istoriia v kartinakh, dopolenie 'Zhivopisnago Karamzina'* (St Petersburg 1844). Alexandra Ishimova's, *Istoriia rossii v razskazakh dlia detei* 2 pts (St Petersburg 1837), was called an 'abridgement of Karamzin' by a reviewer. Four additional parts were added to it by 1840, and a second edition appeared in 1841. Ishimova also wrote *Pervoe chtenie i pervye uroki dlia malen'kikh detei* (St Petersburg 1856), a second part of which was printed in 1858.

16 Stroev, *Razskazy iz russkoi istorii, dlia detei pervago vozrasta* (St Petersburg 1851)

17 See *Sovremennik* XXV Pt 4 (1851) 25-7.

18 N. Timaev, *Kratkoe izlozhenie russkoi istorii* (St Petersburg 1858), and *Kratkaia russkaia istorii* 2 pts (St Petersburg 1865); Ishimova, *Sokrashchennaia russkaia istoriia* (St Petersburg 1868). *Sviataia Rus': Izvlechennaia iz N.M. Karamzina i dr., Soch. Ia. Tiagunov* (St Petersburg 1872 and 1875). For a partial list of other popular histories and textbooks printed in the 1860s and 1870s, see A.N. Tsamutali, *Ocherki Demokraticheskogo napravleniia v russkoi istoriografii 60-70-x godov XIX v.* (Leningrad 1971) 111-12.

19 The Society for the Dissemination of Useful Books described its purpose as follows: 'having constantly taken care of the spreading of useful and moral studies for people and children [the Society] ... has finally put together a whole series of books,' which they sold to the public. See their advertisement in *Vospominaniia o studencheskoi...* 272. Among Suvorin's many contributions to Karamzinia were the books *Tsarstvovaniia Borisa Fedorovicha i Lzhe-Dmitriia* (St Petersburg 1886) and *Velikii kniazi Dimitrii Ivanovich prosvaiem Donskoi* (St Petersburg 1884), each of which was actually a chapter taken from the *History*. Suvorin also published an entire edition of the *History* in 1888-9. On Suvorin, see E. Ambler, *Russian Journalism and Politics, 1861-1881: The Career of A.S. Suvorin* (New York 1972).

20 Ponomarev 44-5. Pletnev described a geographical study which appeared in 1829 – see *Perepiska Ia. K. Grota s P.A. Pletnevym* 730. There was at least one other taken from Karamzin, made up of forty-eight maps and published in 1824 and 1827. See also *Atlas geograficheskii, istoricheskii i khronologicheskii rossiiskago gosudarstva sostavlennyi na osnovanii istorii N.M. Karamzina* (St Petersburg 1844), by I. Akhmatov. A second edition appeared in 1845.

21 Ponomarev 44. See *Leningradskii universitet v vospominaniakh sovremennikov* 23; *Russkii arkhiv* (1862) 7-8

22 *Atenei* 14/15 (1828) 256. A few years later, Tappe also wrote a *Geschichte Russlands, nach Karamzin* 3 pts (Dresden and Leipzig 1828-31). See A.I.

Turgenev, *Khronika Russkogo: Dnevniki* (Moscow-Leningrad 1964) 287, 530-1.

23 Ponomarev 49. Ponomarev also mentioned an English translation of the *History*, and Artsybashev spoke of one as early as 1828, but neither gave a date, translator, or publisher. In fact, there was no English version. According to Viazemsky, the Russian government sent copies to a number of European libraries and each Russian ambassador carried with him a copy of the *History*. For the translation into Chinese, see Peshtich and I.E. Tsiperovich, '*Istoriia gosudarstva Rossiiskogo* N.M. Karamzina na Kitaiskom iazyke,' *Narody Asii i Afriki* 6 (1968) 125-6. These authors also said that there was an English translation.

24 See *Annual Register*, 'Chronicle' (1826) 253; Dickens, ed., *Household Words* X (1855) 533.

25 Dobroliubov, *Sobranie sochinenii...* III (1962) 255; *Karl Marx-Friedrich Engels Werke* XVI (Berlin 1969) 202.

26 See M. Cadot, *La Russie dans la vie intellectuelle française (1839-1856)* (Paris 1967).

27 *Pis'ma Karamzina k Dmitrievu* 274, 278

28 Studies by Rambaud, Lamartine, and others also demonstrate a reliance upon Karamzin. For the French liberal press, see *Pis'ma Karamzina k Dmitrievu* 198-9. *Revue enclyclopédique* VI (1820) 316-25; XIII (1822) 343-56; XVIII (1823) 119-20. The first two reviews were by Depping and Segur, in that order; the third was an announcement of the translation of the second edition, printed in St Petersburg 1818-21. *Bulletin des sciences historiques* I (1824) 177-8; *Moniteur universel* 306 (1820) Wednesday, 1 November, p 1458; *Journal des débats*, Tuesday, 5 December (1820); Sunday, 10 December; Tuesday, 12 December, all on pages 3-4 of a four-page newspaper. The *History* was also very favourably reviewed in Germany. See *Göttingische gelehrte Anzeigen* II 133/4 (1822) 1321-30. This review was translated into Russian for *Severnyi arkhiv* Pt 4, no. 24 (1822) 486-504. I.I. Dmitriev listed several other sources of favourable reviews, though some of his references seem to have been incorrect (or at least this writer was not able to locate them). See his *Vzgliad na moiu zhizn'* (Moscow 1866) 102-3.

The author is indebted to Mr Jean Desmarais, a colleague in graduate school at McGill University, who located and sent to him several of these reviews from Paris in 1969.

29 *Pis'ma Karamzina k Dmitrievu* 206 (5 February 1817)

30 *Literaturnoe nasledstvo* 59 (Moscow 1954) 565-84

31 *Ibid.* 60 (1956) 301

32 'Zapovedi Karamzinistov,' printed in Shtorm, 'Novoe o Pushkine i Karamzine' *Izvestiia akademii nauk SSSP* XIX 2 (1960) 148-9

33 'Pis'ma Dmitrieva k Viazemskomu' 207
34 *Syn otechestva* 6 (1818) 251. Karamzin was delighted when this journal first
    appeared in 1812. Soon afterwards he wrote Grech and congratulated him for
    the patriotism and talent represented in it (12 November 1813). See 'Dva
    pis'ma N.M. Karamzina k N.M. Grechu,' *Russkii arkhiv* (1869/70) 1723-4.
    The first two editions of the *History* were printed in the Grech typography.
35 As a matter of fact, one of Karamzin's admirers, D.V. Dashkov, complained
    to Dmitriev about the cost of the *History* in 1818, and predicted that it
    would be 'lost to many who could not pay the purchase price.' It sounded
    as if he was trying to obtain a free copy from Karamzin through Dmitriev,
    Russkii arkhiv (1869) 589.
36 *Vestnik evropy* 4 (1818) 307, 309; 18 (1818) 123, 125
37 'Pis'mo k P.I. Sh ... vu,' *Syn otechestva* 42 (1819) 81-6 (see also above, n10).
38 *Vestnik evropy* 17 (1819) 4; 2 (1819) 120, 125-31. Kachenovsky was object-
    ing to Karamzin's treatment of Greek and Roman historians. It is ironic that
    this journal, which was founded by Karamzin, became the vehicle for some
    of the harshest criticism of him, see I.A. Kudriavtsev, '*Vestnik evropy* M.T.
    Kachenovskogo ob *Istorii gosudarstva Rossiiskogo* N.M. Karamzina ,' *Trudy
    Moskovskogo gos. istoriko-arkhivnogo instituta* XXII (1966) 210-49.
39 *Vestnik evropy* 5 (1819) 45-50. In his first article, Kachenovsky had said
    that he would continue Schlözer's work in Russian history. See 'Parallel'nye
    mesta v russkoi letopisi,' *Vestnik evropy* 17 (1809) 133.
40 Miliukov, *Glavnyia techeniia russkoi istoricheskoi mysli* 208-9
41 See J.L. Black, 'The *Primechaniia*: Karamzin as a "Scientific" Historian of
    Russia,' *Essays on Karamzin*... 127-47.
42 *Russkii arkhiv* (1869) 972
43 'Pis'ma Dmitrieva k Viazemskomu' 135 (20 March 1820)
44 *Russkii arkhiv* (1866) 1630-1; Pogodin *N.M. Karamzin, po ego*... II 141
45 *Russkii arkhiv* (1864) 1079
46 I.A. Shliapkin, *Pervyi russkii istorik N.M. Karamzin (1766-1826)* (Petrograd
    1917) 23-4. Shliapkin reported from a series of letters sent by A.I. Turgenev
    to his brother Nicholas and to A.S. Kaiserov, in which he constantly lauded
    Karamzin's historical research. On Nicholas Turgenev's reaction, see *Deka-
    brist N.I. Turgenev: pis'ma k bratu S.I. Turgenevu* (Moscow 1936) 203.
47 *Vestnik evropy* 17 (1819) 4-6
48 *Russkii arkhiv* (1866) 1649 (letter to Dmitriev, July 1820). P.I. Shalikov,
    editor of *Moskovskii vedomosti* (1813-38), imitated Karamzin's sentimen-
    talism but was disliked by Viazemsky and others of Karamzin's friends.
49 'Pis'ma Dmitrieva k Viazemskomu' 206, 131; Solov'ev, *Moi zapiski dlia
    detei*... 144
50 *Syn otechestva* 2 (1821) 76. In telling Dmitriev about this poem, Viazemsky

said that 'Kachenovsky resembles an old man whom everyone respects in Petersburg, but who is afraid of the unknown....' 'Pis'ma Dmitrieva k Via-zemskomu' 140; see also 215-16.

51   *Vestnik evropy* 5 (1821) 39042

52   *Pis'ma Karamzina k Dmitrievu* 276; 'Pis'ma Dmitrieva k Viazemskomu' 136, 140

53   *Vestnik evropy* 20 (1819) 277-302. Some of Karamzin's friends were par-ticularly upset about this criticism because they understood that Karamzin, who mentioned the Pole in the *History* (I 1818 n431), had given him finan-cial help which enabled him to complete his studies. See *Moskvitianin* Pt 1 (1823) 273, and *Pis'ma Karamzina k Dmitrievu* 279, 0129.

54   S. Russov, *O kritike g. Artsybasheva na 'Istoriiu gosudarstva Rossiiskogo,'* *sochinenuiu N.M. Karamzinym* (St Petersburg 1829), and *Obozrenie kritiki Khodakovskogo na 'Istoriiu Rossiiskogo gosudarstva,' soch. N.M. Karamzina* (St Petersburg 1820)

55   M.A. Dmitriev, 'O protivnikh i zashchitnikakh istoriografa Karamzina,' *Atenei* 5 (1829) 535. Russov said, 'will posterity believe that ... there would be such bitterness ... against this immortal creation?' *O kritike Artsybasheva...* 104-5

56   The article from *Severnye tsvety* was discussed in *Atenei* 12 (1828) 410. In the same periodical (*Atenei* 11 [1829] 228), a reviewer of contemporary lit-erature in Russia praised Pushkin for bringing Karamzin's historicism into poetry. See 231.

57   See 'Literaturno-esteticheskie positzii *Poliarnoi zvezdy*' in *Poliarnaia zvezda* (Moscow 1823-25), reprint 1960, 803-84. Gnedich had published a speech in support of some of Shishkov's plans; *Pis'ma Karamzina k Dmitrievu* 078-079. See also K. Serbinovich, 'Zametka ob otnosheniia N.M. Karamzina k A.F. Voeikovy,' *Russkaia starina* 1 (1872) 147-9.

58   *Poliarnaia zvezda* (1960 edition) 17, 270

59   *Russkii vestnik* 87 (1870) 506. Interestingly, P.A. Katenin was critical of Bestuzhev because he regarded him as a 'Karamzinian' in literary style. See Tynianov, *Pushkin...* 54.

60   'Pis'ma Karamzina k Viazemskomu' 149; *Pis'ma Karamzina k Dmitrievu* 413. As he said to Dmitriev: 'Both cavaliers of the *Poliarnaia zvezda* sit in the for-tress.'

61   Miliukov 190

62   *Severnyi arkhiv* 23 (1822) 402-34; 19 (1823) 53-80; 20 (1823) 147-60; 22 (1823) 287-97; 1 (1824) 41-52; 2 (1824) 91-103; 3 (1824) 163-72; 15 (1824) 132-43; 16 (1824) 187-95; 19 (1824) 47-53. See also S.L. Ptashitskii, ed. and commentator, 'Ioakhim Lelevel kak kritik *Istorii gosudarstva Rossiiskago*, soch. Karamzina: perepiska s F.V. Bulgarinym, 1822-1830,' *Russkaia starina*

XXII (1878) 633-56, and F. Mocha, 'The Karamzin-Lelewel Controversy,'
Slavic Review XXXI 3 (1972) 592-610.

63 *Pis'ma Karamzina k Dmitrievu* 342, 368. See also Serbinovich 62-3.

64 *Severnyi arkhiv* 23 (1822) 402-3

65 *Pis'ma Karamzina k Dmitrievu* 342. Pogodin rushed to Karamzin's defence
in 1824, but actually sided with Lelewel by the end of his own review. See
'Nechto protiv oproverzheniia g. Lelevela,' *Vestnik evropy* 5 (1824) 19-29.
Bulgarin's journal carried a translation of a favourable review from Germany
in the next issue (no. 24, 1822) and a refutation of it from Bulgarin himself
in the subsequent one (see above, n28).

66 *Vestnik evropy* 11 (1825) 195-6, 191, 204-5

67 *Moskovskii telegraf* 15 (1825) 234-43

68 Viazemsky, *Polnoe sobranie sochinenii* IX (1884) 89; 'Pis'ma Dmitrieva k
Viazemskomu' 157; *Vestnik evropy* 9 (1826) 70

69 Pogodin, 'Nechto protiv mnenie Karamzina o nachale *Rossiiskago gosudarstva*,'
Moskovskii vestnik Pt 7 (1828) 483-90

70 *Vestnik evropy* 4 (1824) 260, 283; 5 (1824) 19. Pogodin, *Istoriko-kriticheskie
otryvki* Bk I (Moscow 1846) 225-70, 271-306. Karamzin said: 'I sent a letter
to M.P. Pogodin, wishing him all possible success...,' a letter which Pogodin
framed and treasured. See *Pis'ma Karamzina k Dmitrievu* 395, 0169 (17
April 1825).

71 *Vestnik evropy* 17 (1829) 8-10; 18 (1829) 98, 103. On Kachenovsky, besides
the standard works on Russian historiography, see Alexander Bourmeyster,
'M.P. [sic] Kachenovskij, l'école sceptique et le cercle de Stankevic,' *Revue
des études slaves* 45 (1966) 115-28.

72 Stroev, 'Piatoe Pis'mo k izdateliu Moskovskogo vestnika,' *Moskovskii vestnik*
23/24 (1828) 389-95. On Karamzin's permission to Stroev to index the *History*, see *Starina i novizna* (1903) 12. Russov, 'Primechaniia na piatoe pis'mo
k Izdateliu Moskovskoe vestnika,' *Syn otechestva* Pt 123 (1829) 239-41; N.
Polevoi, 'Istoriia gosudarstva Rossiiskago (sochinenie N.M. Karamzina), t.
I-VIII,' *Moskovskii telegraf* Pt 27 (1829) 467-500. Polevoi's *Moskovskii telegraf* was suspended in 1834, after nine years of publication, largely because
he incurred the wrath and suspicion of Uvarov. For an extensive, if incomplete, list of the articles, reviews, and arguments over the *History* which permeated Russia's periodical press during the middle third of the nineteenth
century, see Ponomarev, 109-21.

73 *Moskovskii vestnik* 23/24 (1828) 389-93; *Syn Otechestva* Pt 123 (1829) 239

74 'Byl,' in December issue, 1828; cited in Gillel'son, *P.A. Viazemskii* 167

75 *Vestnik evropy* 12 (1830) 266. In his *Povestvovanie*, see for example, II 29
n208; III 67 n496.

76 *Severnyi arkhiv* Pt 13, no. 1 (1825) 60-84; see also Serbinovich 237.

77 A good example of the character of the arguments between contributors to journals can be seen in 'Zamechanie na zhurnal'nyiu kritiki,' *Atenei* (May 1829) 285-97, which is a very sarcastic survey of the *Syn otechestva, Severnyi arkhiv*, and *Severnyi pchela*. The first-named was founded by Grech in 1812; Voeikov helped him in 1820-1 and Bulgarin became joint editor in 1825. Bulgarin also edited the other two, the third-named with the help of Grech. See also Viazemsky, 'O moskovskikh zhurnalakh' (1830), *Polnoe sobranie sochinenii* II (1879) 121-32.

78 Solov'ev, *Moi zapiski dlia detei...* 88-94; Barsukov, *Zhizn' i trudy M.P. Pogodina* III 288-91

79 See Gilman H. Alkire, 'Gogol and Bulgarin's *Ivan Vyzhigin*,' *Slavic Review* XXVIII 2 (1969) 289.

80 See *Pushkin i pis'makh Karamzinykh, 1836-1837 godov* 11-12. Karamzin had hoped to found a salon himself 'for some kind of pleasant studies, neither conversational or academic, but ... to rationalize.' 'Pis'ma Karamzina k Viazemskomu' 94

81 For Constantine's remark, see 'Zapiski A.I. Mikhailovichago-Danilevskago, 1829 god,' *Russkaia starina* 79 (1893) 202-3. For his letter to Karamzin, see *Russkii arkhiv* (1869) 290-2. Constantine once had had a favourable opinion of Karamzin. In 1810, he had listened to the historiographer read from his manuscript and, according to de Maistre, said that his knowledge of Russian history was limited to information provided by Karamzin. 'Pis'ma Karamzina k Viazemskomu' (14 March 1818) 48

82 Ryleev, *Polnoe sobranie sochinenii* (Leningrad 1934) 458

83 For Pushkin's poem, 'Epigramma,' see *Polnoe sobranie sochinenii* I 341. See also 'Pis'ma Dmitrieva k Viazemskomu' 207. Pushkin wrote another, similar epigram which has not yet been dated. See B.V. Tomashevsky, 'Epigrammy Pushkina na Karamzina,' *Pushkin: Issledovaniia i materialy* 208-15. For Pushkin and Karamzin in general, see Tynianov, 212-17, Toibin, and *Russkaia starina* 25 (1879) 380-7. Even in 1824, when Karamzin and Pushkin were at odds, Pushkin wrote Zhukovsky that 'he loved the Karamzin family dearly.' See 'Tri pis'ma A.S. Pushkina k V.A. Zhukovskomu,' *Russkii arkhiv* (1872) 2357.

For Pushkin's defence of Karamzin against Polevoi, see *Polnoe sobranie sochinenii* VII 130-44, 486-7. A later poem, 'Istoriia sela Goriukhina,' has been regarded as an attempt at interpreting Karamzin's *History*. See N. Strakhov, *Zametka o Pushkin i drugikh poetikh* (St Petersburg 1888) 27. Karamzin, in his turn, bemoaned Pushkin's liberalism: 'serving under the sign of liberalism, he wrote and let out poems on freedom, epigrams on the authorities, etc. The police know this. I fear an investigation. Although for a long time I have exhausted all ways to turn that dissipated head...' (letter to Dmitriev, 19 April 1820).

84 'Pis'ma Karamzina k Viazemskomu' 193
85 *Pis'ma Karamzina k Dmitrievu* 280. 'Pis'ma Dmitrieva k Viazemskomu' 133-4. The witness was V.N. Karazin, who reported the incident in *Syn otechestva* Pt 59, no. 11 (1820) 93.
86 *Bulletin des sciences historiques* I (1824) 177-8
87 Pushkin, *Polnoe sobranie sochinenii* VI (1958) 133; Serbinovich 265; *Dekabrist N.I. Turgenev: Pis'ma k bratu S.I. Turgenevu* 250; Kireevsky, 'Obozrenie russkoi slovestnosti za 1829 god,' *Polnoe sobranie sochinenii* II (1911) 21; *Atenei* 5 (1829) 528; Barsukov, *Zhizn' i trudy M.P. Pogodina* Bk II (St Petersburg 1889) 262; Viazemsky, *Polnoe sobranie sochinenii* II (1911) 21; a good general discussion of these arguments in English can be found in Abbott Gleason, *European and Muscovite: Ivan Kireevsky and the Origins of Slavophilism* (Cambridge, MA 1972) 58-61, 71-2.
88 *Neizdannyia sochineniia* 168. Karamzin gave Nicholas two copies of the *History* in 1818 but, in contrast to Alexander and Constantine, the future emperor did not reply, nor is there any evidence to say that he read them. *Russkii arkhiv* (1869) 1835
89 On Uvarov's position, see N.I. Nadezhdin, 'Ob istoricheskikh trudakh v Rossii,' *Biblioteka dlia Chteniia* XX (1837) 112-18.
90 Barsukov, *Zhizn' i trudy M.P. Pogodina* Bk VI (1892) 301. Nicholas Riazanovsky says that Karamzin provided the inspiration for 'Official Nationality' theories. Yet he goes on to show clearly that Pogodin, Shevyrev, Viazemsky, and others took only what they wanted from Karamzin's writings. See *Nicholas I and Official Nationality in Russia, 1825-1855* 178ff.
91 Dobrovsky reviewed Karamzin's *History* favourably. See *Wiener Jahrbücher der Literatur* 43 (1828). Karamzin, in turn, often spoke highly of the Czech. On Karadžič and Karamzin, see Duncan Wilson, *The Life and Times of Vuk Karadzič, 1787-1864* (Oxford 1970) 136.
92 See Riazanovsky and *Biblioteka dlia Chteniia* I 3 (1834) 21, 34.
93 See especially *History* I (1892) 155-7; III 18; IV 50, 248-9; V 183, 224, 237; VI 222-3.
94 *Starina in novizna* IX (1905) 136
95 *Izbrannye sochineniia* II 238
96 M.O. Koialovich, *Istoriia russkogo samosoznaniia po istoricheskim pamiatnikam i nauchnym sochineniiam* (St Petersburg 1884) 154, 159-61; Kireevsky 19; K.S. Aksakov, *Polnoe sobranie sochinenii* I (Moscow 1889) 48-9; Belinsky said in 1846: 'The influence of Karamzin through his *History of the Russian State* is still very conspicuous. This is best evidenced by the so-called Slavo-

phile party.' For Koshelev's opinion, see O.F. Koshelev, *Biografiia A.I. Kosheleva* I (Moscow 1889) 95-8, 107, 196-8. See also Riazanovsky, *Russia and the West in the Teaching of the Slavophiles* 49, and Abbott Gleason, *European and Muscovite* 48, 58-61.

97 Aksakov 4, 8, 12
98 A.S. Khomiakov, *Polnoe sobranie sochinenii* I (1900) 126-7, 237
99 *Ibid.* 41; III 424-5
100 S.T. Aksakov, *Sobranie sochinenii v piati tomakh* I (Moscow 1966) 5. S.T. Aksakov was the father of K.S. and Ivan Aksakov. With Khomiakov and Ivan and Peter Kireevsky they are usually regarded as the founders of Slavophilism.
101 *Pushkin v pis'makh Karamzinykh...* 22-3
102 See Riazanovksy, *Nicholas I and Official Nationality...* 96-123.
103 *Biblioteka dlia Chteniia* VIII 6 (1834) 50-2
104 N.V. Nikitenko, *Moia povest o samom sebe...* 280
105 Ikonnikov I 84-6. See also N. Ya. Aristov, 'Razrabotka russkoi istorii v poslednia dvadtsat' piat let (1855-1880),' *Istoricheskii vestnik* 4 (1880) 665-80.
106 Dobroliubov, *Sobranie sochinenii* I (Moscow-Leningrad 1948) 293, 351; VII 411; Herzen, *Sobranie sochinenii* VII (Moscow-Leningrad 1956) 60-2; VIII 88; XII 74

CHAPTER SIX KARAMZIN AND 'STATIST' THOUGHT
IN NINETEENTH-CENTURY RUSSIAN HISTORICAL WRITING

1 S.M. Solov'ev, *Moi zapiski dlia detei...* 145
2 'Pis'ma M. Pogodina k kniaziu P.A. Viazemskomu,' *Starina i novizna* Bk 4 (1901) 33, 35, 39, 49. See also Barsukov, *Zhizni i trudy M.P. Pogodina* I (1888) 28-32.
3 *Ibid.* VI 42; *Moskvitianin* 2 (1842) 7; *Russkii arkhiv* (1866) 1766-7
4 Pogodin, *Istoriko-politicheskie pis'ma i zapiski v prodolzhenii voiny...* (Moscow 1874) 7. This comment was in the foreword to the fourth volume of his own collected works.
5 Pogodin, *Istoriko-kriticheskii otryvki* Bk I (Moscow 1846) 21-2
6 *Ibid.* 16; *Istoriko-politicheskie pis'ma ... voiny* 250, 254, 202
7 See especially *Istoriko-politicheskie otryvki* 21-34.
8 Barsukov IV 218; 'Pis'ma Pogodina k Viazemskomu' 76. See also J.L. Black, 'M.P. Pogodin and the "Problem" of Poland,' *Canadian Review of Studies on Nationalism* I 1 (Winter 1974) 60-9.
9 *Dnevnik P.A. Valueva, Ministra Vnutrennikakh del (1861-1876)* II (Moscow 1961) 306-7

10 Pogodin, *Istoriko-kriticheskie otryvki* 57, 63-4

11 See, for example, A. Koyré, *La Philosophie et le problème national en Russie au début du XIXe siècle* (Paris 1929) 122-4. Recent studies on Pogodin include *Slovo o Pogodina: Vospominaniia (Sbornik)* (Moscow 1968), and Ulrich Picht, *M.P. Pogodin und die slavische Frage* (Stuttgart 1970). Pogodin did not accept Karamzin's opinions on the origins of the Russian state, though he was a zealous Normanist. Nor did he agree that Ivan IV consciously achieved anything that could be termed 'great' even in the first half of his reign (*Istoriko-kriticheskie otryvki* 227-62). Neither did he agree with Karamzin's insistence that Godunov had arranged for the murder of the tsarevich Dmitry (*ibid.* 273-305).

12 See Polevoi, *Moskovskii telegraf* (1829) 471, and his *Ocherki russkoi literatury* Pt 2 (St Petersburg 1839) 6. A recent article on Polevoi, which outlines his views on Russian history quite well, is that by A.E. Shiklo, 'Problemy russkoi istorii v osveshchenii N.A. Polevogo,' *Vestnik Moskovskogo Universiteta*, series 9, 'Istoriia,' no. 1 (1973) 74-89.

13 Polevoi said that 'Karamzin ... did not create ... a clear idea of the main conditions in ancient Rus',' *Istoriia russkago naroda* I (Moscow 1829) 39. See also I xlii; II 9-11. The study was in its second edition by 1830.

14 Polevoi, *Moskovskii telegraf* Pt 27, no. 12 (1829) 488

15 Miliukov, *Glavnyia techeniia* 239-40

16 *Moskovskii telegraf* (1829) 472, 476. He praised Karamzin's *History* as a 'remarkable creation,' but said that it was a 'chronicle ... and not history' (467, 486).

17 Polevoi, *Istoriia russkago naroda* I 39; V 9-10; VI 18, 22-3. He had accused Karamzin of writing a history only of princes and tsars. *Ibid.* I xxxvi.

18 *Moskovskii telegraf* (1829), 488; 'Vzgliad na istoriia Rossii,' *Biblioteka dlia Chteniia* I 3 (1834) 92

19 See Polevoi, *Russkaia istorii dlia pervonachal'nago Chtenia* Pt I (Moscow 1835) iv, and *Obozrenie russkoi istorii do edinoderzheniia Petra Velikago* (St Petersburg 1846) xlvii. The first six volumes of Glinka's *Istoriia Russkaia* were printed in *Russkii vestnik* 1812-14; the second edition appeared in ten volumes, Moscow 1817-18. The third edition came out 1818-19, and the fourth in fourteen volumes, 1823-5. For Glinka and Karamzin, see Ia. K. Grot, *N.M. Karamzin i F.N. Glinka: Materialy k biografiiam russkikh pisatelei* (St Petersburg 1903).

20 *Atenei* 17 (1828) 73-4; *Moskvitianin*, Bk I, no. 19 (1850) 137

21 N.V. Savel'ev-Rostislavich, 'O neobkhodimosti kriticheskogo (1842) 36-54. See also his *Slavianskii sbornik* (St Petersburg 1845) cccvii-ccix. Polevoi answered Rostislavich's initial changes in *Russkii vestnik* 2 (1842) 39-40.

22 N.G. Ustrialov, *Russkaia istoriia* I (St Petersburg 1838) 19-20. This study went through five editions between 1839 and 1855.
23 Ustrialov, *O sisteme pragmaticheskoi russkoi istorii* (St Petersburg 1836) 25. The *O sisteme* was also added to his five-part *Russkaia istoriia*. See 2nd edition 1841 (I 155-209). In an introduction to his *Istoriia tsarstvovaniia Petra Velikago* I (St Petersburg 1858) xii-xiv, xxviii, he took exception to Karamzin's views on Peter I as they were expressed in the *Memoir*.
24 *O sisteme* 21-2, 40-4, 52, 60-3. Ustrialov interpreted the final collapse of Poland as a major event in Russian history which allowed the 'return' of former Russian lands to the home of their origin. *Russkaia istoriia* Pt IV (1840) 132. See also his 'Izsledovanie voprosa, kakoe mesto v Russkoi Istorii dolzhno zanimat Velikoe kniazhestvo Litovskoe,' *ibid.* V (1841) 210-34.
25 *O sisteme* 48-78
26 Viazemskii, *Polnoe sobranie sochinenii* II (1879) 211-26; Pushkin, *Polnoe sobranie sochinenii* XII (Moscow 1949) 285-6
27 Gillel'son 242-6
28 Nikitenko, *Moia povest' o samom sebe: Zapiski i dnevnik* (1804-1877 gg) I (St Petersburg 1905) 279-80; Dobroliubov, *Sobranie sochinenii v deviati tomakh* IX (Moscow-Leningrad 1964) 210
29 *Biblioteka dlia Chteniia* 6 (1834) 12-14; 11 (1835) 37; 12 (1835) 6
30 Ustrialov, *Nachertanie Russkoi istorii, dlia srednikh uchebnykh zavedenii* (St Petersburg 1839; 2nd edition) vii-ix. See also his *Rukovodstvo k pervonachal'nomu izucheniiu russkoi istorii* (St Petersburg 1840; 2nd edition) 3. On the title page it was noted that this book was recognized by the minister of public instruction for 'district schools.' See also Uvarov, *Desiatiletie Ministerstva narodnago prosveshcheniia, 1833-1843* (St Petersburg 1864) 97-8.
31 Pogodin, *Nachertanie Russkoi istorii, dlia uchilishch* (Moscow 1835) 117, 125, 322. Pogodin prepared several other texts, the most important among them being *Kratkoe nachertanie russkoi istorii* (Moscow 1838) which at 91 pp. was only one-third the length of his text of 1835. However, the short text retained in their entirety the key ideological sections, including the part on the partitions of Poland (86-9).
32 Ustrialov, *Nachertanie...* 90-1; Pogodin, *Nachertanie...* 126-8
33 D.I. Ilovaisky, *Istoriia rossii* Pt 1 (Moscow 1876) v-vi; see also 6-7. Ilovaisky held the same views as Karamzin and other nineteenth-century Russian historians when it came to the relationship between state and people: 'hence there is a natural and inseparable link in the history of any people with the movement of its state structure. The people's mass is none other than ethographical soil which separates itself from the most active people.' See also

M.N. Pokrovsky, *Istoricheskaia nauka i bor'ba klassov* Pt 1 (Moscow-Leningrad 1933) 123-4 and 22-9.

34 K.N. Bestuzhev-Riumin, *Russkaia istoriia* 2 vols (St Petersburg 1872, 1885) here I 4; 'Nravstvennoe chustvo v "Istorii Karamzina",' *N.M. Karamzin: Ego zhizn' i sochineniia: Sbornik istoriko-literaturnykh statei*, ed. V.I. Pokrovsky (Moscow 1908) 108

35 *Russkaia istoriia* I 97-8, 106-7, 217-18, 220, 278-9; *N.M. Karamzin: Ego zhizn' i sochineniia* 112, 121-4; Bestuzhev-Riumin, 'Karamzin kak istorik,' *Biografii i kharakteristiki* (St Petersburg 1882) 258

36 Ilovaisky, *Istoriia Rossii* 6. The title of his text, which was updated and altered several times, was *Kratkie ocherki russkoi istorii, prisposoblennye k kursu srednikh uchebnykh zavedenii* (Moscow 1860).

37 The most important study to date on the 'State School' is that by Klaus-Detlov Grothusen, *Die Historische Rechtsschule Russlands* (Giessen 1962). For the problem of definition and vagueness of terms, see Grothusen 44-7. See also J.L. Black, 'The "State School" Interpretation of Russian History: A Reappraisal of Its Genetic Origins,' *Jahrbücher für Geschichte Osteuropas* Bd 21, no. 4 (1973) 509-30, from which much of the subsequent material in this chapter has been summarized.

38 That the individuals associated with this school of thought constantly argued with each other is clearly demonstrated in Kavelin's criticisms of Solov'ev and Chicherin. *Sobranie sochinenii* I (St Petersburg 1897) 253-308, 507-70. For Solov'ev's rebuttal, see his *Istoriia rossii* Bk I, Vol. II (Moscow 1962) 673-6. In general, however, Kavelin was Solov'ev's greatest supporter. Their disagreements tended to stem from the fact that Solov'ev leaned towards Slavophilism in philosophy, although he attacked that intellectual trend in print. For Solov'ev's own statement to the effect that they had an historical interpretation in common, see 'Iz neizdannykh bumag S.M. Solov'eva,' *Russkii vestnik* 4 (1896) 2.

39 The nineteenth-century scholar, V.O. Kliuchevsky, and the Soviet historian, Illeritsky, both complained about the fatalism implicit in State School writing. Surprisingly, it was the conservative Kliuchevsky in 1862, rather than Illeritsky a century later, who lamented the fact that his friend and mentor, Solov'ev, 'even defended Muscovite centralism and with it unpardonable despotism and petty tryanny.' See Kliuchevsky, *Pis'ma, dnevniki, aforizma i mysli ob istorii* (Moscow 1968) 67 (in a letter to P.P. Gvozdev, January 1862), and M.V. Nechkina, *Kliuchevskii* (Moscow 1974) 16-20, 29-33, 165-68, 532-4.

40 Miliukov, 'Iuridicheskaia shkola v russkoi istoriografii (Solov'ev, Kavelin, Chicherin, Sergeevich),' *Russkaia mysl'*, no. 6, section 2 (1886) 80-1

41 N.I. Rubinshtein said that 'Schlözer and Karamzin represent two different directions in the growth of Russian historical science at the end of the 18th century.' *Russkaia istoriografiia* (Moscow 1941) 150. See also Miliukov, *Glavnyia techeniia* 207, and Grothusen 23.

42 *History* I (1818) xv. V.S. Ikonnikov, 'L. Ranke o trude N.M. Karamzina,' *Chteniia v istoricheskom obshchestve Nestora letopistsa* Bk VI 4 (1902) 77. See also Pogodin, *N.M. Karamzin, po ego...* II 20-6, 54-5.

43 'Pis'ma Karamzina k Turgenevu' 231; Schlözer, *Nestor* III 33, 37, 40; IV v, xxxii, xxxvii

44 On Karamzin as researcher, see J.L. Black, 'The *Primechaniia*: Karamzin as a "Scientific" Historian of Russia,' *Essays on Karamzin...* 127-47. His high re-gard for Krug was made plain in correspondence with Turgenev and in foot-notes to the *History*. As a matter of fact, Karamzin posted manuscripts of the *History* to Krug for examination before they were published. On sending the first volume in 1817, he requested Krug to read it with 'pencil in hand,' commented later that 'each line of your pen is precious to me,' and once wrote that Krug had been enthusiastic about the final product. The opinion of Krug, if indeed that was his opinion, carried some weight. A student of Schlözer's at Göttingen, Krug followed his master's method for criticism and was considered to be one of the finest scholars in Russia by the statist Kavelin. See W. Stieda, 'Nikolai Mikhailovich Karamzin und Johann Philipp Krug,' *Zeitschrift für slavische Philologie* Bd 3 (1926) 281-90.

45 The earliest specific comment to this effect that I have found was that by N. Kalachov in 1876, when he said that Ewers 'was the founder of the historico-juridical school,' a name often used for the statists in the nine-teenth century. See *Arkhiv istoriko-iuridicheskikh svedenii otnosiashchsia do Rossii* Bk I, section 5 (St Petersburg 1876) 11. M.V. Nechkina repeated it in 1927, in one of the few articles written on Ewers, 'Gustav Evers,' in *Russkaia istoricheskaia literatura v klassovom osveshcheniia* I, ed. M.N. Pokrovsky (Moscow 1927-30) 21.

46 *Sobranie sochinenii K.D. Kavelina* I 1006-7; Solov'ev, *Istoriia Rossii* Bk I Vol. I 315; Solov'ev, *Moi zapiski dlia detei...* 60

47 Ewers's works included *Vom Ursprunge des russischen Staats* (Riga and Leipzig 1808); *Kritische Vorarbeiten zur Geschichte der Russen* 2 vols (Dor-pat 1814), which was translated into Russian as *Predvaritel'nye kriticheskie issledovaniia G. Eversa dlia rossiiskoi istorii* (Moscow 1825-6); *Geschichte der Russen* (Dorpat 1816), which was not translated into Russian and a planned second volume of which never appeared. *Das älteste Recht der Russen in seiner geschichtlichen Entwicklung* (Dorpat and Hamburg 1826) was dedicated to A.S. Shishkov and translated into Russian by Ivan Platonov in 1835.

48 See 'Pis'ma Karamzina k Turgenevu' 94, 230; Smirdin III 713-17.
49 Nechkina 28-9. Ewers was no friend of Schlözer's and published an 'unpleasant recollection' of him in 1818. See *Unangenehme Erinnerung an August Ludwig Schlözer* (Dorpat 1818).
50 Ewers, *Das älteste Recht der Russen* 1, 69, 82-3, 130, 192, 202-3, 271-3, 310-11; Schlözer, *Nestor* II (1816) 182-95, 205; Karamzin, *History* I (1818) 54-113 n271.
51 See above, chapter 4, 105, 107; *History* I (1818) 73-8.
52 *Ibid.* xxvi-xxvii
53 *Russkii arkhiv* (1866) 1768
54 See 'Nestor i Karamzin: opyt obstoiatel'nago uiasneniia nekotorye dannykh v Istoriia gosudarstva Rossiiskago,' translated from the German by A. Naumov, *Arkhiv istoriko-iuridicheskikh svedenii...* (1876) 1-46. At least one statist, Solov'ev, defended Karamzin from Ewers's supporters, saying that the *Studien* had been mistaken in several places, and that Karamzin had been correct. See Solov'ev, *Istoriia Rossii* Bk I, Vol. I (1962) n261.
55 Solov'ev, *Moi zapiski dlia detei...* 60; Kavelin, *Sobranie sochinenii* I 949
56 *Sobranie sochinenii S.M. Solov'eva* (St Petersburg 1901) 1389-99. Solov'ev tried to gain government support for his project in the same way that Karamzin had done, but the government, too, thought that a new study on Russian history was superfluous. *Moi zapiski dlia detei...* 143
57 Solov'ev, *Istoriia Rossii s drevneishikh vremen*, published in 29 volumes, 1851-79. All citations used here are from the reprinted version (Moscow 1962-6).
58 *Sobranie sochinenii S.M. Solov'eva* 1434, 1438-9, 1465
59 *Ibid.* 1439; see also 1402-3, 1470.
60 Solov'ev, *Moi zapiski dlia detei...* 60. For Solov'ev's general outlook on life and history, see Grothusen, 'S.M. Solov'evs Stellung in der russischen Historiographie,' *Forschungen zur Osteuropäischen Geschichte* Bd IV (1956) 7-103.
61 *Sobranie sochinenii S.M. Solov'eva* 1122-3.
62 Solov'ev, *Moi zapiski dlia detei...* 55-6, 88-94
63 *Sobranie sochinenii S.M. Solov'eva* 797-902; *Istoriia Rossii*, Bk V, Vol X 10-11; Grothusen, *Historische Rechtsschule* 83.
64 *Sobranie sochinenii S.M. Solov'eva* 1-235. He referred elsewhere to the uselessness of weak governments, especially when speaking of the French Revolution. See *Istoriia Rossii* Bk VII Vol. XIV 440.
65 Besides his study on the fall of Poland which, though the weakest of his scholarly enterprises, was immediately translated into German, see *Istoriia Rossii* Bk XIV, Vol. XXVIII 608-11; Bk VIII, Vol. XVI 437-44; Bk XIII Vol. XXV 151; Vol. XXVI 434ff; *Sobranie sochinenii S.M. Solov'eva* 1516.

66 *Ibid.* 1447, 1415, 1402-4
67 *Ibid.* 1420-2, 1406, 1453
68 *Ibid.* 794
69 *Ibid.* 797-902; *Istoriia Rossii* Bk V Vol. X 10-11; Bk I Vol. I 130-55
70 *Sovremennik* Vol. XXIX section 2 (1851) 46-8
71 *History* X (1892) 232-3, 238-9; Solov'ev, *Istoriia Rossii* Bk III Vol. VI 714-24; Kavelin, *Sobranie sochinenii* I 570-1. See also N.A. Firsov, 'Karamzin ob istorii severvostochnoi Rossii,' *Uchenie zapiski Kazanskago universiteta* 1 (1867) 28-51.
72 G.Z. Elizeev, 'Istoricheskie-ocherki,' *Sovremennik* Vol. LXXX no. 11, section 3 (1860) 68; K.S. Aksakov, *Polnoe sobranie sochinenii* I (Moscow 1861) 253-4. The similarity was a!so noted by V. Zavitnevich in 'Osnovaia ideia truda N.M. Karamzina i ego vospitel'noe znachenie,' *Chteniie v Istoricheskom obsh-chestve Nestora letopistsa* Bk 16, issue 4 (1902) 76. On Elizeev, who wrote under the pseudonym 'Grytsko,' see Tsamutali, *Ocherki demokraticheskogo napravlenniia v russkoi istoriografii* 20-65
73 Solov'ev, *Uchebnaia kniga russkoi istorii* (Moscow 1880) 8th edition 393. This text went through fourteen editions after 1859, the final one appearing in 1915. Near the end of his career, Solov'ev prepared another general text on Russian history for youngsters, *Obshchedostupnye chteniia o russkoi istorii* (Moscow 1874), which was a popularized history of Russia's princes. Elpat'ev-sky's text, *Uchebnik russkoi istorii* (St Petersburg 1892), was in its fourteenth edition by 1915 as well. Victor Abaza's two textbooks were *Istoriia Rossii, narodnoe izdanie* (St Petersburg 1885) and *Rukovodstvo o otechestvennoi istorii* (St Petersburg 1889).
74 Kavelin, *Sobranie sochinenii* I 949-50, 269; on Kachenovsky, see 100-2.
75 Particularly in his contribution to the 'science of self-consciousness,' *ibid.* 262-3
76 *Ibid.* 947-50, 224
77 *Russkii arkhiv* (1872) 467, 2465-6; *Sochineniia I. Zabelina* Pt I (Moscow 1895) 3rd edition 10-11
78 Kavelin, *Sobranie sochinenii* I 25-6, 35, 39, 41-3. He also specifically refuted Solov'ev's contentions about the role of the Tatars in Russian history, *ibid.* 282; for Solov'ev on Ivan III, see *Istoriia Rossii* Bk III Vol. V 7-8. The Soviet historian, Sakharov ('Iz istorii' 79), probably would not have drawn the same conclusions about Karamzin if he had read carefully *History* V (1818) 345; VI (1892) 217-19, 230; VII (1892) 19, 74, 77. Still one of the best overviews of Kavelin's scheme for Russian history is that by V.A. Miakotin, 'K.D. Kavelin i ego vzgliady na russkuiu istoriiu,' *Russkoe bogatstve* 2 (1898) 96-115.
79 *Sobranie sochinenii S.M. Solov'eva* 970
80 *Ibid.* 1122-3, 1126

81 *Ibid.* 1123-4, 971, 7

82 Kavelin, *Sobranie sochinenii* I 280-1, 294; II 938

83 Solov'ev, *Moi zapiski dlia detei...* 144; *Sobranie sochinenii S.M. Solov'eva* 1008

84 *Ibid.* 6, 677-8, 1123; *Istoriia Rossii* Bk VII Vol. XIV 440

85 Solov'ev, *Moi zapiski dlia detei...* 116-17, 158-9

86 Pogodin, *Istoriko-politicheskie pis'ma ... voiny* 257-8

87 See Darrell P. Hammer, 'Two Russian Liberals: The Political Thought of B.N. Chicherin and K.D. Kavelin' (unpublished PHD dissertation, Columbia University 1962) 57, 63. On Kavelin's early liberalism, see Sh. M. Levin, 'K.D. Kavelin o smerti Nikolaia I,' *Literaturnoe nasledstvo* Vol. LXVII (1959) and Daniel Field, 'Kavelin and Russian Liberalism,' *Slavic Review* XXXII 1 (March 1973) 59-78. Solov'ev, too, had detested the despotism of Nicholas's reign. See *Moi zapiski dlia detei...* 116-24.

88 Kavelin, *Sobranie sochinenii* I 637; Kavelin, 'O nigilizme i merakh, protiv nego neobkhodimykh,' *Istoricheskii arkhiv* V (1950) 327

89 See Kavelin's letter to T.N. Granovsky (5 September 1848), *Literaturnoe nasledstva* LXVII (1959) 596; *Istoricheskii arkhiv* V 340; Kavelin, *Sobranie sochinenii* I 512-13, 568-9.

90 *Ibid.* 45, 280. For general information, see *Pis'ma K. Dm. Kavelina i Iv. S. Turgeneva k Al. Iv. Gertsenu,* ed. M. Dragomanov (Geneva 1892), and Hammer 122-85.

91 Solov'ev, '*Istoriia gosudarstva Rossiiskago,* kak vyrazitel'nitsa narodnago zamosoznaniia' in *N.M. Karamzin: Ego zhizn' i sochineniia* 118. See also 'Istoricheskiia pominki po istorike,' *Moskovskii vedomnosti* 254 (1866) 19-20 and *Istoriia Rossii* Bk VII, Vol. XIII 8.

92 Kavelin, *Sobranie sochinenii* I 597-8, 569

93 Solov'ev, *Istoriia Rossii* Bk VII Vol. XIV 440-1. See also 122. On the great man theme and Karamzin, see 'Das Genie in der Geschichte' in Rothe, *N.M. Karamzins europäische reise...* 402-8.

94 *Sobranie sochinenii S.M. Solov'eva* 971, 1916; Karamzin, *Izbrannye sochineniia* II 238

95 *Ibid.* 239; Solov'ev, *Istoriia Rossii* Bk VII Vol. XIV 441

96 *Ibid.* Bk XII Vol XXIV 637

97 *Sobranie sochinenii S.M. Solov'eva* 1497, 1538; Kavelin, *Sobranie sochinenii* I 59, 594-5

98 *Ibid.* 569-84

99 See, for example, *History* III (1892) 125-30, 134; IV 107, 122-3; V 230-5.

100 Solov'ev, *Istoriia Rossii* Bk I Vol. I 257; Karamzin, *History* V (1892) 235. See also 232-5; Kavelin, *Sobranie sochinenii* I 42-3; Chicherin, *O narodnom predstavitel'stve* (Moscow 1866) 361. V.I. Sergeevich, a later member of the

State School, also placed special stress on the *yarlyks* and credited the Tatars for the 'first attempt at political union in Russia.' *Drevnosti russkago prava* II (St Petersburg 1908) 34-8, 252-6

101 D.I. Chizhevsky, *Gegel' v Rossii* (Paris 1939) 288; Chicherin, *Opyty po istorii russkago prava* (Moscow 1858) 371; and *Nauka i Religiia* (Moscow 1879) 63, 512-16. A recent general book on the subject of Hegelianism in Russia is A.N. Volodin, *Gegel' i russkaia sotsialisticheskaia mysl' XIX veka* (Moscow 1973).

102 Chicherin, *Oblastnye uchrezhdeniia v Rossii v XVII veke*. The essay, which appeared in *Russkii vestnik* in 1856, was reprinted in his collection *Opyty po istorii russkago prava*. The latter volume was dedicated to Kavelin. These two books aroused the Slavophiles to action, with I.D. Beliaev leading the assault. Solov'ev and Kavelin continued their defence of Chicherin, and the journals *Russkii beseda, Russkii vestnik*, and *Otechestva zapiski* resounded with their polemics between 1856 and 1858. In these same years, Peter Lavrov began publishing articles on Hegelianism, in which he criticized the dogmatism and acceptance of authority which it represented. Lavrov was therefore also chastising the Statists, although Kavelin was still to support him in vain for the Chair of Philosophy at the University of St Petersburg in 1862. See *Biblioteka dlia Chteniia* 4 and 9 (1858), 4 and 5 (1859) for Lavrov's essays; Nikitenko, *Dnevnik* 175.

103 Chicherin, *Opyty po istorii russkago prava* 369; *O narodnom predstavitel'stve* 389, 482

104 Chicherin, *Nauka i religiia* 125

105 Chicherin, *Opyty po istorii russkago prava* 175, 380; *O narodnom predstavitel'stve* 361; Herzen, *Sobranie sochinenii* XIX (Moscow 1958) 120, 149.

106 Kavelin, *Sobranie sochinenii* I 916

107 Chicherin, *Opyty po istoriia russkago prava* 10-11, 285, 380

108 Chicherin, *O narodnom predstavitel'stve* 282-300, 393-5, 494-5; *Vospominaniia Borisa Nikolaevicha Chicherina: Moskva sorokovykh godov* I (Moscow 1929) 163; Herzen, *Sobranie sochinenii v tridtsati tomakh* XIII (Moscow 1938) 597-9

109 V.O. Kliuchevsky, *Pis'ma, Dnevniki aforizmy i mysli ob istorii* 42, 52; *Vospominaniia B.N. Chicherina: Moskovskii universitet* (Moscow 1929) 22; *Vospominaniia B.N. Chicherina: Puteshestvie za granitsa* (Moscow 1932) 28

110 Chicherin, *Opyty po istorii russkago prava* 369

111 *Ibid.* 285, 389; *O narodnom predstavit'stve* 359, 387; *Vospominaniia ... Moskovskii universitet* III 114

112 Kavelin, *Sobranie sochinenii* I 202-2; Chicherin, *Ocherki Anglii i Frantsii* (Moscow 1858) 160

113 Kavelin, *Sobranie sochinenii* 565, 574, 581, 577

114 Chicherin, *O narodnom predstavitel'stve* 412-13
115 Solov'ev, 'Drevnaia Rossii,' *Sobranie sochinenii S.M. Solov'eva* 795; see also 6.
116 Solov'ev, *Istoriia Rossii* Bk XII Vol. XXIV 637-8
117 See G.W.F. Hegel, *The Philosophy of History*, trans. T.M. Knox (Chicago 1952). Besides Chizhevsky on Hegel in Russia, see Boris Jakowenko, 'Hegel in Russland,' *Der Russische Gedanke: Internationale Zeitschrift* II 3 (1931) 1-8. See also Walter Kaufmann, *Hegel: a Reinterpretation* (New York 1966).
118 Solov'ev, *Moi zapiski dlia detei...* 158, 180; *Istoriia Rossii* Bk IV Vol. VII 296-7; Bk VII Vol. XIII 105-6
119 'Pis'ma K.D. Kavelina- K.K. Grotu (1862-1883),' *Russkaia starina* 92 (1899) 140, 148, 377. Chicherin, *O narodnom predstavitel'stve* 355-7.
120 *Sobranie sochinenii S.M. Solov'eva* 1123; Chicherin, *O narodnom predstavitel'stve* 399

CONCLUSION

1 Viazemsky, *Polnoe sobranie sochinenii* I (1878) 321; O.F. Koshelev, *Biografiia Aleksandra Ivanovich Kosheleva* I (Moscow 1889) 107

Glossary of Russian Terms

appanage: the ancient system of dividing the lands equally among the great prince's sons, who then would succeed to the more desirable principalities as they gained seniority within the ruling family

Boyars: great nobles, or descendants of the former princely families who once had been independent of the great princes in Kiev and Moscow

duma: assembly

druzhina: military retinue of the early princes

dvoriane: (*dvorianstvo*) lesser nobility, landowning gentry, originally the service nobility

Guberniia: province

kolokol: bell, used to call the *veche*, or tribal assembly

muzhik: common man, peasant

obrok: cash payment, made by some serfs to landlord in lieu of labour

Oprichnina: the personal domain set up by Ivan IV as a base from which to destroy an alleged plot on the part of the nobility to seize his throne. Policed by *oprichniki*, sixteenth-century versions of military police responsible only to the ruler, the *Oprichnina* was not subject to the general administration.

otdel: department

pomest'e: an estate held in service tenure only

Raskolniki: dissidents who broke from the Orthodox Church in the seventeenth century; Old Believers

raznochintsy: educated middle, or humbler class; intelligentsia who were not from the nobility

rodovoi byt: tribal existence

Russkaia Pravda: Russian Truth, ancient laws

Stepennaia kniga: sixteenth century historical book, mainly a genealogy of the princes

udel: see appanage

ukaz: decree

veche: ancient tribal assembly, which had the right to elect princes

voevoda: an appointed governor in mediaeval Russia.

votchina: hereditary estate

yarlyk: Tatar decree or commission giving Russian princes specific powers or duties

Select Bibliography

Because there have been so many studies on Karamzin published over the last two centuries, this bibliography necessarily is a selective one. In the first place, it contains works that deal exclusively with Karamzin. The vast literature on such individuals as Pogodin, Pushkin, Uvarov, S.M. Solov'ev, Kavelin, Chicherin, Viazemskyi, Zhukovsky, and many others who figure prominently in the book has been left to the notes. Russian-language studies on Karamzin have been included only if they are recent and relative to the topic at hand. The key Russian-language general works and the memoirs of such people as M.A. Dmitriev, N.I. Grech, F.N. Glinka, A.S. Griboedov, A.I. Turgenev, Ivan Dmitriev, P.A. Viazemsky, D.N. Bludov, Catherine Pavlovna, de Maistre, A.V. Nikitenko, and others of Karamzin's contemporaries can also be found only in the notes.

Thus, this list encompasses bibliographical sources, biographical works, and a résumé of Karamzin's own published works and letters. A list of recent books and articles on Karamzin in the Western languages, with a few Russian-language additions, follows. For further interest, a list of Karamzin's works which have been translated into English, and where to find them, accompanies the bibliography.

A BIBLIOGRAPHICAL WORKS

Bibliografiia russkoi bibliografii po istorii SSSR: *Annotirovannyi perechen' bibliograficheskikh ukazatelei, izdannykh do 1917 g.* (Moscow 1957)

Black, J.L. 'The Soviets and the Anniversary of N.M. Karamzin' *The New Review: A Journal of East European History* VIII (October 1968) 139-47

Cross, A.G. 'Karamzin Studies: For the Bicentenary of the Birth of N.M. Karamzin (1766-1966)' *Slavonic and East European Review* XLV 104 (1967) 1-11

Istoriia russkoi literatury XVIII veka: Bibliograficheskii ukazatel' ed. V.P. Stepanov, Ju. V. Stennik and P.N. Berkov (Leningrad 1968)
Istoriia russkoi literatury XIX veka: Bibliograficheskii ukazatel' ed. K.D. Muratovoi (Moscow-Leningrad 1962)
Istoriia istoricheskoi nauki v SSSR: dooktoiabr'skii period: Bibliografiia (Moscow 1965)
Garrard, J.G. 'Karamzin in Recent Soviet Criticism: A Review Article' *Slavic and East European Journal* XL (January 1967) 464-72
Mezhov, V.I. *Jubilei Lomonosova, Karamzina i Krylova: Bibliograficheskii ukazatel' knig i statei, vyshedshikh po povodu etikh jubileev* (St Petersburg 1871)
Ponomarev, S.I. *Materialy dlia bibliografii literatury o N.M. Karamzine: k stoletiiu ego literaturnoi deiatel'nosti (1783-1883)* (St Petersburg 1883)
Rothe, Hans 'Die Entwicklung der Karamzinforschung seit ihren Anfängen' *Zeitschrift für slavische Philologie* XXXIV 1 (1968) 129-48; XXXIX 2 (1969) 385-96
Vengerov, S.A. *Istochniki slovaria russkikh pisatelei* II (St Petersburg 1910)

B BIOGRAPHICAL WORKS
Bulich, N.N. 'Biograficheskii ocherk N.M. Karamzina i razvitie ego literaturnoi deiatel'nosti' in *Simbirskii jubilei Nikolaia Mikhailovicha Karamzina: 1 dekabria 1766-1866 goda* (Simbirsk 1867) 37-143
Grot, Ja. K. 'Karamzin v istorii russkogo literaturnogo iazyka' *Trudy Ja. K. Grota* II (St Petersburg 1899) 46-98
Longinov, M. 'Nikolai Mikhailovich Karamzin: biograficheskii ocherk,' *Moskovskaia universiteta izvestiia* 3 (1867) 228-40
Pogodin, M.P. *N.M. Karamzin, po ego sochineniiam, pis'mam i otsyvam sovremennikov: Materialu dlia biografii* 2 vols (Moscow 1866)
Shugarov, M. 'Eshche o gode rozhdeniia Karamzina,' *Russkii arkhiv* (1866) 1504-7
Sipovskii, V. 'O predkakh Karamzina,' *Russkii starina* XCIII (1898) 431-5
Starchevskii, A. *Nikolai Mikhailovich Karamzin* (St Petersburg 1849)
Tikhonravov, N.S. 'Chetyre goda iz zhizni Karamzina, 1785-1788' *Russkii vestnik* 4 (1862) 732-49

C KARAMZIN: PUBLISHED WORKS AND CORRESPONDENCE
'Al'bom N.M. Karamzin (napisannyi dlia kn. Ekaterinu Pavlovnu 1811)' *Letopisi russkoi literatury i drevnosti* I Bk 2 (Moscow 1859) 161-92
Detskoe Chtenie dlia serdtsa i razuma vols 9-15, 17-18 (Moscow 1787-9)
[2nd edition, Moscow 1819]
'Dva pis'ma N.M. Karamzina k V.V. Izmailovu' *Russkii arkhiv* (1869) 599-600

'Imperator Nikolai Pavlovich i Karamzin v poslednie ego dni, ikh perepiska'
    Russkii arkhiv (1906) 122-7
'Iz bumag Karamzina' *Starina i novizna* Bk 2 (St Petersburg 1898) 1-26
    [extracts from *Neizdannyia sochineniia ... Karamzina*]
Karamzin, N.M. *Istoriia gosudarstva Rossiiskago* 12 vols (St Petersburg 1818-29).
    For the purpose of this book, I used a microfiched copy of the original and
    bound copies of the editions of 1892 and 1897.
– *Izbrannye proizvedeniia* ed. Vl. Murav'ev (Moscow 1966)
– *Izbrannye sochineniia N.M. Karamzina* Pt I ed. Lev Polivanov (Moscow 1884)
– *Izbrannye sochineniia Karamzina* 2 vols (Moscow-Leningrad 1964)
– *Polnoe sobranie stikhotvorenii* I ed. Iu. Lotman (Moscow-Leningrad 1966)
– *Sochineniia Karamzina* 3 vols, ed. A. Smirdin (St Petersburg 1848)
– *Sochineniia* 9 vols (Moscow 1820) 3rd edition
– *Zapiska o drevnei o novoi Rossii* ed. Richard Pipes (Cambridge, MA 1959)
Moskovskii zhurnal ed. N.M. Karamzin (Moscow 1791-2), 2nd edition
    (Moscow 1802-3)
Neizdannyia sochineniia i perepiska Nikolai Mikhailovicha Karamzina ed.
    K.S. Serbinovich (St Petersburg 1862)
'N.M. Karamzin-general-ad'iutantu P.V. Golenishchevu-Kutuzova,' *Russkaia
    starina* LXXVIII (1893) 632
Panteon inostrannoi slovestnosti 3 vols, ed. N.M. Karamzin (Moscow 1798)
    [2nd edition, Moscow 1818]
'Perepiska Karamzina s Lafaterom, 1786-1790,' *Zapiski imperatorskoi akademii
    nauk* LXXIII Bk 1 (St Petersburg 1893) appendix I, 1-67
Perevody Karamzina vols 7-9 (St Petersburg 1834-5)
*Pis'ma N.M. Karamzina k A.F. Malinovskomu i pis'ma A.S. Griboedova k S.N.
    Begichevu* ed. M.N. Longinov (Moscow 1860)
'Pis'ma N.M. Karamzina k A.I. Turgenevu 1806-1825' *Russkaia starina* XCVII
    (1899) 211-38, 463-80, 707-16; XCVIII (1899) 225-38
'Pis'ma A.M. Kutuzova' *Russkii istoricheskii zhurnal* Bk 1 (1917) 131-40
'Pis'ma N.M. Karamzina k V.N. Karazinu, 1818 g.' *Russkaia starina* 3 (1900)
    684, 4 (1900) 138
'Pis'ma Karamzina k D.N. Bantysh-Kamenskomu' *Russkaia starina* LIV (1871)
    525-8
'Pis'ma Karamzina k E.F. Murav'evoi,' *Russkii arkhiv* 3 (1867) 455-66
Pis'ma N.M. Karamzina k I.I. Dmitrievu ed. Ja. Grot, P.P. Pekarsky (St Peters-
    burg 1866)
'Pis'ma N.M. Karamzina k kniaziu P.A. Viazemskomu (1810-1826),' *Starina
    i novizna* Bk 1, section 1 (St Petersburg 1897) 1-20
'Pis'ma N.M. Karamzina k grafu S.P. Rumiantsevu' *Russkii arkhiv* (1869) 587-99
'Pis'ma N.M. Karamzina k S.S. Uvarovu' *Syn otechestva* XLIV 8 (1818) 79-80

'Pis'ma N.M. Karamzina k S.S. Uvarovu' ed. M.I. Gillel'son *XVIII vek: sbornik 8*
(1969) 351-4
'Pis'ma N.M. Karamzina k V.A. Zhukovskomu,' *Russkii arkhiv* (1869) 1383-6,
1827-36, (1870) 1682-90, (1875) 493-497, (1900) 5-54
'Pis'mo N.M. Karamzina k P.M. Stroevu,' in N. Barsukov *Zhizni' i trudy P.M.
Stroeva* (St Petersburg 1878) 46, 48-53
'Pis'mo N. Karamzina k popechiteliu Vilenskogo universiteta kniaziu A. Char-
toryiskomu' *Russkaia literatura* 2 (1967) 116
'Poslednie snosheniia N.M. Karamzina s N.I. Novikovym. Ikh perepiska 1816 g.'
Russkii arkhiv (1890) 367-75

D RECENT BOOKS AND ARTICLES ON KARAMZIN
Anderson, Roger B. 'The "Split Personality" of the Narrator in N.M. Karamzin's
Pis'ma Russkogo puteshestvennika: A Textual Analysis' *Études slaves et est
européenes* XIII (1968) 20-31
– 'Karamzin's Concept of Linguistic "Cosmopolitanism" in Russian Literature'
Studies by Members of SCMLA, XXXI 4 (Winter 1971) 168-70
– 'Karamzin's 'Bornholm Island': Its Narrator and Its Meaning' *Orbis Litterarum*
XXVIII (1973) 204-15
– 'Karamzin's *Letters of a Russian Traveller:* An Education in Western Sentimen-
talism' in J.L. Black, ed. *Essays on Karamzin: Russian Man-of-Letters, Political
Commentator, Historian, 1766-1825* (The Hague 1974) 22-39
Bächtold, R. *Karamzins Weg zur Geschichte* (Basel 1946)
Bittner, Konrad 'Der junge N.M. Karamzin und Deutschland' *Herderstudien* X
(1960) 81-94
– 'Herdersche Gedanken in Karamzins Geschichtsschau' *Jahrbücher für
Geschichte Osteuropas* VII Pt 3 (1959) 237-69
Black, J.L. 'N.M. Karamzin's Views on Peter the Great' *The New Review:
A Journal of East European History* VI (December 1966) 20-37
– 'Karamzin's Scheme for Russian History' in *Eastern Europe: Historical Essays*
ed. H.C. Schlieper (Toronto 1969) 16-33
– 'Karamzin, Napoleon and the Notion of 'Defensive War' in Russian History,'
Canadian Slavonic Papers XII (January 1970) 30-46
– 'Interpretations of Poland in Nineteenth Century Russian Nationalist-
Conservative Historiography' *The Polish Review* XVII 4 (Autumn 1972) 20-42
[on Karamzin, Pogodin, and Solov'ev]
– 'The "State School" Interpretation of Russian History: A Reappraisal of Its
Genetic Origins' *Jahrbücher für Geschichte Osteuropas* XXI (1973) 509-30
– 'The *Primechaniia*: Karamzin as a "Scientific" Historian of Russia' in J.L.
Black, ed. *Essays on Karamzin: Russian Man-of-Letters, Political Commentator,
Historian, 1766-1826* (The Hague 1974) 127-47

– *Essays on Karamzin: Russian Man of Letters, Political Commentator, Historian, 1766-1826,* (The Hague 1974)
Brang, Peter '"Natal'ia, boiarskaia doch" und *Tatiana Larina,' Zeitschrift für slavische Philologie* XXVII (1959) 348-63
– *Studien zu Theorie und Praxis der russischen Erzählung, 1770-1811* (Wiesbaden 1960)
Cross, A.G. 'Karamzin and England' *Slavonic and East European Review* XLIII 100 (1964) 91-114
– 'N.M. Karamzin and Barthélemy's *Voyage du jeune Anacharsis' Modern Language Review* LXI (July 1966) 467-72
– 'Problems of Form and Literary Influence in the Poetry of Karamzin' *Slavic Review* XXVII (January 1968) 39-48
– 'Karamzin in English: A Review Article' *Canadian Slavic Studies* III (December 1969) 716-27
– 'N.M. Karamzin's *Messenger of Europe (Vestnik Yevropy*), 1802-03' *Forum for Modern Language Studies* V (January 1969) 1-25
– *N.M. Karamzin: A Study of His Literary Career, 1783-1803* (Carbondale, Ill. 1971)
– 'Karamzin's First Short Story?' in *Russia: Essays in History and Literature* ed. Lyman H. Legters (Leiden 1972)
– 'Karamzin's Versions of the Idyll' in J.L. Black, ed. *Essays on Karamzin: Russian Man-of-Letters, Political Commentator, Historian, 1766-1826* (The Hague 1974)
Derzhavin i Karamzin v literaturnom dvizhenii XVIII-nachala XIX veka, XVIII vek, sbornik 8 (Leningrad 1969). Contains eighteen articles on Karamzin, including the Russian-language version of the last-named Cross article
Dewey, Horace W. 'Sentimentalism in the Historical Writing of N.M. Karamzin' *American Contributions to the 4th International Congress of Slavicists* (Moscow 1958)
Garrard, J.G. 'Karamzin, Mme de Staël, and the Russian Romantics' *American Contributions to the 7th International Congress of Slavists* (Warsaw 1973) II *Literature and Folklore* ed. Victor Terras (The Hague 1973) 221-46
– 'Poor Erast, or Point of View in Karamzin' in J.L. Black, ed. *Essays on Karamzin: Russian Man-of-Letters, Political Commentator, Historian, 1766-1826* (The Hague 1974)
Gotting, Doris 'Die äesthetischen Kriterion der Dichtungsauffassung Karamzins' *Aus der Geisteswelt der Slaven: Dankesgabe an Erwin Koschmieder* (Munich 1967) 189-217
Harder, H.B. 'Eine unbekannte Übersetzung Karamzins aus Matthisson' *Ost und West* (1967) 1-10
Ivanov, M.V. 'Problemy istorii i frantsuzskaia revolutsiia v tvorchestve Karamzina 1790-x godov' *Russkaia literatura* 2 (1974) 134-42

Kisliagina, L.G. *Formirovanie obshchestvenno-politicheskikh vzgliadov N.M. Karamzina (1785-1803)* (Moscow 1975)

Kośny, Witold 'Zum Problem der historischen Erzählung bei N.M. Karamzin' *Die Welt der Slaven* XIII 3 (1968) 252-82

Kanunova, F.Z. *Is istorii russkoi povesti (Istoriko-literaturnoe znachenie povestei N.M. Karamzina)* (Tomsk 1967)

'Kharakter izobrazheniia evropeiskoi deistvitel'nosti v *Pis'makh iz Frantsii* D.I. Fonvisina i "pis'makh russkogo puteshestvennika" N.M. Karamzina,' in M.V. Arsen'eva *Voprosy istorii literatury i metodiki ee prepodavaniia* (Murmansk 1971) 50-60

Kisliagina, L.G. 'K voprosu o razvitii sotsial'no politicheskikh vzgliadov N.M. Karamzina v 90-x godakh XVIII burzhuaznaia revoliutsiia' *Vestnik Moskovskogo universiteta* 5 (1968) 33-44. This article was translated into English for J.L. Black, ed. *Essays on Karamzin: Russian Man-of-Letters, Political Commentator, Historian, 1766-1826* (The Hague 1974) 91-104

Kudriavtsev, I.A. '*Vestnik Evropy* M.T. Kachenovskogo ob *Istorii gosudarstva Rossiiskogo* N.M. Karamzina' *Trudy Moskovskogo gos. istoriko-arkhivnogo instituta* 22 (1966) 210-49

Luzianina, L.N. '*Istoriia gosudarstva rossiiskogo* N.M. Karamzina i tragediia Pushkina *Boris Godunov* (k probleme Kharaktera letopistsa)' *Russkaia literatura* 1 (1971) 45-57

– 'Ob osobennostiakh izobrazheniia naroda v *istorii gosudarstva Rossiiskogo* N.M. Karamzina' *Uchenye zapiski Leningradskogo universiteta* Seriia filologicheskikh nauk, 76, no. 355 (1971) 3-17

Martynov, I.F. 'English Literature and Eighteenth-Century Russian Reviewers' *Oxford Slavonic Papers* new series IV (1971) 30-42 (on Karamzin as reviewer of English literature)

McGrew, R.E. 'Notes on the Princely Role in Karamzin's *Istoriya gosudarstva Rossiiskogo*' *American Slavic and East European Review* XVIII (1959) 12-25

Mitter, W. 'Die Entwicklung der politischen Anschauungen Karamzins,' *Forschungen zur osteuropäischen Geschichte* II (1955) 165-284

Mocha, F. 'The Karamzin-Lelewel Controversy' *Slavic Review* XXXI 3 (September 1972) 592-610

Nebel, Henry M., Jr *N.M. Karamzin: A Russian Sentimentalist* (The Hague 1967)

– *Selected Prose of N.M. Karamzin* (Evanston, Ill. 1969)

Neuhäuser, R. 'Karamzin's Spiritual Crisis of 1793 and 1794' in J.L. Black, ed. *Essays on Karamzin: Russian Man-of-Letters, Political Commentator, Historian, 1766-1826* (The Hague 1974) 56-74

– *Towards the Romantic Age: Essays on Sentimental and Preromantic Literature in Russia* (The Hague 1974)

Orlov, P.A. 'Respublikanskaia tema v zhurnale Karamzina Vestnik evropy (k voprosu ob evoliutsii mirovozzreniia pisatel'ia)' *Nauchnye doklady vysshei shkoly: filogicheskie nauki* (1969) 15-24

– *'Povest* N.M. Karamzina "Marfa Posadnitsa"' *Russkaia literatura* 2 (1968) 192-200

Pamp, F. 'Charles Bonnet und Karamzin' *Revue de littérature comparée* XXX (1956) 87-92

Pavlovich, S.E. 'Evropeiskaia zhizn' 1789-1790 godov v *Pis'makh russkogo puteshestvennika* Karamzina' in *K istorii realizma i romantizma v russkoi i zarubezhnoi literature* (Saratov 1969) 7-17

Peshtich, S.L. and I.E. Tsiperovich *'Istoriia gosudarstva Rossiiskogo* N.M. Karamzina na kitaiskom iazyke' *Narody Asii i Afriki* 6 (1968) 125-6

Pipes, Richard *Karamzin's Memoir on Ancient and Modern Russia* (Cambridge, MA 1959)

– 'Karamzin's Conception of the Monarchy' *Harvard Slavic Studies* IV (1957) 35-58. Reprinted in J.L. Black, ed. *Essays on Karamzin: Russian Man-of-Letters, Political Commentator, Historian, 1766-1826* (The Hague 1974) 105-26

Regemorter, J.-L. van 'Deux Images idéales de la paysannerie russe à la fin du XVIIIᵉ siècle' *Cahiers du monde russe et soviétique* IX 1 (1968) 5-19 [on Karamzin and Radishchev]

Rothe, Hans 'Karamzinstudien' I, II *Zeitschrift für slavische Philologie* XXIX (1960) 102-25, XXX (1962) 272-306

– 'Marginalien zum "griechischen Geschmack" in Russland 1780-1820' *Festschrift für Margarete Woltner zum 70. Geburtstag* (Heidelberg 1967) 205-18

– *N.M. Karamzins europäische Reise: Der Beginn des russischen Romans* (Berlin 1968)

– 'Karamzin and His Heritage: History of a Legend' in J.L. Black, ed. *Essays on Karamzin: Russian Man-of-Letters, Political Commentator, Historian, 1766-1826* (The Hague 1974) 148-90. Translated from the German by D.K. Buse, Laurentian University

Toibin, I. *'Istoriia gosudarstva Rossiiskogo* N.M. Karamzina v tvorcheskoi zhizni Pushkina' *Russkaia literatura* 4 (1966) 37-49

Vatsuro, V.E. 'Podvig chestnogo cheloveka' *Prometei* 5 (1968) 8-51 [on Pushkin and Karamzin]

Verkhovskaia, N. *Karamzin v Moskve i Podmoskov'e* (Moscow 1968)

Wedel, W. 'Radishchev und Karamzin' *Die Welt der Slaven* IV (1959) 38-65

– 'A.N. Radishchevs, *Reise von Petersburg nach Moskau* und N.M. Karamzins, *Reisebriefe eines Russen'* I, II *Die Welt der Slaven* IV (1959) 302-27, 435-44

E   KARAMZIN'S WORKS: ENGLISH TRANSLATIONS

These titles are listed according to the year in which they were written, and refer to recent, readily accessible translations. For a general discussion of the enthusiasm for Karamzin among English-language readers during the nineteenth century, see the article by Cross, 'Karamzin in English: A Review Article,' and that by T.A. Bykova, 'Perevody proisvedenii Karamzina na inostrannye iazyki i otliki na nikh v inostrannoi literature' *XVIII vek: sbornik 8* (Leningrad 1969) 324-42.

1786-87: *On Shakespeare and His Tragedy, 'Julius Caesar' (O Shekspire i ego tragedii 'Iulii Tsezar'*); translated by Henry M. Nebel, Jr, for his *Selected Prose of N.M. Karamzin* (Evanston, Ill. 1969) 155-60

1791-2: *Letters of a Russian Traveller (Pis'ma russkago Puteshestvennika)*; translated by Florence Jonas (New York 1957), but much abridged. Several extracts from the *Letters* were included in H.B. Segel, ed., *The Literature of Eighteenth Century Russia* I (New York 1967) 341-51, and in Leo Weiner, ed., *Anthology of Russian Literature* II (New York 1903) 27-33.

1792: *The Churchyard (Kladbishche)* Weiner II 33-4

1798: *Poor Liza (Bednaia Liza)*, Nebel 53-72, Segel II 76-93, Weiner II 34-7; Carl R. Proffer, ed., *From Karamzin to Bunin: An Anthology of Russian Short Stories* (Bloomington 1969) 53-67

1792: *Natalie, the Boyar's Daughter (Natal'ia boiarskaia doch')*, Nebel 73-116

1793: *The Island of Bornholm (Ostrov Borngol'm)*; Nebel 117-32, Segel II 94-105

1794: *What Does an Author Need? (Chto nuzhno avtoru?)*, Nebel 165-70

1794: *Julia (Juliia)*, Nebel 133-53. This work was not printed until 1796.

1797: *Preface to the Second Book of Aonides (Predislovie)*; Nebel 165-70

1797: *A Word about Russian Literature (Un Mot sur la littérature russe)*, Segel I 430-41. Written in French for the émigré periodical, *Le Spectateur du Nord*, it contained some comments about the French Revolution. Appeared first in Russian in 1801; reprinted in French as an appendix to *Pis'ma N.M. Karamzin k I.I. Dmitrievu* 473-83

1802: *My Confession: A Letter to an Editor of a Journal (Moia ispoved': Pis'ma k izdateliiu zhurnala)*, Nebel 171-84

1802: *Why is There so Little Writing Talent in Russia? (Otchego v Rossii malo avtorskikh talantov?)*, Segel I 454-8, Nebel 191-6

1802: *Society in America (Obshchestvo v amerike)*; translated by J.L. Black for the *Laurentian University Review* IV 3 (1972) 43-4. This short essay appeared first in the *Messenger of Europe*, 1802, and was reprinted in 1818.

1802: *The Book Trade and Love of Reading in Russia (O knizhnoi torgovle i liubvi k chteniia v Rossii)*, Nebel 185-90, Segel I 449-53. It was also included in Marc Raeff, ed., *Russian Intellectual History: An Anthology* (New York 1966) 113-16.

1802: *Love of Country and National Pride* (*O liubvi k otechestvu i narodnoi gordosti*), Segel I 442-8, Raeff 107-12

1802: *On Events and Characters in Russian History That are Possible Subjects of Art* (*O sluchaiakh i Kharakterakh v Rossiiskoi istorii kotorye mogut byt' predmetom Khudozhestv*), Segel I 459-69

1803: *The Emotional and the Cold: Two Characters* (*Chuvstvitel'nyi k Kholodnyi: Dva Kharaktera*), Nebel 197-214

1803: *An Englishman's Letter from Quebec* (*Pis'mo odnogo anglichanina iz Kvebeka*), translated by Helena Debevc-Moroz for the *Laurentian University Review* IV 3 (1972) 45-6

1811: *Memoir on Ancient and Modern Russia* (*Zapiska o drevnei i novoi Rossii*), Richard Pipes *Karamzin's Memoir on Ancient and Modern Russia* (Cambridge, MA 1959). First printed in Russian in 1870

1815: *Foreword to the 'History of the Russian State'* (*Predislovie*), Raeff 117-24, Weiner II 37-40. Partly written as early as 1803, not printed until 1818

1818: *A Note about N.I. Novikov* (*Zapiska o N.I. Novikove*), Segel I 470-2

1818-26: *History of the Russian State* (*Istoriia gosudarstva Rossiiskago*), extracts translated by Helena Debevc-Moroz for J.L. Black, ed. *Essays on Karamzin: Russian Man-of-Letters, Political Commentator, Historian, 1766-1826* (The Hague 1974) 199-220

1819: *Opinion of a Russian Citizen* (*Mnenie russkago grazhdanina*), translated by J.L. Black for *Essays on Karamzin: Russian Man-of-Letters, Political Commentator, Historian, 1766-1826* (The Hague 1974) 193-6

1825: *Thoughts about True Freedom* (*Mysli ob istinnoi svobode*); translated by Helena Debevc-Moroz for J.L. Black, ed., *Essays on Karamzin: Russian Man-of-Letters, Political Commentator, Historian, 1766-1826* (The Hague 1974) 197-8. Not published in Russian until 1862

Appendix

LETTER FROM KARAMZIN TO ALEXANDER I 1801*

Sir!
Having received with reverence the token of royal grace, I hasten to express to
you my sincere gratitude as its executor. Sir, I appreciate the value of what you
so graciously did for me. If I genuinely have any talent, I will dedicate it from
now on with even greater zeal to our dear Fatherland, whose glory is inseparable
from the glory of the Monarch. The History of Russia will be the object of my
diligent labours. How fortunate I will consider myself if fate allows me to depict
also that common joyful feeling following the age of Catherine the Great with
which the Russians saw Alexander ascend the throne, and all their hopes and
happy fulfillment of these hopes!

With eternal gratitude and sincere respect, I have the honour,

Sir! to remain your
most humble servant,
Nicholas Karamzin.

Moscow
8 April 1801

---

* This letter was reprinted as the frontispiece of the 1892 edition of Karamzin's *History*.
Karamzin was thanking Alexander for gifts sent to him in response to the writer's 1801
odes to Catherine and Alexander.

KARAMZIN TO I.I. DMITRIEV*

Tver, 20 March 1811
My Dear Friend!
Yesterday we were fortunate to dine with the Sovereign for the last time here. He departed during the night. Besides four dinners, my wife and I were in the inner rooms twice and during the third time, with the Grand Duchess and the Prince present. I read to him from my history for more than two hours. After that I talked to him a lot – and about what? *About Autocracy!* Unfortunately, I was not in agreement with several of his ideas, but was honestly surprised with his intelligence and humble eloquence. My heart was always drawn to him because it guessed and felt the kindness in this monarch; now I love and respect him by my inner conviction in the beauty of his soul. Pray to God that he will be happy with the happiness of Russia! That is the foremost wish of my heart, which is attached to him and to the Fatherland! Saying goodby to us, he invited me to come to St Petersburg, and added that we will have no need for a rented house; that the Anichkovsky Palace is big enough – that the Grand Duchess doubtlessly will accommodate us with pleasure in her house. I feel the value of his favour. Tell him, my good friend, at the appropriate moment, that I, by duty and by inclination, am devoted forever to the monarch, who is that rarity with refined, elegant qualities of the soul. His last words were: 'What is the message to Ivan Ivanovich?' [Dmitriev]. The Grand Duchess even wanted me to give my letter to you to the sovereign! 'There is a post for that,' I answered with a low bow. Let others forget themselves: the thing for me to remember is who is the Sovereign and who is the subordinate. He talked to me several times about you, about your health, and doesn't wish to believe that you were once a diligent walker. He listened to my History, it seems, with unfeigned attention and pleasure; he didn't want to break into our reading at all. Finally, after conversation, looking at his watch, he asked the Grand Duchess: 'Guess the time, it is after 11.' In short, I should be quite satisfied....

N. Karamzin

---

* This letter and the four following were translated by Elizabeth Gorky, Modern Language Department, Laurentian University, from *Pis'ma N.M. Karamzina k I.I. Dmitrievu* (St Petersburg 1866), and 'Pis'ma N.M. Karamzina k kniaziu P.A. Viazemskomu, 1810-1826,' *Starina i novizna* (1897).

KARAMZIN TO I.I. DMITRIEV, 13 JUNE 1813

Moscow,
And you, my dear friend, have experienced a cruel loss! It is terrible to be deprived of a loving mother. I know how much she loved you, and how you loved her. God and time will comfort you in this natural and, I dare say, proper sadness. Besides the social calamity, we will have sympathy with you. It is sorrowful and sickening. I wept profusely; I also wept here on viewing the ruins. Moscow no longer exists; all that remains are her ashes. Not only were the houses burned: the very morals of the people are changed for the worse, or so they assure one. They are noticeably rude, loud and insolent, which they were not before. The government must institute beneficial measures....

N. Karamzin

KARAMZIN TO I.I. DMITRIEV

Moscow, 15 June 1813
And you also my dear friend suffered a cruel blow! It is hard to lose a tender mother...

There is no Moscow; only small parts of it left. Not only were the houses burned down, but people's morality itself had changed into evil, or so that is what some people say. Bitterness is noticeable; one sees impudence which did not exist before. The government is in need of extraordinarily wise measures. However, it is not my business; there is God. He knows better than we do. ...
My concern is to long for my son, to feel sorry for a friend and to get ready for Petersburg, so that I can embrace you and can publish my History with the permission of the Sovereign...

N. Karamzin

KARAMZIN TO P.A. VIAZEMSKY

Tsarskoe Selo, 21 August 1818
Dear Friends! Our hearty thanks for the good news: you are in good health and so are we. You, dear Prince, were getting into the carriage to go to Cracov; I hope that you enjoyed returning better than going. Cracov is not Rome, nevertheless, it has its own antiquities, and is Slavic as well. One can look at it with pleasure

and curiosity. Soon you will have a female visitor in Warsaw, the widowed Empress, and after that a guest – the Emperor, who is on a return trip.

We are much more fond of the Emperor than ever before, for his kind favours and affection towards us. Today we are dining with him, probably for the last time before he goes. After dinner he is going to Peterhof, to Petersburg and, on the 20th, abroad. Madame de Staël did not have such a strong effect on me as she did on you. It is not surprising – ladies have a stronger influence on young men than on the old, and as far as I am concerned she is a woman in this book – although a rather clever one. To give Russia a constitution in the modern sense is the same as to dress some important person in a dunce's cap – or to teach your scholar Linde the three R's by the Lancasterian method. Russia is not England, nor even the Polish Kingdom. It has its own great and amazing national faith, and can sooner fall than glorify itself more. Autocracy is its soul and life, as Republican rule was the life of Rome. In this case, experiments won't do. Nevertheless, I am not preventing anyone from thinking differently. One clever man once said, 'I don't like young men who don't like liberty; but I don't like middle-aged men who do love liberty.' If what he said is not nonsense, then you should love me, and I you. Posterity will see what is better or what was better for Russia. For me, the old man, it is much better to go to a comedy than to the Hall of National Assembly, or to the Chamber of Deputies, even though I am a republican and will die as one.

You are complaining about flies; we are complaining about rain, nevertheless, we are hoping that some day the clouds will break and that we will be able to live in Tsarskoe Selo until October. In the city we will have another apartment in the house of Kat. Fed. Murav'eva....

N. Karamzin

KARAMZIN TO P.A. VIAZEMSKY

St Petersburg, 31 December 1825
Dearest Friends! Let God send to you and to us a good New Year! Wishing you good health and well-being for the year 1826. Embracing you tenderly, all of you, from young to old.

My emotional fever has not quite gone as yet, I mean an exaltation provoked by extraordinary circumstances.

What we Karamzins have lost in Alexander, no one can restore to us. You, my dear Prince, are talking about a habit of mine; I am talking about kindred souls. There was no blindness on my part, but there was a great love. How can one read without tender emotions the things the cleverest Frenchmen and Englishmen write about Alexander? For us it is better to observe an eloquent silence. The Russian version makes me sick. I shall not write a single word, but perhaps will say something at the end of the twelfth volume, or in a review of our latest history in a year or two – if I am still alive. Or else I may have to talk to Alexander himself in the Elysian Fields. There are many conversations he and I did not finish in this world.

There is so much sorrow and anxiety in the families [of the Decembrists]. I still don't have a detailed and clear idea about this vicious and senseless plot. It is true that secret societies did exist and that their goal was the overthrow of the government. From important to unimportant things now: most of the [Decembrist] members honoured me with their hatred, or at least did not like me. But I am not, it seems, an enemy either to the Fatherland or to humanity. One hears that the repentance of several of them is sincere and complete. Poor mothers, wives, children, infants! Without having any political influence, I am praying for Russia. God saved us on December 14th from a great misfortune. It was as bad as the French invasion. In both instances, I see a heavenly ray of hope. Again, I am able to write my History. I am alive, alive. I am myself again. I tenderly embrace you for offering to us your city and country living quarters. Sometimes, I really think about Moscow, about Dresden for the children's education, about the shores of the Rhine. But first of all I would like to publish the twelfth volume of my historical epic. As God wishes: I believe in Him seriously, having lived in this world close to 60 years, neither heartless nor blindfolded. However, either here or there – there is not much difference. I can stay in Petersburg also.

I am concerned about Ivan Ivanovich [Dmitriev], not having heard from him in a long time.

Forgive me, dears, forever yours,
N. Karamzin

DIPLOMA PRESENTED TO KARAMZIN BY ARZAMAS*

From the Arzamas society of unknown people to the respected and well-known Historiographer of all Russia, to the Knight of Anna, the glory of Mr Karamzin, kind salutations and a friendly handshake:

It is known to us that your Honour is occupying himself with writing the famous adventures of the Russian people, and that you are giving of yourself towards the

* Translated by Elizabeth Gorky from 'Diplom, podnesennyi Obshchestvom 'Arzamas' k N.M. Karamzinu,' *Starina i novizna* 12 (1907) 334-5. The text of the diploma was written in Zhukovsky's hand, and the others signed it.

vision of Russia's glory, which until now has been in a state of conversational coma, and in a state of death in a coffin built for her by all kinds of good-for-nothings, like Mr Leclerc and Mr Levesque, and by some embittered sons and stepsons of Russia.

It is known to us that your Honour, with the greatness of the geese of Arzamas, is strolling along the silky pastures of Russian words and that you honour with your glance neither the quagmire of nonsense which features the *Gathering* [Beseda], nor the academic backstreets of absurdity.

It is known to us that your heart, that heavenly treasure, by its pureness is like the barely feathered white gosling, one that is only beginning to straighten out its wings and gaily paddle in the clear waters of the Motherland, and that your disposition is just as clear as the sky that is shining in spring beauty over the gosling.

It is known to us that all of the undersigned love you with unhypocritical love, everyone separately and all of us together, we love you for ourselves and for the motherland, to which you are an honour and glory.

It is known to us, thanks to God, that the father of our country also loves you and that he was kind enough to distinguish you among all other of his children with his respect. You quite properly deserve the Tsar's heart, and his deed brings honour to him and reveals his greatness.

It is known to us that your Honour also received decorations from the esteemed Tsar which mark his respect, and that you, as a very good son of Russia, felt gratitude towards the Tsar for this act.

And because of that, and for nothing else but this and that, we felt an urge to present you with a visible specimen of this mark of distinction, this ribbon with a cross and this star that goes along with it; let the star shine on your chest as a sign of our love; and you, dear Honourable one, be for us the evershining Star of glory, friendship and everything there is in Arzamas – which is the best in the world.

> Svetlana [Zhukovsky]
> Kassandra [Bludov]
> Eolova Arfa [A.I. Turgenev]
> Starushka [Uvarov]
> Gromovoi [Zhikharev]
> Ibikov zhuravl' [Vigel']
> Vot [V.L. Pushkin]
> Asmodei [Viazemsky]
> Chu!!! [Dashkov]
> Akhill [Batiushkov]

Index